Albany County Public
Library
Sources of Materials
FY12

■ County Sales Tax
■ City Sales Tax
■ Foundation
■ Friends
■ Cash Gifts from Public
■ Replacement Fees
▫ Donated Items

THE NATURE OF THE
FUTURE

DISPATCHES FROM
THE **SOCIALSTRUCTED WORLD**

MARINA GORBIS

Free Press
New York   London   Toronto   Sydney   New Delhi

*f*P

Free Press
A Division of Simon & Schuster, Inc.
1230 Avenue of the Americas
New York, NY 10020

First Free Press hardcover edition April 2013

FREE PRESS and colophon are trademarks of Simon & Schuster, Inc.

For information about special discounts for bulk purchases, please contact Simon & Schuster Special Sales at 1-866-506-1949 or business@simonandschuster.com.

The Simon & Schuster Speakers Bureau can bring authors to your live event. For more information or to book an event, contact the Simon & Schuster Speakers Bureau at 1-866-248-3049 or visit our website at www.simonspeakers.com.

Designed by Jill Putorti

Manufactured in the United States of America

10   9   8   7   6   5   4   3   2   1

Library of Congress Cataloging-in-Publication Data
Gorbis, Marina.
The nature of the future: dispatches from the socialstructed world /
by Marina Gorbis.
    p. cm.
Includes bibliographical references and index.
1. Online social networks—Economic aspects. 2. Social change. I. Title.
HM742.G67 2013
303.4—dc23

                                                    2012025670

ISBN 978-1-4516-4118-9
ISBN 978-1-4516-4120-2 (ebook)

To my mother, whose light continues to shine
To Greg, whose restless search for meaning is an inspiration
To Chris, my best friend and partner in this dance

Contents

THE NATURE OF THE
FUTURE

1

Putting the Social Back into Our Economy

My mother never heard the term *social capital,* but she knew its value well. In the Soviet Union, where she lived and where I grew up, no one could survive without it, and she leveraged her social capital on a daily basis. It enabled her to provide a decent life for her family, even though she was a widow without much money, excluded from the privileged class of the Communist Party. We never worried about having enough food. My sister and I always wore fashionable clothes (at least by Soviet standards). We took music and dance lessons. We went to the symphony, attended good schools, and spent summers by the Black Sea. In short, we enjoyed a lifestyle that seemed well beyond our means.

How was my mother able to provide all these things on the meager salary of a physician in a government-run clinic in Odessa, Ukraine? Social connections were a powerful currency that flowed through her network of friends and acquaintances, giving her access to many goods and services and enabling our comfortable, if not luxurious, lifestyle. Even when no meat could be found in any store in the city, my mother was able to get it, along with a wealth of other hard-to-find foods, from the director of the supermarket who was the husband of a close colleague of hers. I was accepted into music school because my mother treated the director of the school in her off-hours. We were able to get Western medicines because a friend was the head of a large local pharmacy.

Our apartment was always filled with people my mother was counseling, diagnosing, treating, and prescribing medicines for. No money ever changed hands; that was too risky. She had lived through the era of Stalin's purges, and the memory of his fabricated charges against Jewish doctors, who he claimed were trying to poison the Soviet leadership, was still vivid in her mind. She was too afraid to build a private underground medical practice. "With my luck, I would be the first to be caught," she would say with a nervous laugh.

All those people who regularly visited us, or whose houses she visited to provide care, were my mom's substitute for money, providing not only food, medicines, and clothes but also intangibles of information, services, and emotional support. When my mother died shortly after emigrating to the United States in 1990, the only material possessions she left me and my sister were her wedding ring, some books, and a few pieces of clothing. But she also left thousands of grateful friends and former patients whose lives she had touched.

Our story was not unique. All around us, amid empty stores, low salaries, dismal productivity numbers, and fraying infrastructure, people seemed to live normal middle-class lives. An economist would have had a hard time explaining our lifestyle by analyzing economic statistics or walking around the stores and markets in Russia in the 1960s and 1970s. In fact, visitors to the Soviet Union always marveled at the gap between what they saw in state stores—shelves empty or filled with things no one wanted—and what they saw in people's homes: nice furnishings and tables filled with food.

What filled the gap? A vast informal economy driven by human relationships, dense networks of social connections through which people traded resources and created value. The Soviet people didn't plot how they would build these networks. No one was teaching them how to maximize their connections the way social marketers eagerly teach us today. Their networks evolved naturally, out of necessity, that was the only way to survive.

Today, all around the world, we are seeing a new kind of network or relationship-driven economics emerging, with individuals joining forces sometimes to fill the gaps left by existing institutions—corporations, governments, educational establishments—and sometimes creating new products, services, and knowledge that no institution is able to provide. Empowered by computing and communication technologies that have been steadily building village-like networks on a global scale, we are infusing more and more of our economic transactions with social connectedness.

The new technologies are inherently social and personal. They help us create communities around interests, identities, and common personal challenges. They allow us to gain direct access to a worldwide community of others. And they take anonymity out of our economic transactions. We can assess those we don't know by checking their reputations as buyers and sellers on eBay or by following their Twitter streams. We can look up their friends on Facebook and watch their YouTube videos. We can easily get people's advice on where to find the best shoemaker in Brazil, the best programmer in India, and the best apple farmer in our local community. We no longer have to rely on bankers or venture capitalists as the only sources of funding for our ideas. We can raise funds directly from individuals, most of whom we don't even know, through websites like Grow VC and Kickstarter, which allow people to post descriptions of their projects and generate donations, investments, or loans.

We are moving away from the dominance of the depersonalized world of institutional production and creating a new economy around social connections and social rewards—a process I call *socialstructing*. Others have referred to this model of production as social, commons-based, or peer-to-peer.[1] Not only is this new social economy bringing with it an unprecedented level of familiarity and connectedness to both our global and our local economic exchanges, but it is also changing every domain of our lives, from finance to education and health. It is rapidly ushering in a vast array of new opportunities for us to pursue our passions, create new types of businesses and charitable organizations, redefine the nature of work, and address a wide range of problems that the prevailing formal economy has neglected, if not caused.

Socialstructing is in fact enabling not only a new kind of global economy but a new kind of society, in which amplified individuals—individuals empowered with technologies and the collective intelligence of others in their social network—can take on many functions that previously only large organizations could perform, often more efficiently, at lower cost or no cost at all, and with much greater ease. Socialstructing is opening up a world of what my colleagues Jacques Vallée and Bob Johansen describe as the world of impossible futures, a world in which a large software firm can be displaced by weekend software hackers, and rapidly orchestrated social movements can bring down governments in a matter of weeks. The changes are exciting and unpredictable. They threaten many established institutions and offer a wealth of opportunities for individuals to empower themselves, find rich new connections, and tap into a fast-evolving set of new resources in everything from health care to education and science.

Much has been written about how technology distances us from the benefits of face-to-face communication and quality social time. I think those are important concerns. But while the quality of our face-to-face interactions is changing, the countervailing force of socialstructing is connecting us at levels never seen before, opening up new opportunities to create, learn, and share. Consider a few examples of amplified individuals who are pioneering this transformation.

Opening Up Biology for the Masses

Eri Gentry always had a strong interest in health and well-being. She read health books and magazines as a teenager and moved on to academic papers on medicine in college. She got hooked on research into aging and life extension, and in the process, discovered the SENS Foundation, a brainchild of the noted British anti-aging researcher and scientist Aubrey de Grey. SENS was located close to where she lived in Arizona, so Eri started volunteering there, doing a variety of tasks, from talking to real estate brokers to helping get visas for overseas scientists visiting the lab. She was dismayed to learn how top-heavy many scientific efforts are and that too often scientists themselves are undervalued and underrewarded. She became a true advocate for scientists. "Such important research should be scientist-driven and have as little overhead as possible,"[2] she says. Thus was born her desire to uplift scientists who are eager to do research, often for very little money, and at the same time to make science, particularly biology, more accessible to the masses.

While working at SENS, Eri and a biomedical researcher, John Schloendorn, started a nonprofit company called Livly to pursue research in immunotherapy treatments for cancer. Realizing that Arizona was not the best place for a start-up, the team decided to move to Silicon Valley. Eri looked into renting a biotech incubator space there, but the rents were exorbitant—more than $6,000 per person per month. Instead, she rented the cheapest house with a garage she could find in Mountain View, and she and John moved in.

The team soon turned their garage into a biotech lab. They acquired most of their equipment from biotech companies that were going out of business and were willing to get rid of their gear for pennies on the dollar. Eri and John would sometimes drive to Los Angeles to pick up equipment and attend a biotech conference on the way. Word about their lab spread quickly. Many people came by to visit, among them Peter Thiel, a venture capitalist famous for his early investment in Facebook. Thiel decided to invest in Immune-Path,[3] a start-up created by Schloendorn that specializes in stem cell therapeutics for diseases of the immune system.

Eri took a different path. The community of people interested in doing biology research quickly outgrew her garage and started meeting in larger spaces, including the Institute for the Future (IFTF). BioCurious, as the group became known, evolved into many things:

a physical space where people come to learn, share ideas, and collaborate on projects; a place for hackers to come together and apply their skills to biology; a community for interested amateurs to learn about and to participate in biology research. Today the members are a diverse group—scientists, philosophers, engineers, programmers, designers, amateurs and professionals, young and old. Eri sees Bio-Curious as a "space for people to innovate biology in a world where change is sorely needed."[4]

One of the projects developed by some of the members of the BioCurious community is an open PCR (polymerase chain reaction) machine. A PCR machine is critical for DNA analysis and is a foundational tool for virtually all of modern molecular biology research. Traditional PCR machines cost between $4,000 and $10,000, but two of the BioCurious cofounders, Josh Perfetto and Tito Jankowski, developed a PCR machine that sells for around $600. Along with Mac Cowell, a cofounder of DIYbio.org, another non-profit dedicated to engaging people in biology research, Josh created another project called Cofactor Bio that sells kits to enable people to do all kinds of genetic and biological testing on their own.[5] You can, for example, specify which genes you want to test for, such as the gene associated with quick metabolization of caffeine or the gene associated with natural marathon-running abilities, and they will send you a kit to do the testing.

After a year of operating out of the garage, Eri and her co-conspirators turned to Kickstarter, a crowdfunding platform where strangers can contribute money to underwrite projects in the arts, music, and science. With contributions ranging from $3 to $2,500 and over two hundred backers, BioCurious managed to raise enough money to start a community lab in Sunnyvale, California, where members have access to lab equipment and a community to help them pursue their research interests in biology.

BioCurious and other DIY biology efforts come at an important time and serve a critical role in the evolution of biological research. Disciplines such as synthetic biology and genomics are truly trans-disciplinary, that is, they require knowledge from multiple disciplines, including genetics, bioinformatics, chemistry, and biology. In most academic settings, these disciplines are highly specialized. Even in neuroscience departments, researchers might be highly specialized in biological, microbiological, cognitive, and other types of neuroscience. And people with different specializations find it difficult to talk to each other. Meanwhile, the stores of biological and genetic data we are accumulating are growing exponentially. To take advantage of this data and to speed up the rate of scientific discoveries, we need people from different disciplines to talk to each other in a similar language. Communities such as BioCurious provide a place for people to develop a common language and work together.

At the same time, tools for doing self-diagnosis, self-tracking, and biological research are becoming increasingly available to individuals. BioCurious encourages and enables people to acquire the necessary knowledge and tools to do such research, to become experts on their own bodies, and to participate in broader research by contributing their own data to a large pool of community information. Eri's goal is to engage more and more people in biological research—to bring biology to the masses.

Eri also helped shape Genomera, a platform for open-source clinical trials. Traditional clinical trials are lengthy and expensive and are done only by large R&D labs or government organizations. Genomera allows virtually anyone to run a clinical trial. Say you want to investigate whether drinking green tea affects your energy level or cuts down on your food cravings. You can propose a clinical trial to the Genomera community, and Genomera will help you recruit study participants, provide you with templates for running the study, and give you assistance with data analysis. Greg Biggers, the founder of Genomera, envisions it not only as a platform for conducting research but also as a social platform—a place where people can find others interested in similar issues, share research ideas, and help improve methodologies. Far from the way traditional clinical trials are conducted, where subjects never see each other, much less talk to each other, Genomera's approach is to create a community of participant researchers who are socially connected.

Genomera and efforts like it play an important role in crowd-sourcing health information and in enabling highly personalized treatment choices. People are increasingly tracking data about themselves, and genetic testing is becoming routine. Combine that with years of data from doctors and aggregate personal data across thousands, if not millions, of people, and it becomes possible to determine which nutritional supplements would be helpful given your individual profile and which foods, drugs, and treatments are most likely to work for you.

BioCurious, Genomera, and platforms for social production of science open up a much larger terrain for investigation. Right now R&D dollars and investments are directed to a narrow set of discoveries that can produce large monetary payoffs for pharmaceutical companies and R&D labs. However, there are many questions that need answers but may not have a huge monetary payoff even though they could make an extraordinary impact on individuals and society as a whole. Efforts like BioCurious and Genomera democratize what we investigate and who does the investigating. At the same time, they drastically reduce the costs of running clinical trials—that is, the costs of innovation. The cost of running a clinical trial with Genomera is close to zero. And here is another benefit of Genomera and open platforms like it: the data they collect is available to anyone to review, analyze, and add to.

There are now hundreds of community labs such as BioCurious and Genomera around the world. Think about the collective impact of their efforts on research!

Combating Global Organized Crime

In 2001 Paul Radu, a young Romanian journalist, got a press fellowship from the Alfred Friendly Foundation to work on an investigative team at the *San Antonio Express-News*. While at the newspaper, he embarked on an investigation of a transnational group involved in helping Americans adopt children from Eastern Europe, including Romania and Ukraine. His investigation specifically focused on

Orson Mozes, the head of Adoption International Program, based in Montecito, California. Paul pored over court records and IRS filings, searched adoption forums, and conducted interviews in Eastern Europe and the United States. He uncovered numerous unsavory and sometimes illegal practices, including failure to disclose medical problems of adopted children, mistreatment of and threats against prospective parents who complained or asked too many questions, and separations of siblings without disclosure of that information to the adoptive parents.

Paul had completed the investigation and was ready to publish his exposé in September 2001, but his story was pushed aside by the events of 9/11. Few people were interested in adoption scams involving Eastern Europe. When the story finally appeared as a lead article in the *San Antonio Express-News* in October 2001,[6] it didn't garner much attention. Nevertheless the experience taught Paul the value of local information and sources, the importance of doing painstaking and often boring forensic reporting work, and the long life that archived online stories can have, with direct impact occurring possibly years after a story is published.

For seven years after its publication, Paul's article on Mozes was posted and reposted on adoption bulletin boards and in discussion forums. Parents who were looking for children and those who had had direct experience with Mozes kept bringing Paul's article back into the conversation. Finally, in 2008, Mozes was arrested for the crimes described in the 2001 article. It took a long time, but publication of the article disrupted Mozes' ablity to do business as usual. "What's more important is not that he was arrested," says Paul, "but that for seven years he tried moving his business to Azerbaijan and to various places, and these people, these local journalists, would always find my story. Or some parent who was interested in adopting would find it. So then I realized that archived information has a lot of power. If it's proper information, if it's sourced correctly, if it's put in a good form, if it's backed by documents, then it can have impact for a very long time."[7]

Paul and his colleagues apply these lessons in a new journalism venture focused on creating a truly global investigative journalism platform. The Organized Crime and Corruption Reporting Project (OCCRP) is a virtual organization that brings together journalists with local knowledge and local connections from different parts of the world. Members of OCCRP collaborate online and in person to decide which investigations to launch. They allocate small amounts of money to groups of reporters, and sometimes citizen journalists, to conduct research in their locales. Working on shoestring budgets, these journalists interview people locally in their native language, go through bank records and company registrations, and collect reports from local media sources. That is, they do the same kind of work Paul was doing in Texas. They understand that organized crime is a global business representing millions of dollars in profits, with a huge network of people and assets.

Organized crime operations use familiar business structures—companies, banks, networks of employees—to conduct illegal activities. They thrive on exploiting jurisdictional boundaries—differences in regulatory, legal, accounting, and cultural norms—often setting up operations in areas where illegal activities can be well hidden from authorities. Unfortunately, because of these jurisdictional differences and constraints, it is often difficult or impossible for local authorities to uncover the whole network and see the larger picture. For example, during a drug bust in Argentina, the authorities might be happy to seize millions of dollars' worth of cocaine and arrest a few people. However, the culprits are likely to be part of a much larger network that involves people in Eastern Europe and elsewhere. "The criminal enterprises of today represent a multibillion-dollar set of networks that prey on every aspect of global society, distorting markets, corrupting governments, and draining huge resources from both," says Paul. "Criminal syndicates have unprecedented reach into the lives of ordinary people, and journalists need to do a better job of putting the transnational puzzle together and of presenting to the public the threat posed by such criminal enterprises."[8]

This type of globally networked criminal activity can go unnoticed and unchallenged in today's media environment. In many Eastern European countries and other parts of the world, oligarchs and corrupt officials own most of the media outlets. In the United States, drops in advertising revenues have led many mainstream media outlets to cut funding for serious investigative journalism. With slow economic growth and falling government revenues, there is also less money for regulatory authorities to conduct in-depth investigations.

This is where organizations like OCCRP can fill the void. The OCCRP global network of journalists is able to weave together fine-grained hyperlocal knowledge into a high-resolution view of global crime and corruption. Such organizations will increasingly assume the role of de facto regulators and drive demand for greater levels of transparency in political and financial systems.

A case in point is an OCCRP investigation in 2010 that uncovered shady offshore business practices popular in Eastern Europe among corrupt politicians, criminal elements, and wealthy individuals eager to avoid paying taxes.[9] Journalists from the United States, Slovakia, Romania, Ukraine, and several other countries came together to investigate one individual, a Romanian businessman named Laszlo Kiss, who was helping many such individuals set up companies in Cyprus, the Seychelles Islands, and Delaware. Among other things, the investigation made transparent how some of the key political figures in Romania were funneling government projects to offshore companies in which they had direct interests. Around one month after the report was released, Laszlo Kiss was arrested; nine months later, his associate Ian Taylor was forced to halt operations. As a result of the OCCRP investigation the New Zealand government shut down over one thousand companies belonging to the network. Not a small accomplishment for a handful of underpaid journalists! The reporters who worked on the project ultimately won the Daniel Pearl Global Investigative Journalism Award for their work.[10]

The creation of archives, databases, and software tools is a big part of the OCCRP effort. Paul's hope is to establish a global information resource that will make it easy for not just skilled investigative journalists but also citizen journalists and others to participate in disrupting global organized crime. As he puts it, "For many years organized crime has been successful in exporting crime all over the world. Ponzi schemes, trafficking in persons, value-added tax fraud, carbon credits fraud, credit card skimming, and many other crimes have been exported from country to country while law enforcement and citizens were not prepared to confront them because they didn't have enough information. Investigative journalists and databases created by investigative journalism organizations may act in a preemptive way in order to stop the migration of crime. This can be done through the construction of databases where [information on] individuals, organizations involved in crime, and emerging crime models would be stored and indexed so that crime syndicates would not be able to conduct business as usual."[11] Paul's first lesson from Texas has proven invaluable: when information is properly archived, sourced, and indexed, it will have a lasting value in disrupting corruption.

Building a Collaborative Video Library of Human Experience

In 2002 David Evan Harris, like so many other college students, was spending his junior year abroad, traveling through Tanzania, India, the Philippines, Mexico, and the United Kingdom. In each of these places he lived with local families, sharing their intimate spaces and daily lives. He stayed in a bamboo house in the Philippines, a former squatter settlement in Mexico City, and a mansion in New Delhi. As with many young people having their first overseas adventure, the experience left an indelible mark on David. "I went from thinking of those countries as nations of abstract numbers of millions of people to thinking of them as individuals,"[12] he says. Unlike many college students who return from abroad and go back to their regular lives, however, David parlayed his experience into a global social enterprise—part art project, part anthropological resource, part social movement.

The Global Lives Project is a collaboratively built video library of human life experience. For its first major undertaking, the Global

Lives team captured twenty-four continuous hours in the lives of ten people in different parts of the world. How were the ten people selected? In the early 2000s, David saw an email asking what the world would look like if it had only one hundred people. Based on proportional distribution, only one person would have a computer, only one would have a college degree, thirty-three would not have access to clean drinking water, and so on. When reading the emails, David was struck by the contrast between what he was reading and the demographics of his social network, mostly college-educated middle class Americans. It inspired him to select ten people who would be representative of the global population.

For the first shoot, of James Bullock, a cable car operator in San Francisco, David's collaborator was Daniel Jones of Kalamazoo, Michigan, someone David had met during his days as a climate change activist. Daniel had studied film and had gone on to get his first documentary production gig after college. The company he was working for went bankrupt, though, and instead of getting a severance paycheck he got a package of video production equipment. Daniel offered to fly to San Francisco to do the first shoot, and he and David split the cost of the airplane ticket plus gasoline and food expenses for the day. When the film was shot, Daniel edited it for the first DVD to be distributed to potential supporters. One of his friends, who worked at AOL at the time, created a website so they could show the film to people in other countries and invite them to participate.

The next shoot took a while to organize, as David moved to Brazil to do graduate study in sociology. Not far from his apartment he stumbled upon the Museum of the Person, a museum of people's life stories, with more than seven thousand stories captured on video, ranging from stories of rural farmers to stories of most of the recent presidents of Brazil. One of the directors of the museum, Jose Santos, became David's mentor and supporter, along with others on the museum's staff. The Museum of the Person not only agreed to coproduce a second Global Lives shoot in Brazil, the staff also connected David with partners in Japan and the United States.

But Global Lives as a sustainable project did not become a reality until two other shoots took place, one in Malawi and one in Japan. David himself did not go to either of these locations, and this is where the model came together: self-organized teams of volunteers using the platform of Global Lives to create something independently that fits into the larger narrative of the project. Helio Ishii, a Japanese Brazilian filmmaker whom David had met through his university in Brazil, asked David if he could try to organize a shoot in Japan. So David emailed everyone he knew who had ever been to Japan and asked if anyone knew a filmmaker or a photographer there interested in social change. Remarkably he got twenty responses from people in Japan who wanted to help, including one at the United Nations University and one at Temple University's Japan campus. Right around the same time, Jason Price, an American anthropology graduate student whom David had met briefly and who had been a Peace Corps volunteer in Malawi, offered to do a shoot in Malawi. So the two shoots happened without David's on-site participation. The filmmakers were far more skilled than he was and had much better video equipment than he had. "All of a sudden, I was working with all of these people who were way out of my league and who were really interested in it and wanted to do it. At that point, I had my first sensation of, 'Oh, my! It will really happen. We will get the ten done.'"[13]

Since that time the Global Lives Collective has completed shoots in ten countries and has organized a number of exhibits around the world. Global Lives videos have been displayed as art installations in various museums, art spaces, and festivals, with footage of people's lives around the globe playing simultaneously, inviting audiences to "confer close attention onto other worlds and simultaneously reflect upon their own." The exhibits provide powerful immersive experiences for audiences, but what is equally instructive is how the videos themselves are created.

For its first three years of operation, the Global Lives Project had no paid staff.[14] Instead, hundreds of volunteers from around the world, who make up the Global Lives Collective, organized themselves to create the videos. These volunteers include filmmakers, photographers, programmers, engineers, architects, designers, students, and scholars. Collectively they have donated thousands of hours to bring this project into being. Online volunteers have subtitled all 240 hours of footage and translated them into English and other languages.

Today Global Lives is a 501(c)(3) nonprofit organization with a shared office and only one full-time staff member, but it has a huge network of contributors creating an amazing archive of human life experiences globally. With the motto "Step out of your world" and a mission "to collaboratively build a video library of human life experience that reshapes how we as both producers and viewers conceive of cultures, nations and people outside of our own communities,"[15] the project continues to attract more and more eager contributors.

From the Margins to the Mainstream

The range of ways in which individuals like Eri, Paul, David, and many others are creating value, developing new solutions, and providing new kinds of resources is breathtaking. These efforts are touching every domain of our lives. Take education as one example. Content that was once the purview only of credentialed teachers, accessible only in classrooms, and locked up in expensive textbooks is becoming accessible to everyone around the globe. It is available in free online encyclopedias like Wikipedia, in free courseware like MIT's OpenCourseWare, and on platforms such as Academic Earth, which offers free online video lectures from such top-notch universities as University of California, Berkeley; Harvard; and Stanford.

In addition, new tools and technologies are turning the whole world into a classroom, making learning possible anytime and anywhere. Think of a simple app on your iPhone such as Yelp Monocle.[16] When you point the phone at a particular location, it displays "points of interest" in that location, such as restaurants, stores, and museums. But this is just the beginning. What if, instead of restaurant and store information, we could access historical, artistic, demographic, environmental, architectural, and other kinds of information embedded in the real world? This is exactly what a project from the University of Southern California (USC) and the University of California, Los Angeles (UCLA) called HyperCities is doing; it is layering historical information on the actual city terrain. As you walk around with your cell phone, you can point to a site and see what it looked like a century ago, who lived there, what the environment was like. Not interested in architecture? Passionate about botany and landscaping instead? The Smithsonian's free iPhone and iPad app, Leafsnap, responds when you take a photo of a tree leaf by instantly searching a growing library of leaf images amassed by the Smithsonian Institution. In seconds it displays a likely species name along with high-resolution photographs of and information on the tree's flowers, fruit, seeds, and bark. We are turning each pixel of our geography into a live textbook, a live encyclopedia.

Developments such as these, which I'll discuss more fully in the following chapters, are being replicated all around the world in many areas from space research to manufacturing, from banking to the arts. These initiatives may appear to be founded on a combination of passion, naïveté, and blatant disregard of the "real world," so it is easy to dismiss them as marginal, only for the tech-savvy or the rebellious ones. But I invite you to look at this emerging world through the eyes of an immigrant, the eyes through which I look at the world.

I came to the United States as an eighteen-year-old, young enough not to have been fully embedded in the social institutions and language of the adult life of work, family obligations, and worries of my home country but old enough to have devoured its history, literature, and thinking. Being an immigrant, I got used to feeling at home and yet slightly estranged in many places. Over the years, I have experienced my foreignness as both a blessing and a curse— a curse when no matter how hard I try, traces of my accent come through in a conversation. No introduction of mine ever skips the question, "So, where are you originally from?" I've come to appreciate my otherness only later in life, when I realized that it is precisely this otherness that allows me to question the conventional wisdom, "the way things have to be," and "the right way to do things." I bristle when I hear from "experts" that teenage rebellion is a normal part of adolescent development. Normal where? Maybe in the West, but not in many other parts of the world where young people do not have the luxury of an extended childhood or a desire to live in nuclear families. I laugh at scientific studies showing that girls are not as good at math as boys are. I never heard this growing up in the Soviet Union, with a sister who was a math whiz and surrounded by girls who were outperforming boys in math in high school.

After college, while I was working in Europe for a refugee agency, a friend said to me, "You are like Pippi Longstocking. She always comes back from some faraway land and tells everyone how people there live differently." I don't think she meant the comment as a compliment, and I certainly viewed my foreignness more as something of a curse at the time. But in my work as a futurist, now directing the Institute for the Future in Palo Alto, California, I have come to view my immigrant history as a blessing. After all, we are all immigrants to the future; none of us is a native in that land. Margaret Mead famously wrote about the profound changes wrought by the Second World War, "All of us who grew up before the war are immigrants in time, immigrants from an earlier world, living in an age essentially different from anything we knew before."[17] Today we are again in the early stages of defining a new age. The very underpinnings of our society and institutions—from how we work to how we create value, govern, trade, learn, and innovate—are being profoundly reshaped by amplified individuals. We are indeed all migrating to a new land and should be looking at the new landscape emerging before us like immigrants: ready to learn a new language, a new way of doing things, anticipating new beginnings with a sense of excitement, if also with a bit of understandable trepidation.

This book is about the new territory we are migrating to, the landscape of which is only beginning to emerge. In *The Second Curve: Managing the Velocity of Change,* the futurist and former president of the Institute for the Future, Ian Morrison, argues that any period of big technological transformation is characterized by two curves.[18] The first is the incumbent curve: the way things have been done, the way we've organized before, often quite successfully. This curve may still show a reasonable pace of growth, and sometimes a lot of money can be made along this curve. Looking long term, however, this way of doing things is on the decline. Today this incumbent curve is the curve of institutional production, a model that has been dominant throughout the past century in which most value creation and resources were concentrated and flowed through large hierarchical institutions: banks, corporations, large universities. The second curve is the nascent one, and it is the curve of socialstructing, the new way of organizing our activities. Many socialstructed efforts have not yet achieved scale, and the activities on this second curve may seem to exist on the margins. We can see only signals of this emerging curve today, and many of the signals may appear strange and disorienting; they simply don't fit into the way we have always done things. Yet we ignore these signals from the new land at our peril. They are beacons of the things to come, a land of exciting opportunity, open to us all.

My core contention in this book is that the innovations rapidly emerging through socialstructing are not merely fringe developments but are the early manifestations of a new economy that will increasingly replace the institutional production we have come to rely on in so many areas of our lives. A number of industries are already being profoundly disrupted by the rise of socialstructing, such as publishing and the music business. Over time this emerging socialstructed economy will likely become mainstream, but that might be a long-term process. I believe we can all benefit right now, though, by learning about the ways the new economy is rapidly evolving and by taking part in it.

A socialstructed economy may seem foreign to many now, but there is no reason for anyone to feel like a stranger in it. There is a place for everyone. Participation requires no special knowledge of technology. The tools for connecting have become so readily accessible, cheap or free, and so easy to use that anyone can learn to use them after brief immersion. We can find health and other kinds of traditionally expensive professional advice at low or no cost, find new avenues for creative expression and social connection, and engage in more meaningful work. But even more fundamentally, we can rekindle our basic human drive to be part of something larger than ourselves, something that isn't primarily about profit-driven productivity, and can begin to restore the value of personal connections, and the sharing of our time, talents, and resources, to a central and deeply satisfying place in our lives.

The institutional, corporate structure of our economy and the stripping out of the social and the distinctive human touch in production are relatively recent phenomena. We are well adapted to the more social, participatory way of doing things that is at the heart of socialstructing, despite how novel and daunting it may seem. This is one reason I am confident that current developments will go mainstream. As I explore in the next chapter, we have now achieved something of a perfect storm of technologies: we have built a deep technology infrastructure for mass participation and collaboration, at the same time robotics and automation technologies are taking humans out of most rote tasks, not only in manufacturing but also in the service economy, making more and more of the traditional jobs we've relied on obsolete. Now is the right time for all of us to understand the potential of the new socialstructed world emerging and to begin participating in it.

Social Technologies, Social Economy

Recently I have been feeling like a hypocrite. On the one hand, I am a great admirer of amplified individuals like Eri Gentry, Paul Radu, and David Evan Harris who are bypassing traditional institutions to create value for so many communities. On the other hand, when my college-age son and his friends tell me that they really don't see why they need to go to college and sit through boring lectures rather than just read the same material online at their leisure, I find myself urging them to stay in college (an institution), find one or two amazing professors, make friends for life, and get a degree because without one it is so hard to get a job.

My ambivalence is not unique. As I mentioned in the previous chapter, we are living simultaneously in two worlds, one in which almost everything is still done through formal institutions, whether corporations, large R&D labs, banks, universities, or governments, and another in which people are joining up to create something new outside of traditional boundaries, in the process displacing these decades-old institutions. It is a period in which many sectors, from music to publishing to education, are witnessing the demise of the institutions that had come to dominate their industries' landscapes. Many people involved in these sectors are feeling disruptions firsthand. Their career trajectories no longer look promising, and the skill requirements and expectations of compensation for their efforts are changing.

We should have no doubt about the power of the forces at work. Just consider the dramatic disruptions already in full swing in the media business and the music industry. In its bleak "State of the News Media 2011" report, the Pew Project on Excellence in Journalism points out that 20 percent of the journalists working for American newspapers in 2001 were gone by the end of 2009, and by the end of 2011 that number had increased to 30 percent.[1] Meanwhile, both individual and group blogs as well as citizen journalism sites are proliferating. Sites such as Newswire21.org filter and shape stories submitted by citizen reporters. Similarly, the Public Insight Network (PIN), an initiative of American Public Media, turns citizens into experts to share their knowledge and observations. Professional journalists take that information, distill it, and pass it on to reporters and editors. Citizens also tell PIN about stories the media should be covering, stories that matter to them and are not necessarily known to professional reporters. In one of the boldest experiments in the social production of news, AOL's Patch, a network of hyperlocal news sites, is recruiting thousands of bloggers to create local content.[2]

The situation appears paradoxical: we have fewer professional, paid reporters and fewer large newspapers, yet more people are writing and reporting news, there is more local coverage, and we have many more channels through which to access news. For decades, local and regional newspapers depended on large global wire services (many of which are cutting staff) for access to national and international news. These news aggregators were central points for the collection and distribution of news. Because they served so many markets, they had the resources to fund a network of reporters around the world covering major news events and distributing their stories to thousands of newspapers worldwide. However, these outfits didn't cover many local stories, and the range of their coverage was also limited. The model is clearly under strain as groups ranging from Newswire21.org to PIN to the OCCRP are reinventing news services by distributing the job of news gathering and reporting to larger networks, sometimes turning ordinary citizens into reporters, in some cases aided by professional journalists. They are doing this at low cost and are able to cover a much greater range of stories while giving voice and access to local stories that are usually ignored by syndicated media. The net result is a larger network of people involved in the production and distribution of news.

A similar disruption has been taking place in the music business. In 2009, recorded music revenues in the United States and the European Union declined to 42 percent of their high-water mark in 2000, representing a net loss of $20.2 billion.[3] But data collected for the U.K. music industry shows that while music labels have earned less, artists themselves saw a huge increase in revenues.[4] Swedish researchers came up with similar calculations for the Swedish music industry.[5] So as revenues are moving out of institutional music production and distribution, more musicians are making money from their music than at any other time in history. Technology has made it possible for almost any artist to get heard and reach audiences, with no company or intermediary making editorial or managerial decisions.[6]

These disruptions in the media world are just the beginning of a transformation in fields as diverse as health, education, and banking. To understand why this is happening, why the shift is irreversible, and what it means for the long term, we need to understand the nature of the technology infrastructure we have been building globally for the past forty years.

John Culkin summed up his colleague Marshall McLuhan's perspective on technologies as follows, "we shape our tools, and thereafter they shape us."[7] We've put in place a new technology infrastructure, and now this technology is reshaping the landscape of our lives. Like the invention of the steam engine, which ushered in the Industrial Revolution, the architecture of the Internet, with its unique distributed communication nodes, is revolutionizing our social and economic landscapes, reshaping how we live, produce, trade, and innovate.

Distributed Communications, Distributed Value Creation

In the 1960s, Paul Baran, one of the founders of the Institute for the Future, worked at the RAND Corporation, a large nonprofit think tank. The 1950s and 1960s witnessed the height of the Cold War, with nuclear confrontation between the United States and the Soviet Union seemingly imminent. The two countries were accumulating nuclear arsenals, and each was engaged in planning for nuclear attack scenarios and their aftermath. One of the critical needs for maintaining a functioning society in the face of such attacks was to preserve a vital communications infrastructure for postattack coordination.

In any kind of serious confrontation, centralized switching communications facilities (including critical physical transportation hubs) are likely targets of attack, and with their destruction the whole system would be rendered unusable. To make the system more resilient, Baran proposed moving from a centralized communications infrastructure, where all data flowed through central switches, to a highly distributed system in which data was broken into small bits (packets) that would move through distributed relay nodes in an ad hoc and emergent manner. Baran and others envisioned a network of unmanned nodes that would act as switches, routing information to its final destination. The simple diagram below illustrates his vision.

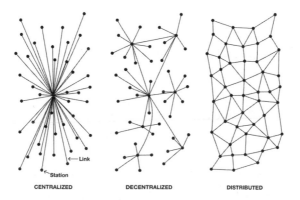

CENTRALIZED   DECENTRALIZED   DISTRIBUTED

The nodes would use a scheme Baran called "hot-potato routing,"[8] which Donald Davies, a scientist working independently at the same time at the National Physical Laboratory in the United Kingdom, called "packet switching."[9] When a node receives a packet, it stores it, determines the best route to its destination, and sends it to the next node on that path. To make this work, large data chunks are broken up into micro-size ones and then reassembled at the point of destination. Whenever a node is damaged, there are other nodes that can be activated to pick up the load, creating multiple routes. As a result, the whole system is much harder to bring down. The whole is self-healing, emergent, and highly resilient. Most importantly, the distributed system, unlike the centralized one, does not need any centralized management.

This model became the foundation of what we have come to know as the Internet: a decentralized, highly distributed communications infrastructure that has become intricately woven into every aspect of our lives. For the past forty years, we've been putting this technology infrastructure in place. Now, just as McLuhan foresaw, this foundational technology infrastructure is reshaping our lives. We are quickly finding out that when we go from a centralized communications infrastructure to a distributed one, when we connect everything and everyone, the result is not just to make things faster, better, and bigger. The social system itself acquires a fundamentally different quality: it becomes more diversified, more emergent, and often unpredictable.

The centralized nodes in Baran's diagram are equivalent to our institutions: corporations, universities, banks, centralized governments, and large philanthropies. They have been, for better and worse, central nodes through which most resources flowed—money, people, ideas, technologies. They have been core mechanisms for the production and creation of measurable value. Our distributed technology infrastructure, however, is increasingly de-gridding not only our communications but also our social and economic landscapes, with value flowing not through centralized nodes but through many more and much smaller nodes: us, individuals. This is the essence of the process I call socialstructing. It is a new form of value creation that involves microcontributions from large networks of people utilizing social tools and technologies to create a new kind of wealth. Socialstructing at social and economic levels is mirroring the transformation in our fundamental technology infrastructure, bringing with it the large-scale de-institutionalization of production and value creation. In this era, amplified individuals like Eri Gentry, David Evan Harris, and thousands of others are becoming micro-institutions—nodes in a distributed network who can assemble the needed resources and networks to accomplish things that previously no one or only large institutions could do. If the incumbent curve involves institutional production, the emergent curve involves socialstructed creation.

Elements of Socialstructing

Shaped by technologies we are only beginning to deploy, the very underpinnings of our society and institutions—from how we work to how we create value, govern, trade, learn, and innovate—are being reshaped. All the systems built on top of the distributed technology infrastructure—governance, education, manufacturing—are undergoing this transformation. By looking at what people like David Evan Harris, Paul Radu, and Eri Gentry are doing, we can begin to understand some of the key elements of socialstructed creation, which we should all become fluent in.

Microcontributions

Similar to small packets of data that flow through the distributed communications infrastructure, small bits of work—microcontributions—coming from many people, mostly volunteers, are at the core of socialstructing. Such microcontributions may take different forms: a hundred people coming together for a hackathon to create new apps in bursts of inspired activity, or people simply sharing some of their health data, which takes hardly any time at all. Facebook, Twitter, Google, Flickr, and many other stalwarts of today's digital economy are enablers and beneficiaries of such microcontributions. They couldn't exist without our content, our unpaid, albeit fun, labor. It is we who create Facebook profiles and post to them, we who share our thoughts on Twitter, we who upload our pictures to Flickr, we who put our medical data on PatientsLikeMe. Without us making these daily microcontributions, none of these platforms could exist. This is the kind of work we will increasingly be called upon to do. And because much of this participation has more in common with playing a game than carrying a briefcase to the office, it is beginning to redefine the very meaning of work.

Is helping to classify galaxies on the online platform Galaxy Zoo work or play? Are people involved in Foldit, a game in which they are individually solving puzzles but collectively uncovering the mechanisms of protein folding, doing serious research or just playing? Are people contributing to these platforms volunteers, co-creators, producers, or all of the above? One thing is certain: they are not employees. They are social producers engaging in a new type of value creation. The work these people are doing is often not reflected in productivity numbers or GDP measurements. Yet they are producing great value, social and economic, and their activities are critical to solving many of the smallest and largest problems facing our society today.

Nonmonetary Rewards

While people are most often making these microcontributions free of charge, they do receive payment in the form of fun, peer recognition, and a sense of belonging. Clearly people are motivated by many things other than money, and socialstructing capitalizes on these incentives. Participation in socialstructed ventures is driven at heart by intrinsic rather than monetary motivations—the motivation to belong, to be a part of something meaningful, to have fun, or, as described by the game researcher Jane McGonigal, to "achieve an epic win."[10] There is now a wealth of literature on what brings people pleasure and why people do things for free—and why they often perform better when they do things for free than when they are paid. Such data is coming from experts in many disciplines—from psychologists such as Daniel Pink, behavioral economists like Dan Ariely, and game researchers such as Jane McGonigal.

McGonigal calculates that collectively around the globe we spend three billion hours a week playing online games. Why do we spend so much time this way? She writes, "Games make us happy because they are hard work that we choose for ourselves, and it turns out that almost nothing makes us happier than good, hard work that we choose for ourselves."[11] As she points out, when we play games, we are working at the "edge of our abilities." If the task is too easy, it's boring; if it's too hard, it's demotivating. Gamers thrive by continuously upping the level at which they are playing, trying, failing, mastering, and moving to the next level.

This is why we've increasingly seen the "gamification" of the Web—using game mechanics and overlaying games on Web platforms in order to engage people to do serious work but in a way that does not look or feel like work, such as sharing ideas, solving problems, and engaging customers. Some of these platforms are enriching idea pools and the innovation landscape as they bring many people with diverse backgrounds and points of view into the conversation. For example, Foresight Engine, a game-like platform for collective foresight, developed by the Institute for the Future, ran a twenty-four-hour online idea-generating game for the Myelin Repair Foundation, which focused on developing drug therapies for multiple sclerosis patients. More than four hundred players—including corporate executives, teachers, engineers, students, and patients across five continents, as well as academic, government, and industry scientists—joined in generating more than three thousand ideas. They contributed, collaborated, and built on each other's ideas, creating value and receiving intrinsic rewards for their contributions.

Technology-Enabled Sociality

Clearly social media platforms and tools are critical to the success of many socialstructing efforts. They are important not only for communicating and transmitting data and information but also for establishing social connections in the group. Paul Radu and his colleagues use online forums and social media tools daily to coordinate activities, engage in conversations, and plan strategies. The same is true for Global Lives and BioCurious. It is fair to say that if the technologies we've developed weren't so centrally social in nature, these novel forms of collaboration wouldn't be flourishing. For Greg Biggers and his colleagues, the whole point of Genomera was to create social connections in the process of conducting clinical trials. Such social connectivity and community building are at the very core of socialstructing.

In the past we've been advised to leave the personal and social at the door when we go to work. But the new work is all about the social and personal. It draws on the power of personal connections and the diversity of personal tastes, talents, and quirks. This sociality isn't about typical socializing, though sometimes that is certainly a strong draw; it does not necessarily involve face-to-face socializing or long-term engagement, although these are often motivations or indirect results of such efforts. In many socialstructed efforts, people become connected and gain knowledge of each other by accessing each other's digital trails and identities, finding similarities online, checking out online reputations, and collaborating online on common projects. Our technology infrastructure, in fact, enables a new type of technology-driven social connectivity—connectivity that sometimes, but not necessarily, facilitates deeper social relations. More often, such connectivity enables ad hoc and temporary connections for the purpose of filling a particular need or carrying out a specific project.

Community Organizers, Not Managers

Myriad management books have been written advising us how to motivate people and organize them for optimal performance, using clearly defined hierarchies and clear boundaries between responsibilites. Yet none of the people I profile in this book as pioneers of socialstructing operates by these rules or has been schooled in them. In fact, most of them have chosen their paths precisely because they couldn't see themselves fitting into larger formal organizations. Paul Radu spent years in the punk rock music scene; David Evan Harris honed many of his skills in political organizing, including as a volunteer for Greenpeace; Eri Gentry never wanted to work in a large organization. What the pioneers of socialstructing are doing looks less like management and more like community organizing. Yes, good old-fashioned community organizing, but with a new set of tools and motivations. And their efforts are more akin to social movements than to managed organizations. Much of the motivation for building and contributing to socialstructs comes from a sense of urgency and greater purpose. This drive has often grown out of a particular vulnerability or personal experience of founders, making them into powerful advocates for their causes. Alex Carmichael, a cofounder of the community health site CureTogether, for example, suffered from a painful condition her doctors could not diagnose. Her insight—if I have this condition, there must be thousands of others who are suffering like I am and are probably hungry for information—ultimately led her to create CureTogether. She turned this vulnerability into something that thousands of others can identify with.

The Internet offers the unique opportunity for those whose voices have been underrepresented or unheard—people who have suffered alone, been embarrassed alone, or felt like they are the only ones facing a particular challenge—to come together and coalesce into communities whose voices are strong and who have impact. This is a powerful force that many leading social producers are tapping into.

Large Network Participation

Much has been written about collective intelligence emerging from the collaboration of large groups of people. In his book *The Wisdom of Crowds,* James Surowiecki cites a number of academic studies documenting the fact that for many problems, large groups of nonexperts are capable of coming up with wiser solutions than small groups of experts.[12] Bernardo Huberman of the Hewlett-Packard Social Computing Lab has shown that culling the wisdom of crowds is an effective way to predict the failure or success of new product introductions, new movie releases, as well as company stock positions.[13] Many things can influence the wisdom of crowds: the diversity of the participants, commonly held biases, the tightness of connections among members of the group, and so forth. Yet on many tasks it is clear that, when appropriately harnessed, large networks of people can perform better than a few experts.[14] One of the reasons for the superior performance of large networks is the sheer diversity of knowledge, expertise, and viewpoints they bring together. Another reason is that networks are often able to amplify the efforts of experts. For example, in a recent Science Hack Day—a gathering of scientists, programmers, designers, and artists organized by another amplified individual, my colleague Ariel Waldman—a nuclear scientist brought the idea of converting data from particle accelerators into music, but he didn't have the software or design expertise to do this himself. At Science Hack Day, he found a team of volunteers that included designers, programmers, and writers who helped him complete the project.

So impressive is the power of these socialstructed initiatives that many existing organizations are, not surprisingly, trying to tap into the vast potential of socialstructing to reinvent themselves or extend their capabilities. They are building social production platforms for a variety of purposes: to expand the internal ideas pipeline, generate customer and employee engagement, or reach new markets and audiences. They are often using gaming tools to create these social production factories. One example is OpenIDEO.com, created by IDEO, a well-known design firm, which asks people to post solutions to challenges, such as how to improve maternal health using mobile technologies. Community members can contribute in a variety of ways, from providing inspirational observations and photos to designing business models and snippets of code. People participating in OpenIDEO can provide feedback every step of the way, from framing the challenge to prototyping and encouraging the conversation.

Or consider the Lost Ladybug Project, created by entomologists at Cornell University. This project asks participants to find ladybugs in their area, photograph them, and upload the images to the project's website. Hunting ladybugs and taking pictures of them is fun for the participants, but they are also helping scientists understand changes in the distribution of the ladybug population in the United States, where over the past twenty years several native ladybug species, once very common, have become extremely rare while others have greatly increased both their numbers and range.

There is a host of other such examples, and the list is growing. Taken together these efforts represent a new way for us to create, work, and collaborate.

Scale Disrupted

Come to a workshop at the Institute for the Future and you will surely see the drive for scale in action. In many of our workshops we engage participants in an exercise we call Foresight to Insight to Action. The workshop starts with Institute staff presenting forecasts: visions or scenarios of the future that focus on disruptive shifts in technology, society, economics, or other domains. We then engage the participants in thinking about potential implications of the forecast for their organization and what actions they need to take to get to a desirable future. At the beginning of the exercise I always encourage people to think expansively and not to filter out ideas. During the early stages of brainstorming, quantity is more important than quality. The exercise itself should be fun, and the goal is to free the mind to explore a wide range of possibilities. As the workshop progresses we start to sort through these ideas to see if there is a fit with the organization's goals, capabilities, and long-term strategy. At that point, most of our participants, particularly from large corporations, bring a familiar filter, a kind of mantra, to the process: *How big is the opportunity?* For most companies, if the opportunity is not at least half a billion dollars in sales, the idea is simply not worth pursuing.

They are not to blame for focusing on scale. In fact, in pursuing scale, organizational managers are fulfilling their duty. After all, scale is exactly what their organizations were created for. Their purpose, which drives all of the management goals, is the achievement of maximum scale at minimum cost in order to increase profits. This is the fundamental rationale for large organizations, as the Nobel Prize–winning economist Ronald Coase pointed out in his seminal 1937 paper "The Nature of the Firm."[15]

Coase posed the question, *Why do we need corporations? Why not just produce and trade as individual agents?* His explanation was that large corporations (and organizations in general) allow us to minimize transaction costs, the costs of planning and coordinating production activities that involve many people and resources distributed across locations. In this sense, large organizations can be seen as a kind of technology for scaling up activities while minimizing the costs of doing so.

Before the invention of large corporations people were not sitting around doing nothing. They were of course producing all kinds of goods and services, but their activities were limited in scale. They produced relatively small quantities and sold or traded primarily with others in close geographic proximity—neighbors, family, or tribe. It was during the early mercantile era, in the seventeenth century, that "chartered companies" such as the Dutch East India Company first appeared, allowing producers to reach larger markets and achieve greater profits. They hired more people, invested more capital, built larger production facilities, invested in advertising, and created organizations and management structures for coordinating increasingly complex transactions.

We almost cannot conceive of a world without hierarchical organizational charts, mission statements, departments, and clear sets of corporate rules and incentives. In his book *Life Inc.* Douglas Rushkoff, a writer and media expert, points out that corporatism, or the corporate way of thinking, has permeated our culture, language, philanthropic organizations, schools, and media.[16] Yet if we consider the totality of human history and our experience of creating, producing, and trading, for most of that time we have organized these activities outside of large institutional, particularly corporate boundaries. It was not until the twentieth century that large corporate institutions became the dominant structure for economic activities.

We can think of the twentieth century, with its emphasis on productivity, scale, and scientific management, as the era in which we conquered scale. Take just one example. Between October 1, 1908, and September 30, 1909, the first full year of production of the Model T, Ford produced 14,161 cars; at its height in 1923, yearly production of the Model T reached 2,055,299.[17] By 2008, Ford was producing over five million automobiles with about 200,000 employees. That's about 20,000 cars per employee—more than the total company production in 1909![18]

Scale, usually measured by market size, is the key filter we have come to rely on in judging the prospects for any given venture. It is the dominant metric used by banks and venture capitalists in deciding whether to fund companies, and we've increasingly applied it to our government and social undertakings as well. Just read President Obama's educational policy and you will see the emphasis on investments in innovations that can be "scaled up" to reach thousands of schools and millions of students.[19] The message is that something that works in only one or a few schools is not worth investing in. Large philanthropic organizations similarly look for projects that can be scaled beyond one community and one endeavor. We have become so good at realizing the benefits of scale that in many areas production costs are so low that it makes economic sense to overproduce, even if that means destroying a substantial portion of unsold goods (and incurring additional environmental costs, of course). Clothing and food retailers, car and equipment manufacturers habitually overproduce and destroy unsold merchandise.

Today, however, the rules of scale are being disrupted. We can now achieve scale without the need for large organizations. Writer, professor, and new media expert Clay Shirky has made a compelling case that the connective technologies and communication tools we have at our disposal are radically driving down transaction costs, particularly the costs of coordinating, managing, and distributing goods and services.[20] In some cases those costs are close to zero. So the primary economic justification for many institutions no longer exists. A case in point: Boing Boing, a popular blog, employs fewer than ten people but reaches millions of readers weekly.[21] Twitter employs fewer than five hundred people and had 200 million accounts as of January 2011.[22]

The ability of individuals and groups to achieve scale cheaply is effectively disrupting whole areas of business and will continue to do so in more and more areas. Shirky has argued that there are two kinds of economic activities for which the new organizational forms are particularly well suited. First are activities that are too small for a larger organization to engage in because operating costs are simply too high for the payoffs. Economists would say that they fall beneath the Coasean floor. Health is a good example of this. Right now R&D dollars are directed to a narrow set of discoveries that can produce high monetary payoffs for pharmaceutical companies; however, we could find treatments for many conditions that would not have huge monetary payoffs but that would have a huge impact on individuals or society at large. This is where new initiatives like Genomera come in. Creating neighborhood bulletin boards and discussion forums, blogging about local topics, and running small community-based labs like BioCurious are all examples of things that are simply not economically viable for larger institutions but which have generated significant value for individuals and groups.

The other activities for which the new organizational forms have an advantage are those that lie above the Coasean ceiling, activities that are simply too big for one organization to undertake. Projects such as Galaxy Zoo and Foldit fall into this category. The Galaxy Zoo project put online more than a million high-resolution scans of the universe, accessible to anyone, and asked people to help classify galaxies by shape. Without human volunteers, it would have taken researchers years to process the photographs, but with thousands of participants helping out, the first classification project was finished in a few months. Foldit is a project that engages thousands of players in a video game with the purpose of collectively helping scientists to understand the mechanisms of protein folding, again something that would be hard for any one organization to do.

The Displacement of Automation

Socialstructing has arrived at an auspicious time. As we move into the new century, we are achieving the ultimate dream of generations of industrialists and efficiency theorists, from Henry Ford to management guru and father of the Total Quality Movement, W. Edwards Deming: industrial production at massive scales with very little human labor. This is the meaning of high productivity.

You can see this dream in action when you visit the FANUC robotics factory in rural Japan. The factory has no air-conditioning or heating, and sometimes as much as a month goes by without a single visit from a supervisor. At this so-called lights-out factory, robots are building other robots twenty-four hours a day, seven days a week, with hardly any human assistance, and they are doing so at rates no human labor force could achieve: about fifty robots per twenty-four-hour shift.[23] The FANUC factory is the epitome of what we've been striving for in institutional production: massive output with minimal costs for planning, coordination, and maintenance. What, after all, minimizes transaction costs more than a factory operated by robots that work nonstop? Compared to machines, humans are quite inefficient. We are idiosyncratic and often unpredictable, our output is not always uniform, we have moods, we get sick and have family problems, and we don't always get along. We humans are actually a deterrent to efficiency and scale. Talk to any farmer trying to run a large agribusiness operation and you will hear that human equipment operators—the people driving tractors, applying fertilizers, and clearing fields—are the major source of inconsistency and productivity losses on the farm. There are vast differences in the productivity of the same field based on who operates the machinery or labors in the field. This is why agricultural equipment manufacturers are working to automate as many parts of the farm operation as possible, from seeding and fertilization to irrigation and the clearing of crops.

For close to a century we have found ways to eliminate human idiosyncrasies from production—that is, to reduce transaction costs by shaping our work processes to increase uniformity, predictability, and consistency. We invented specialization, training each individual to do one task or focus on one area of knowledge and expertise to achieve the greatest mastery. We developed processes that can operate across populations, groups, often geographies. We focused on mass production, producing uniform products for large groups. These are not bad things, by the way. They have made automobiles affordable for virtually every American and have helped create a growing middle class worldwide. They have put more food on many tables. They have made education accessible to multitudes. They have also given us management tools to minimize tensions in the workplace and allow people to work side by side regardless of their beliefs, backgrounds, or personal characteristics. But the end result of the drive for uniformity, consistency, reliability, and scale is the advanced manufacturing facility of today, where you see hardly any humans.

In the next ten years the dream of taking humans almost entirely out of massively scaled production processes will become reality. Smart machines that are much better suited to producing at a massive scale will largely displace people from most tasks that are repetitive and mechanistic. This will be true not just for manual manufacturing labor but also for repetitive white-collar and service work in which grand scales can be achieved, such as rote language instruction and phone sales. Whether hammering nails on an assembly line or answering the same question over and over again, humans simply do not have a competitive advantage over machines in performing repetitive tasks.

Not surprisingly, we are already beginning to see smart machines at work in many domains. South Korea has placed robots in classrooms to assist with language learning. The plan is to have 8,400 robots in schools by 2013.[24] The MIT-Manus robotic system helps with stroke rehabilitation; it can help a patient move her arm 800 to 1,000 times in a forty-five-minute session, compared with 60 to 80 times for a physical therapist.[25] And software is replacing armies of lawyers in tasks requiring the search and analysis of legal documents. Such software can even extract relevant concepts and deduce patterns of behavior from data.[26]

This drive to automation is pushing masses of people out of jobs. David Autor, an MIT economist who studies American labor trends, concluded in a 2010 study that there has been a dramatic decline in mid-skill white-collar clerical, administrative, and sales occupations and mid-skill blue-collar production, craft, and operative occupations.[27] This shift is likely irreversible, which is why we are increasingly going to be called on to capitalize on our unique human skills to engage in the new types of production that socialstructing is facilitating. Those unique human skills that differentiate us, at least for now, from smart machines include:

- *Sensemaking:* the ability to determine the deeper meaning or significance of what is being expressed

- *Social and emotional intelligence*: the ability to connect to others in a deep and direct way, to sense and stimulate reactions and desired interactions

- *Novel and adaptive thinking*: proficiency at coming up with solutions and responses beyond the rote or rule-based

- *Moral and ethical reasoning:* the ability to filter ideas through nuanced sets of values[28]

These are the skills we all should be honing as the transition from institutional to socialstructed production unfolds. When everything that can be decoded, standardized, and programmed can be done better by machines, it is important that instead of competing with machines we hone what we are really good at: the emotional, idiosyncratic, and, yes, social. We've already seen these skills in action in Eri Gentry's creation of BioCurious, Paul Radu's spearheading of the Organized Crime and Corruption Reporting Project, and David Evan Harris' launching of the Global Lives Project, and we'll see them at work in many more cases of ingenious projects in the rest of the book.

Back to Social

This brings me back to my mother and how she was able to rely on social relationships to get so many of the goods and services my family needed. In the absence of money, relationships were her avenues for access to resources. While many experts dismiss the kinds of informal economies my mother lived in as marginal, these are the economies humanity has supported for most of its history. In fact, this is how half of humankind lives today, as the eminent sociologist Teodor Shanin points out. Shanin has invented a field of study called peasantology to understand how people survive in informal economies. In many such economies relationships serve as virtually the only capital people rely on in the course of their daily lives. One of the consequences of the development of the market economy is the excising of relationships and everything that goes along with them—the social, the local, the familiar, and the personal—from our economic lives. It is not particularly efficient to spend time searching for and building the right relationships to fulfill our every need. In the drive for efficiency, modern economies have replaced many social and interpersonal interactions with highly institutionalized ones that revolve around a single form of exchange: money. Instead of taking care of our elderly, we hire others or pay institutions to take care of them; instead of getting advice from those close to us, we pay for counseling sessions with professionals. We pay career coaches, fitness trainers, travel advisors, financial planners—whole armies of professionals performing functions that were previously performed by social contract within one's social community or extended family. When you live in relative abundance and have money, you simply don't have to rely on social connections to meet your needs.

The professionalization and institutionalization of so much of our production has resulted in great economic growth. Institutional production creates the need for more products and more services. All those personal trainers and babysitters need equipment, cars to commute to work in, bank accounts and financial services. Not surprisingly, then, the institutional and money-based production economy brought growth and great efficiency to our economic life in the twentieth century. Not only did it create need for more products and services, but it also made their provision more efficient. Large institutions, from banks to corporations, aggregated resources across people and geographies, making the production, purchase, and delivery of products and services easy and efficient, if devoid of social context. Along the way we developed a host of management theories and practices that have become bibles to generations of working men and women.

But the need for institutional structures to create value and achieve scale is evaporating. Amplified by a new level of collective intelligence and tapping resources embedded in social connections with multitudes of others, we can now achieve the kind of scale and reach previously attainable only by large organizations. Instead of taking the personal and social out of our transactions, we are using our technology-enabled social connectivity to achieve scale in new ways. Though the disruptions under way in the institutional economy are painful, tapping into the promise of the emerging social economy will not only help us cope with the disruptions but will also enrich our lives.

Certainly the development of the socialstructed economy is going to take many years, and it will move faster in some areas than in others. The process is analogous to that of "punctuated equilibrium" in biological evolution, a concept proposed by Stephen Jay Gould and Niles Eldredge, two evolutionary biologists. They argued that new species are likely to originate at the edge of a population, where a small group can easily become separated geographically from the main body and undergo changes that can create a survival advantage over the dominant group. Then, in a dramatic "punctuation," the new species displaces the old.[30] We are in the early stages of such a punctuated equilibrium in our economy, with new species, new socialstructs, forming on the edges. Those that thrive will do so because they will be more agile, more resilient, and more powerful than our legacy institutions. They will be filling gaps left by such institutions and better satisfying our basic human desires for connection and meaning.

In the chapters that follow, I describe how this is already beginning to happen in finance, education, governance, science, and health, and how together today's innovations are likely to transform our society and our lives. But before we dive into these transformations, let's talk about money.

What about Money?

Magic is an identifiable sociological process by
which individual fantasies become social reality.
EDWARD CASTRONOVA, "ON MONEY AND MAGIC"[1]

Whenever I talk about socialstructing, the inevitable question is *Why are people doing this?* What the questioner means is *Why are people spending their time doing something for free? And if they spend more and more time this way, how will they support themselves? What will they live on?* Clearly we can't survive on happiness, social connections, and goodwill alone. Or can we?

Some people believe they can and are putting their beliefs into action. If you eat at a Karma Kitchen restaurant, at the end of the meal you get a bill for $0.00, along with a note that says, "Your meal was a gift from someone who came before you. To keep the chain of gifts alive, we invite you to pay it forward for those who dine after you." You can pay forward by donating money or by volunteering at the restaurant, preferably both. Everyone working at Karma Kitchen is a volunteer, and the restaurant bills itself as a "volunteer-driven experiment in generosity."[2] It is part of a long-lived and well-documented tradition of "gift economies," found in societies all around the world for millennia. Let's remember that the current money-based economic system is not a natural system, it is not somehow preordained, and it is not the only possible system. Money is a necessary element of only one type of economy—the market, commodity-based one. There are other ways of organizing our economic lives that do not involve money.

For example, in the early 1900s the anthropologist Bronislaw Malinowski studied the people of the Trobriand Islands in Melanesia and found that they lived in an economic system that revolves around reciprocal gift exchanges.[3] Trobriand Islanders are among thousands of inhabitants of the Massim archipelago off the eastern coast of New Guinea involved in what is known as Kula exchange. As a part of this exchange system, members travel by canoe from island to island on long expeditions, sometimes hundreds of miles, in order to exchange two key types of valuables: red shell-disc necklaces and white shell armbands. These are referred to as Kula gifts, and they are invested with a richness of meaning. Each gift has a name and a history, a personality, so to speak, with stories of its past and the times when it was possessed by famous people as well as adventures it has encountered while being traded. Necklaces are traded to the north, circling the ring of exchange in a clockwise direction, while white armbands are traded in the southern direction, or counterclockwise. If the opening gift was a shell armband, then the closing gift must be a necklace, and vice versa.

While he saw Kula expeditions as fundamentally nonutilitarian "in that they [the Kula valuables] are merely possessed for the sake of possession itself, and the ownership of them with the ensuing renown is the main source of their value,"[4] Malinowski also saw that the exchanges play a vital part in how the society functions. First, they are essential to establishing friendly relations among the inhabitants of the different islands, helping to maintain peace. Second, they provide the occasion for other types of trading, of yams, fish, pottery, and other commodities important for people's daily existence. And third, because the expeditions require a good deal of work and coordination—for example to build canoes—they also serve as a kind of technology for organizing the society and reinforcing the status and authority of its leaders. The hereditary chiefs own the most important shell valuables and assume the responsibility for organizing the ocean voyages, and this power structure helps maintain the social order.

One critical feature of gift economies such as Kula is that ownership often has a different meaning from that in a market economy. For the participants in Kula exchanges, Malinowski explained, "to possess is to give and here the natives differ from us notably. A man who owns a thing is naturally expected to share it, to distribute it, to be its trustee and dispenser. And the higher the rank the greater the obligation."[5] Chiefs are expected to be the greatest givers because among the Trobriand Islanders, "the main symptom of being powerful is to be wealthy, and of wealth is to be generous. . . . Generosity is the essence of goodness."[6] In gift economies ownership is not about permanent possession, it is about giving. And it is vital to the system that the gifts keep circulating. "It seems almost incredible at first," Malinowski writes, "but it is the fact, nevertheless, that no one ever keeps any of the Kula valuables for any length of time. Indeed, in the whole of the Trobriands there are perhaps only one or two specially fine armshells and shell necklaces permanently owned as heirlooms, and these are set apart as a special class, and are once and for all out of the Kula."[7]

Malinowski makes clear that this doesn't mean the Islanders are always satisfied with the transactions; there are sometimes squabbles, resentments, and even feuds. But most of the feuding is about who is more generous, as Islanders try to outdo each other in generosity.

Versions of gift economies can be found throughout human history, and they still exist in many places around the globe. Native Americans living in the Pacific Northwest practiced the potlatch ritual, in which leaders gave away large amounts of goods to their followers in order to strengthen group relations. Many Pacific Island societies prior to the nineteenth century were essentially gift economies, and some still are. On the island of Anuta, one of the Solomon Islands, inhabitants consider each other family. According to a tradition of

Aropa, which roughly translates as "compassion, love, and affection,"[8] all land and other resources, including food, are shared.

But we don't have to look to such older or faraway cultures to see gift economies in action. Eric S. Raymond, a hacker and open software advocate, writes that the "society of open-source hackers is in fact a gift culture. Within it, there is no serious shortage of the 'survival necessities'—disk space, network bandwidth, computing power. Software is freely shared. This abundance creates a situation in which the only available measure of competitive success is "reputation among one's peers."[9] One gains a reputation (social currency) in the open-source community by contributing code, making revisions, and adding to code others have developed.

Another contemporary example of a gift economy can be seen at the Burning Man gathering, a week-long annual event held in the Black Rock Desert in northern Nevada, which is partly an experiment in community living and partly an exercise in radical self-expression and self-reliance. Among the governing principles of the festival are gifting and decommodification.[10] Except for a few charities and fuel, sanitation, and coffee vendors, no cash transactions are permitted at the event. Instead of cash, participants (or "burners," as they are called) gift each other various goods and services—massage, yoga lessons, food, and any other items and skills they bring with them and are willing to give to others. The spirit of gifting and generosity is infectious, and many burners go out of their way to share and give away food they make.

We don't have to participate in the open-source software movement or go to Burning Man to experience gift economies. We already participate in them on a daily basis in many ways. We don't pay for love, for dinners at our parents' homes, for our children's affection. We don't think of these as commodities that can be traded for money, yet they bring enormous value and meaning into our lives—so much so that it's fair to say we wouldn't be able to survive without them.

Another alternative to money exchange that is alive and well today is bartering, which some economists consider a form of gift exchange. Barter exchanges are utilitarian, they involve goods and services that have obvious practical utility rather than being primarily symbols of social meaning. The values of items and services being traded are clearly articulated, and an exchange of estimated equal value is generally demanded.

The important point is not whether gift and barter exchanges are the same or different, but that we have alternatives to draw on to complement or to take the place of the money economy. The core distinction between money and nonmoney economies, whether gift or barter, is that in the latter, exchanges of goods and services are socially embedded—they serve social as well as practical needs and they are laden with social connectivity and meaning.

In a commodity economy, by contrast, the drive for efficiency results in social connections being minimized or taken out of the equation. When I buy an iPad, I have no idea who the people are in the long supply chain that went into making it. If I buy it online, I don't even make a connection with a salesperson. As the economist Duran Bell puts it, "The commodity economy requires the substitution of social relations with commodity relations. Complex relationships among people are replaced by complex relations among commodities and among people as commodities."[11] Instead of worrying about creating a bond during a transaction or ensuring reciprocity, we buy what we need independently of whether we know or like the person behind the transaction.

According to Bell, in a gift economy the most important technology is the "technology of social relations."[12] The relationships of a group with other groups, as well as intragroup relations, are critical to the well-being of the social unit in a gift economy. "To increase the benefits of trade, the decision makers in the gift economy attempt to make improvements in the technology of social relations, given the technology of production."[13] By contrast, Bell argues, the managers in a perfectly competitive enterprise aim to reduce unit costs by making improvements in the technology of production, rather than the technology of social relations.[14] In a gift economy, the leaders must direct their attention to improving the conditions for social exchanges and to encouraging more exchanges; this is how they gain status. They must be social designers. When Eri Gentry organizes BioCurious meet-ups—a form of a gift economy—she gives serious thought to the social technology of the events: the setting, the mix of participants, the process that will elicit the most interesting conversations. The meet-ups must be enjoyable, otherwise people won't keep coming. A manager in a typical money-based economy, by contrast, must worry primarily about the efficiency of output. If a worker is too slow and can be replaced by someone more productive, or by a machine, the manager would be remiss to not do so. Social considerations are secondary, if not wholly irrelevant.

From a market perspective, gift or barter economies are not particularly efficient. Finding the right people with the right resources to conduct exchanges with can be quite cumbersome. Worrying about social conditions and social design often goes against the drive for efficiency and productivity. What is efficient from the market perspective may not be efficient from the social perspective and vice versa. And, for the past few hundred years we have been perfecting a system for market efficiency—to achieve the most productive generation of products and services. Money and the various financial mechanisms we have developed in the process have been an important enabler and by-product of this system. Money is what brings efficiency into an economy concerned with large-scale production of goods and services. Money is also what substitutes for social connections in the process of conducting economic activities. But the new technologies are enabling us to bring social connections back into our economic transactions, making our economy more socially, if not more economically, efficient.

Beyond Money: New Forms of Exchange, New Kinds of Currency

In a dusty jar stashed deep in a cupboard in my kitchen lie old treasures picked up during travels around the world over almost forty years: Soviet *rubles* with portraits of Lenin looking proud, Italin *lire* (devalued faster than I was able to turn them into something else on the next trip), Argentine *australes* (a short-lived currency of the 1980s), and my most recent acquisition, *hryvnia,* a new currency of independent Ukraine. Occasionally I get the jar out. I think of it as a kind of scrapbook that brings back memories of places I've been to, stories I've heard, people I've met. The coins and notes are also reminders of fragility, of how quickly something valuable can turn into a plaything, as most of the once powerful currencies in my jar are nothing more than play money today. This doesn't really surprise me. When I was growing up, my grandfather often took out and counted a thick stack of official-looking papers, carefully wrapped in a towel. The papers—large, green, colorful—did not look anything like money and they had an ominous name, *obligatsii* (Russian for "obligations" or "guarantees"), otherwise called *tsennye bumagi,* or valuable papers. Soviet citizens were required to accept them as payment or partial payment for their work in lieu of cash during the lean years after World War II. In the 1960s and 1970s Grandpa regularly scoured local papers to see if any of the *obligatsii* had come due, that is, whether the government would convert any of the papers he had into *rubles,* actual money. Of course, none of his *obligatsii* would ever be converted into anything of value. Eventually most of the colorful papers were thrown away, their magical powers vanishing in a pile of trash.

So there is nothing magical about money, or, as the noted economist and games researcher Edward Castronova astutely observes in an essay titled "On Money and Magic," we are the ones who "imbue money with magic."[15] Castronova argues that in order to give money or any currency its magical power, a group needs to collectively agree on and believe that a particular thing—a piece of paper, an ounce of gold, or a Kula necklace—has value and that it can be exchanged for goods and services within the group. Throughout human history, in fact, we've imbued different things with such magical powers. From 9,000 to 6,000 B.C. humans primarily used cattle as money; with the advent of agriculture, plant products, such as grain, became the currency. As recently as the middle of the twentieth century, cowrie shells were still being used as money in some parts of Africa; in fact the cowrie is the most widely and longest circulating currency in human history. So money in its current paper form isn't a necessity, and its role is likely to diminish as digital money replaces it.[16]

It is precisely because we are the ones who imbue money with value, and because the creation and circulation of money requires a social contract—a social agreement of its value—that a group of any size can potentially create a currency. And people have been doing this for a while. The WIR (Wirtschaftsring-Genossenschaft) is one of the oldest independent complementary currency systems. Popular in Switzerland, it serves small and medium-size businesses. It was created in 1934 by two businessmen in reaction to currency shortages after the stock market crash of 1929, with the purpose of encouraging "participating members to put their buying power at each other's disposal and keep it circulating within their ranks, thereby providing members with additional sales volume."[17] The WIR bank has become a nonprofit serving the interests of its clients and remains fully operational even in times of general economic crisis.[18] In fact, the WIR may have contributed to the remarkable stability of the Swiss economy, as it dampens downturns in the business cycle.[19]

More recently, currencies have been created to fulfill special local needs. BerkShares are a local currency launched in the Berkshires region of Massachusetts in 2006. The BerkShares website lists over four hundred businesses in Berkshire County that accept the currency. As of 2011, over 2.7 million BerkShares have been circulated, issued through a network of thirteen branch offices from five participating banks. BerkShares have a fixed exchange rate with U.S. dollars (1 BerkShare = U.S.$0.95). However, Nick Kacher of the New Economics Institute has suggested pegging the BerkShare value to one gallon of maple syrup instead in order to insulate the region from the instability of the U.S. economy.[20] The oldest and largest local currency in the United States is the Ithaca HOUR created in 1991 in Ithaca, New York, by Paul Glover, an author and community activist, as a way to maintain a vibrant and self-reliant local economy. One Ithaca HOUR is valued at $10, and local residents can use the currency as payment for local services.

The Internet is making the creation of alternative currencies such as BerkShares and Ithaca HOURs easy because it powerfully facilitates the community building that enables groups to come together and set up currencies that are exchangeable within a group and increasingly between groups. As a result, such currencies are proliferating and taking on intriguing new virtual forms. In 1996, for example, Liu Jia, who came from mainland China to study at MIT, created an online community named MITBBS, which is a bullentin board for Chinese students and families to discuss issues associated with studying abroad.[21] The community is now widely recognized as an important resource for helping Chinese people living in the United States.[22] MITBBS has an estimated 300,000 registered users and covers over three hundred topic boards, ranging from news about China to job hunting, investment, health advice, soccer, and education. MITBBS has developed its own virtual currency, called MB, which stands for *bi,* the word for "coin" in Chinese. Within the confines of the community, MITBBS has created a thriving economy in which the MB facilitates content creation and exchanges of knowledge, services, and goods. Like money, the MB is an information resource that communicates how much each site member has "worked" or, more accurately, contributed to the MITBBS community.[23] Participants earn MBs in many ways, such as contributing a post on a board, being selected by a board administrator for an outstanding post, working as a board administrator, contributing business information to the site's Yellow Pages, or even winning one of the weekly MShow fashion competitions among members' avatars. There is no official means for exchanging MBs for real currencies, or vice versa. Instead the MB can be used for gifting to other users, betting on the site, or buying virtual items for decorating users' avatars.[24]

Another example of an online platform using virtual currency, but with a purpose very different from the MB, is the Nitro site created by Bunchball,[25] a gamification company that is using principles of gaming to drive customer engagement for communications and advertising purposes. Among its clients are Warner Bros., Comcast, Victoria's Secret PINK, and the USA Network. Bunchball's Nitro platform integrates game-like features into various companies' online sites and media channels, allowing visitors to earn points for different activities on the site. It awards users points for contributing to the site and lets them exchange the points they earn for access to content on the site, including movies, TV shows, and other media. The aim of the platform is to increase customer loyalty and engagement.[26]

One of Bunchball's first projects was Dunder Mifflin Infinity, a game based on the television show *The Office* that lets users "work" for the show's fictional corporation. The game has a virtual currency, Schrutebucks, which can be exchanged for virtual goods, such as items users can display on their virtual office desks. Casual users can play simple flash games to earn small numbers of Schrutebucks, while more hardcore fans can go for big earnings by uploading music videos they create themselves. The site became a big hit for NBC, the network that airs *The Office,* and has surpassed its original purpose of promoting the TV show to become a moneymaking project, garnering advertising from the likes of Visa and Toyota.

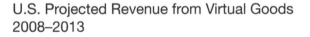

U.S. Projected Revenue from Virtual Goods
2008–2013

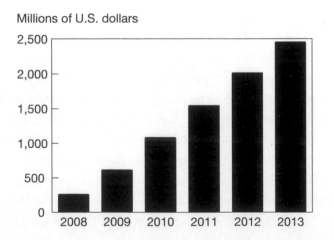

Millions of U.S. dollars

The growth of virtual currencies, and the revenue generated by the purchasing of virtual goods, is increasing at an astonishing rate, and the trend is expected to continue (as you can see in the table on page 50).

Whether virtual or physical, alternative currencies can play important roles in local and national economies. In the midst of the economic crisis in Greece, for example, many Greek cities have created their own currencies and are using them to facilitate bartering. The city of Volos, to cite one instance, has a widely popular Local Alternative Unit to pay for such goods and services as language classes, babysitting, computer support, and home-cooked meals and to receive discounts at some local businesses. As the *New York Times* reports, "Part alternative currency, part barter system, part open-air market, the Volos network has grown exponentially in the past year, from 50 to 400 members. It is one of several such groups cropping up around the country as Greeks squeezed by large wage cuts, tax increases and growing fears about whether they will continue to use the euro have looked for creative ways to cope with a radically changing economic landscape."[27]

Alternative currencies can be created by an individual, a community, a corporation, or a nonprofit organization; they can also be created by national, state, or local governments, or they can arise naturally as people begin to use a certain commodity as a currency, such as points obtained in an online game (Schrutebucks) or a community forum (MB). Key to the appeal of many alternative currencies is that they are created to facilitate social connections. They are also appealing to many communities because they take the control of currency away from the centralized government institutions and put it directly into the hands of smaller groups. This looming possibility of individuals and groups having the power to take control of curency scared the Chinese government so much that in 2007 it issued a directive to assert control over virtual currency markets. The directive read, "The People's Bank of China will strengthen management of the virtual currencies used in online games and will stay on the lookout for any assault by such virtual currencies on the real economic and financial order."[28]

This directive was in reaction to the growth of a virtual currency named the Q coin, traded by close to a billion Chinese Instant Messenger users. The Q coin was so popular that many Chinese online stores and gaming sites accepted it, and it could be exchanged in some physical stores for real goods. Secondary markets for trading in Q coins started to grow, all of this apparently threatening the Chinese government's ability to control its own financial markets and, consequently, its own economy.

The emergence of alternative currencies brings the power to manage our economic interactions into people's hands and away from the dictates of central banks and governments. Because the creation and successful circulation of currencies requires a social contract, as I mentioned earlier, groups designing virtual currency platforms are not only enabling the creation of currencies, they are also designing social norms that facilitate the earning and circulation of these currencies. In short, they are designing new types of social and economic interactions. The design elements they put into alternative currency platforms can encourage greed and hoarding, or gift-giving and generosity. Ithaca HOURs are designed to facilitate local spending; MBs are designed to encourage the sharing of knowledge; Q coins are designed to encourage greater use of IM. Each of the platforms facilitates certain types of interactions and rewards participants for certain types of behaviors. In the words of Castronova, designers of virtual platforms that enable people to accumulate alternative currencies are creators of the "new magic." They are designers of a new social reality who can craft new kinds of interactions just as they do in creating online games.[29] As the media theorist and author Douglas Rushkoff writes in his essay "Economics Is Not Natural Science," "The marketplace in which most commerce takes place today is not a pre-existing condition of the universe. It's not nature. It's a game, with very particular rules, set in motion by real people with real purposes."[30] And today the ability of groups to create new kinds of currencies is giving us the power to change the global economic game and to create new games.

But creating alternative currencies is only one way we are beginning to bring the social back into our economic relationships. We are also doing this by sharing goods and becoming patrons and lenders (bypassing banks and other financial institutions). In the process we are rediscovering just how generous we can be and how much satisfaction we can find in trading and sharing with one another.

Sharing and Bartering Platforms

Recently, after a major accident that totaled my car, I decided to go "carless." Visions of spending a Saturday at a dealership, being bombarded with complicated options, and haggling over prices made the idea quite appealing. At dinner with several friends who also happened to be our neighbors, I mentioned the agreement my husband and I made to share one car, walk more to work (luckily we live close to both of our offices), and use public transportation more when needed. It also meant that when my husband was away on his various weekend kayaking expeditions, I would simply not have a car. To my surprise, several of the neighbors offered to lend me their cars for use on such weekends. At the same time, I found out about Getaround, a peer-to-peer car-sharing and rental service that allows you to rent or borrow cars from your neighbors. You simply sign up, put in your zip code, and the map of everyone in your neighborhood who has signed up to rent his or her personal car appears with details on model, price, availability, and rental terms. A colleague of mine who uses the service told me that he has started renting from the same neighbor regularly and has gotten to know her well. Now every time he picks up the car, she leaves a batch of cookies for him on the front seat. Plus, he has had great conversations with her! My recent car renting experience at the airport was nothing like that. In a long line of tired and irritated customers, there was no pleasant neighborly chitchat and no one brought freshly baked cookies.

Platforms for sharing goods and resources of all of kinds are flourishing. Like the inhabitants of the Trobriand Islands described by Malinowski, people everywhere are beginning to see the value of goods not only in terms of possession but in terms of circulation: giving what we have to others and in the process increasing our social network and reputation in communities we are sharing with. New Internet platforms make this easy, allowing people to take an excess of many things (cars, space, domestic appliances, clothing) and put them to use by someone else, and in the process, promote new levels of social connectivity on a scale we haven't seen before. In her book *What's Mine Is Yours,* Rachel Botsman describes the emergence of this form of "collaborative consumption."[31] Sites such as Shareable and magazines like *Good* track thousands of platforms and profile ways that sharing, bartering, trading, renting, and swapping are enabling the same pleasures of ownership but with reduced personal cost and burden, and with lower environmental impact. There is now hardly a domain of life without a platform for people to share or swap.

Here is a brief list of some of these:

- CouchSurfing is a hybrid hospitality exchange and social networking website with a mission to "create inspiring experiences."[32] The service is particularly popular with young people who can't afford to pay for accommodations when they travel. It lists individuals around the globe who are willing to provide sleeping accommodations to travelers free of charge. As of December 2011, CouchSurfing had over 3.5 million users.[33]

- Neighborgoods facilitates the lending and borrowing of everyday items within a community. It not only helps to save money and resources but also connects neighbors in a meaningful way, ultimately creating stronger communities. People post items they are willing to share, thus making it easy to find needed items in your neighborhood.[34]

- Landshare is one of a growing network of yard-sharing programs around the world. Services connect people who have unused or underutilized plots of land with those who have the skills and desire to grow their own fruits and vegetables. Since its founding in 2009, Landshare has grown to over 65,000 members in the United Kingdom, Australia, and Canada.[35]

- RelayRides and other neighbor-to-neighbor car-sharing services act as the middleman between vehicle owners and people temporarily in need of a car. By renting out their underused vehicles to their neighbors, owners can make up to $7,000 a year, according to the website. Users can utilize the website to search through a database of thousands of privately owned cars to find the one closest to them. Renting a car can cost as little as $5 an hour.[36]

- 65hours is one of a number of time banks that communities have set up to allow their members to accumulate hours for various community activities—taking care of the elderly, babysitting, driving residents. These hours then can be exchanged for services within the community.[37]

- Bag Borrow or Steal is a site brought into the spotlight in the *Sex and the City* movie that offers designer handbag rentals. Rental is by the week or by the month, with the option to buy. Similar sites exist for clothing and accessories.[38]

- Real Milk is one of the cow- and goat-share programs that have grown out of the raw milk movement. In these programs farms offer people the chance to buy a "share" of a dairy animal, giving them direct access to a portion of the milk produced. Real Milk serves as a directory for cow- and goat-shares across the United States.[39]

At the Institute for the Future we've had our own very satisfying experience in resource sharing. A few years ago my colleagues and I realized that we have a lot of underoccupied open space on one of our floors. We use this space primarily for workshops and large meetings, but the rest of the time it is empty. With the recession in full swing, many people did not have jobs or offices to work in, so we decided to regularly open up the space to coworking. We sent out invitations on various social media sites for people to sign up to cowork in our space on a specified day. We provided Wi-Fi, coffee, tables, and chairs; if you wanted a place to work, you were welcome to sign up and come in and work with us. Two of our staff members acted as hosts and agreed to be at the coworking space during the day. As it turned out, many more of the staff wanted to participate; some moved their work from their permanent desks, others dropped in for periods of time. No wonder—the people who came in were quite interesting. Some were members of our extended community of researchers, scientists, entrepreneurs, and students. Others were people we'd never met before, including a graduate student working on her dissertation in sociology, a green energy consultant, two people working on a business plan for a new venture, and a venture capitalist. Ideas flowed, interesting conversations took place, connections were made. Everyone on staff agreed that it was great for us to be doing this. We turned a resource that was standing idle into something that could help others at virtually no cost to us. Plus we created a lot of goodwill and hopefully sparked some ideas for our staff and for our visitors and made some lasting connections.

We now hold open coworking days nearly every month. We also actively support meet-ups, hack days, and science bar days, various types of informal gatherings of people with similar interests (science, biology, coding, 3-D printing) who come together to share ideas, meet others, and do projects together. We often provide these communities with space and access to our facilities on weekends and in the evening. Our only requirement is that one of our staff members is sufficiently interested in the subject to want to act as a host and that the group leaves the space in the same shape they found it in. We have learned so much from these gatherings that we believe we couldn't do our work without them.

From Banks to Social Finance

In 2009 Robin Sloan, a strategist at Current TV, left his job and decided to pursue something he's been passionate about for a long time: writing. But rather than take a traditional publishing route, writing a book proposal and looking for funding from potential publishers, he turned to Kickstarter, a platform for artists, designers, musicians, and other creative types to get funding for their projects. Here is how he began his call for funding:

> Hello friends, Snarkmarket readers, Twitter pals, and internet gremlins!
>
> I'm writing a book: a detective story set halfway between San Francisco and the internet. And the more people who reserve a copy, the better each one will be![40]

Robin was asking for quite modest contributions: $1 would get you a PDF copy of his novel; for $3 you would get a PDF plus "behind the scenes updates"; for a whopping $39 contributors would get a "super occult value pack—four copies of the book to give one to a friend, donate one to the library, leave one in a coffee shop with a line of hexadecimal code scribbled across the title."[41] He was asking for a total of $3,500, but within a month he had raised $13,942 from 570 backers, including friends and family, readers of his blog, and his Twitter followers. Robin's story is an example of a quiet revolution in finance as lending and patronage break out of banks and traditional financial institutions into social networks.

A rapidly proliferating number of online platforms make it possible for people to raise money, to find borrowers and lenders, to aggregate their financial information, make smart financial decisions, and complete other transactions that previously only banks or venture capital firms were able to do. With the rising popularity of social financing peer-to-peer websites like Prosper, Lending Club, and Kickstarter, anyone with a computer and an Internet connection is a prospective lender, borrower, or patron.

Kickstarter is only one of a number of sites that enable micropatronage, people supporting projects of interest to them through donations, rather than loans or investments. Instead of earning profits, they get returns in the form of mementos and a feeling of a personal connection to a project or a person. As Perry Chen, one of the cofounders of Kickstarter, explains, the platform is "somewhere between commerce and patronage."[42] Since the early days of Kickstarter, a host of musicians, designers, artists, gamers, and scientists have used the platform to raise money for their projects. In fact in 2011, the amount of money raised on Kickstarter for art projects surpassed the funding given to artists by the National Endowment for the Arts.[43] With over 63,000 projects raising some $250 million as of the middle of 2012, Kickstarter has emerged in only a few years as a major platform for crowdfunding everything from a small music video project to a new venture.[44] In one of its largest drives to date close to 70,000 people donated a whopping total of $10 million to allow a team of entrepreneurs to produce the Pebble E-Paper smart watch, which communicates with the Android and iPhone and is loaded with apps that let you do everything from listen to music to read your emails on your watch.[45] That amount rivals what many entrepreneurs would be able to raise from venture funds.

The number of such micropatronage platforms is rapidly growing. They include Indiegogo, whose goal is to help people run campaigns to raise money for various causes; Sellaband, a music website that allows artists to raise money from their fans and community in order to record a professional album; and SciFund, a platform for raising money for science projects.

Membership in peer-to-peer lending groups is also climbing fast, and so is the money involved. Analysis by Ken Lemke, who runs the independent website lendstats.com, shows that total loan volume in peer-to-peer lending has gone through the roof.[46] Prosper, a San Francisco–based peer-to-peer lending platform, grew over 30 percent in 2011, to 1.19 million members who have facilitated over $280 million in loans.[47] Lending Club, another peer-to-peer lending platform, has more than doubled its volume of loans, top-ping $919 million. It issued almost $60 million in new loans in July 2012 alone.[48] Peer-to-peer borrowers usually get loans at lower rates than they would from banks or credit cards, and investors often get higher returns than they would from traditional bank products such as certificates of deposit. Returns on investment in some of the peer-to-peer lending institutions over the past three years average out to about 10 percent.[49] "Lending Club's CEO Renaud Laplanche says that if his company sustains its current growth rate, within seven years it will be bigger than Citibank, one of the largest banks in the United States."[50]

Social lending sites are not only providing funding but are making it easier for borrowers to reach their target audience, and as success stories proliferate, the already burgeoning popularity of these websites is likely to change the landscape of the money economy. In fact, micropatronage is on its way to socialstructing the way we finance everything from education to health.

Micropatronage of Education

ScholarMatch is the brainchild of the writer and social activist Dave Eggers. It is an online platform founded in 2010 where potential donors can meet graduating high school seniors who have been accepted to college but need assistance paying their tuition. Students write stories about themselves, their aspirations, accomplishments, and needs. Potential donors choose the student they want to support, and once they donate the money, they will be sent periodic updates about that student's progress throughout the academic year. Since its inception in 2010 until April 2012, sixty-four students have received a total of $130,000 in scholarship money. Most of these students are the first in their family to attend college.[51]

Structured Lending among Family and Friends

Never do business with family or friends, goes the saying. Well, platforms such as LendFriend are trying to prove the saying wrong.

The founders claim that many loans between friends and family end in disaster because there aren't clear expectations between the borrower and the lender. To remedy this, LendFriend promises to make such loans work better by adding documentation, legal standing, and a repayment process to these arrangements. Unlike Lending Club or Prosper, two peer-to-peer lending sites that arrange loans between strangers who lend money to one another anonymously, LendFriend facilitates a loan between two people who already know each other.[52]

Microloans for Health

Lend4Health enables borrowers to get interest-free microloans for biomedical treatment of children and adults with autism spectrum and related disorders, and it may expand to include other conditions for which people can seek loans in the future. Lend4Health hits the sweet spot for those who want to do good and help others. Lenders can check personal profiles of those needing money for medical treatment and even monitor their medical progress. In the United States, where medical bankruptcies are extremely common and the ranks of the uninsured have swelled, websites like Lend4Health, YouCaring.com, and Fundly provide a safe, low-risk alternative for people seeking loans or funding for medical treatment.

Microventure Funding

Venture capital has traditionally been a closed enterprise, allowing only a select few with large sums to make the go/no-go decisions about innovations. Not anymore. A number of microventure platforms are popping up, opening up the field to average people. Grow VC is one example. It is a new community fund for technology start-ups. For a subscription fee, members can get a micro-investment plan for as little as $20 per month. Micro-investments are aggregated and facilitated by Grow VC partners. Individuals can also make "work investments" in start-ups, investing their time and expertise in return for equity compensation. Grow VC profiles start-ups that are looking for investment—detailing the individual entrepreneurs, their history, and traction with investors so far. It is not only a place for people to invest but also a place to foster relationships between entrepreneurs and various experts who might be able to help them.

Personalized Loans for Entrepreneurs

Since 2005 Kiva has helped Internet users give microloans of $25 or more to business owners in impoverished countries.[53] The first project was launched in a Ugandan village, and now the San Francisco–based nonprofit has become a microlending powerhouse. With under a hundred employees the company has loaned a total of $333,992,925 as of July 2012 to groups and individuals in sixty-one countries.[54] In 2009 Kiva began domestic lending, partnering with Opportunity Fund in the Bay Area and other microlenders around the United States. It has helped people start small businesses and make necessary repairs to equipment in order to keep their businesses going. Donors on the site can choose specific projects and individuals to invest in and are provided regular updates on their projects. Many develop personal relationships with the people they lend money to, in addition to receiving repayment on the money they loaned.

All these platforms are imbuing money and calculations about money—who should get loans, what repayment terms should be—with social meaning. They are taking purely economic relations and enveloping them, in many cases complicating them, with social relations.

Socialstructing Wealth

Having to talk to your neighbor and maintain a good relationship with him in order to borrow his car is not efficient and can be very tricky. Yet getting to know him may help expand your social net-work and may come in handy in case of an emergency or when you require assistance. Sharing platforms and alternative currencies do not necessarily result in efficient production of more goods and ser-vices. They may actually complicate economic transactions, some-times slowing them down. But they also produce social value, and that value is not captured by traditional GDP data or other economic statistics. We don't measure the value of a lawnmower being loaned to a neighbor; this value registers in economic statistics only when the lawnmower is produced and purchased. The transactions facili-tated by social platforms are creating a different kind of value and a different kind of wealth, which is not necessarily measurable in monetary terms. This wealth is in part a matter of how we *feel* when we engage in these transactions. Socially embedded transactions in-crease our levels of connectedness and engagement with others. And this, according to Jonathan Haidt, a professor of psychology at the University of Virginia and the author of *The Happiness Hypothesis,* is one of the main contributors to happiness.

Haidt points out, "We are, in a way, like bees: our lives only make full sense as members of a larger hive, or as cells in a larger body. Yet in our modern way of living we've busted out of the hive and flown out on our own, each one of us free to live as we please. Most of us need to be part of a hive in some way, ideally a hive that has a clearly noble purpose."[55]

A great deal of research in neuroscience and happiness psychol-ogy supports Haidt's argument. Elizabeth Dunn, a professor of psy-chology, and her colleagues at the University of British Columbia showed that spending more of one's income on others predicted greater happiness.[56] Dunn's studies also show that participants who were randomly assigned to spend money on others experienced greater happiness than those assigned to spend money on them-selves. Her work and other studies suggest that beyond the point at which people have economic security, happiness doesn't scale with money, even very large amounts of money. We are more happy spending money on social experiences than on buying things. In parallel, behavioral economics is showing that money isn't as powerful a motivator for performance as once thought. Daniel Pink, a best-selling author of books on work, creativity, and motivation, shows that while monetary rewards work well to motivate us to do tasks that are mechanical or rote in nature, such as adding up columns of figures or turning the same screw the same way, they don't work well for tasks that require a higher quotient of cognitive skill. In fact, in these cases there is a negative correlation between greater monetary reward and increased performance.[57] Pink and others time and again remind us that it is intrinsic rewards—the desire to master, discover, belong, be a part of something meaningful, something larger than oneself—that are the most powerful motivators for performance, much more powerful than money and other carrot-and-stick approaches.

Daniel Ariely, a behavioral economist, writes in his book *Predictably Irrational,* "People will work more for a cause than for cash."[58] Like Duran Bell, the economist who contrasted commodity and gift economies, Ariely in his TEDxBlackRockCity talk during the Burning Man festival in 2011 pointed out two different frameworks people use to negotiate exchanges: the economic and the social.[59] In the economic mode, we're willing to give away goods and services only if we get something we value in exchange. In the social mode, we give goods and services because it's socially expected of us to do so. And the mere act of putting a price tag on a good or a service makes people switch from the social to the economic mode, thus reducing their natural inclination toward altruism and generosity. This is because when money is mentioned, we immediately apply market norms to the situation and often revert to critiquing the offer: Is it a good deal? Is it worth my time? Am I being cheated out of more money? However, when no money is involved, people apply social norms to the situation and will often work harder. You will probably work a lot harder preparing a meal for your friends whose judgment and approval are important to you than if someone paid you money to make a meal for strangers. You would probably enjoy the former a lot more too.

When we are spending billions of hours contributing to Wikipedia, Twitter, and thousands of other social platforms, donating money to hundreds of thousands of projects, sharing our health experiences and expertise, we are in our social mode. We are doing this without receiving financial rewards because we are driven to connect with others, to do some good, and to express the richness of who we are. We are "working" hard; in fact we may be saving the best of ourselves for these unpaid activities. Many of the volunteers participating in the Global Lives Project—videographers, translators, editors, production assistants, and others—are professionals in the advertising and film industries who get paid a lot of money in their regular careers. Yet many report that doing Global Lives shoots is the most meaningful experience in their lives. They put all of themselves into their Global Lives projects in a way that they don't in their "day jobs."

In the process of socialstructing money, we are also socialstructing the meaning of wealth away from the possession of stuff and toward valuing relationships and connectedness. This is what many leading activists, academics, and political leaders are beginning to understand. We are hearing calls to rethink our reliance on traditional measures of progress, such as GDP. Once thought of as a quaint concept pioneered by the tiny kingdom of Bhutan, the Gross Happiness Index, a measure of the overall well-being of a country, including health, education levels, and life satisfaction, is increasingly moving to the mainstream. Former president of France Nicolas Sarkozy established the International Commission on the Measurement of Economic Performance and Social Progress, which recommended a shift in economic emphasis from simply the production of goods to a broader measure of overall well-being, which would include the benefits of health, education, and security.[60] The commission was chaired by Joseph E. Stiglitz, a Nobel Prize–winning economist and professor at Columbia University, no slouch or touchy-feely dreamer. The New Economic Foundation (NEF), an influential think tank, following the path of a growing number of academics and politicians, has called for a new measure of progress it calls National Accounts of Well-being.[61] It uses comprehensive data from a survey of twenty-two European nations examining both personal and social well-being. Personal well-being looks at people's experiences, such as positive and negative emotions, satisfaction, vitality, resilience, self-esteem, and a sense of purpose and meaning. Measures of social well-being include two main components: supportive relationships and a feeling of trust and belonging. According to NEF, these indicators together give us a "picture of what we all really want: a fulfilling and happy life."[62] NEF, Stiglitz, Sarkozy, and others who advocate broadening our definition of well-being follow in the footsteps of prominent Scottish Enlightment thinkers, among them none other than Adam Smith.

Many see Adam Smith as the father of free market economics and a key proponent of consumerism. However, in his treatise "The Theory of Moral Sentiments," written in 1759, Smith cautioned his readers about the dangers of status-driven consumerism. The political economist Michael Busch points out, "Consumerism has led to a growth of status consumption and want-creation, both of which increase consumption without contributing to happiness. Adam Smith observed that lasting happiness is found in tranquility as opposed to consumption. In their quest for more consumption, people have forgotten about the three virtues Smith observed that best provide for a tranquil lifestyle and overall social well-being: justice, beneficence and prudence. Applying the virtues to modern society may decrease overall consumption but will lead to a more satisfied life."[63]

The prevailing free market economic theory argues that we humans are perfectly rational economic actors who make economic decisions purely on the basis of the monetary rewards we'll receive. But neuroscience and the new sciences of behavioral economics and happiness psychology are opening our eyes to the reality that this is a grossly oversimplified conception of human beings. We are not simply self-interested economic actors; we are citizens and members of communities, and we are driven by many intrinsic, often intangible rewards that traditional market economics does not take into account.

As we socialstruct our economy, we will also need to socialstruct our thinking—how we view wealth, efficiency, equity, abundance, and well-being. It's a tall order but something we have begun to do already.

This fundamental change from a rational economic paradigm to a social economy will ripple through all the domains of daily and institutional life over the coming decades. In the next four chapters I will take you on a more detailed tour of these ripple effects as people socialstruct education, governance, science, and health. I start each chapter with a fictional scenario so that you can imagine yourself as an immigrant to that particular future. How will people learn ten or twenty years from now? How will we govern ourselves? How will we innovate business models, conduct scientific research, and manage our health? Each of the fictional future stories or vignettes I present takes signals from today—events, developments, data points, or innovations that may appear small or on the fringe but are already here—and brings them together to paint a picture of a larger future transformation. Looking at signals and learning to pattern them to foresee directions of larger transformations are indispensable skills for doing futures work. A signal may be an innovation in the lab, a new product, a new practice, a new policy or strategy. In short, it is something that catches our attention at one scale and in one locale and points to larger implications for other locales or even globally. In the next four chapters I will use signals from today to make the future possibilities more real and tangible.

I want to caution that any particular organization or project I write about may not ultimately be successful. The long-term fate of many cannot be known. What is more important is how they represent the bigger story that is surely unfolding. In the early stages of any transformation, many efforts will fail, but in the process they lay the groundwork for a bigger disruption. Just think about the dot.com bubble and how it led to a recession in the early 2000s in much of the IT industry. Some thought that the IT industry was dead, but the information and communications technology revolution is still in full swing, and many of the business models and projects that seemed to be dead in 2000 are being successfully implemented today. So consider the signals I point to in this book simply as illustrations of possibilities that are likely to be realized by many others who may not even exist today.

As a futurist I firmly believe that no one can predict the precise shape the future will take or which specific organizations or individuals will be successful. However, I also believe that we can see important directions of change that are driven by a confluence of larger trends and that it is important for us as individuals and as a society to understand these shifts and explore how they may reshape our lives, our organizations, and our routines. Such endeavors allow us to better prepare for the future and at the same time shape a more desirable future. Perhaps you will even be one of those making this new world happen.

The Whole World's a Classroom

If you want to build a ship, don't gather people together to collect wood and don't assign them tasks
and work, but rather, teach them to long for the endless immensity of the sea.
                    ANTOINE DE SAINT-EXUPÉRY

Future Scenario 2021: Free-Range Architecture

With a heavy heart, Andy Rhimes decided to take a year off from his architecture program in college—and he wasn't sure if he would ever go back. He had dreamed of becoming an architect since he was sixteen, when he attended a lecture by Frank Gehry, a pioneer of poststructuralist architecture. The ideas Gehry talked about— especially that form need not follow function—and the beautiful, challenging, and weird building designs he showed to illustrate his point captured Andy's imagination. The concept that city buildings could be a form of artistic, even philosophical expression ignited in him a burning desire to become an architect. He started collecting pictures of buildings he found interesting and proceeded to devour books on architecture. He discovered Gaudí, Koolhaus, I. M. Pei, Saarinen, and many other pioneering architects and their creations. Ecological design particularly interested him, and he aspired to build affordable and ecologically sustainable housing.

Getting accepted into one of the top architecture schools in the country was a dream come true. The summer before classes started, Andy imagined himself working on cool projects with fellow students and having deep conversations with his professors about the nature of architecture and the role of the architect in society.

But seven months into his college experience, after numerous nights staying up to finish a project that didn't seem relevant or interesting, and numerous mornings struggling to stay awake in class, he took stock of the situation. Yes, he had met a few great professors and some interesting students. And he enjoyed weekends spent drinking with his dorm mates (a requirement if one wanted to be part of campus social life). He had learned some new things, but the joy of discovering architecture was somehow gone. His days were filled with too many tasks that didn't seem to be getting him where he wanted to be. In the rush to please his teachers, get good grades, and have a social life, studying had become less about learning and more about doing stuff for others. Andy hadn't read a book for pleasure in months. He wistfully remembered those free hours when he could just read or tinker in his workshop and think. "That's it!" he realized. That was the hardest thing for him to accept: he didn't have time to think! And thinking was what he desperately wanted to do.

Eventually he made the painful phone call he had been dreading for months. He told his parents that he needed to take a year off to figure things out. "I am dedicated to architecture. I am very self-directed," he said, fighting back tears. "But this is just not working for me. All I feel is stressed out and overwhelmed all the time. I just don't want to live like that anymore." They struck a deal: Andy would take a year off and work, then either transfer to a different college or figure out an alternative way to become an architect.

Over the summer Andy got a job at Burger Barn. He was reading lots of books and had regained some control over his time, which afforded him opportunity to think. One thing he realized he desperately needed and wanted was a mentor, someone to guide him in his studies and to tell him what was important to know. He wanted someone to point him to the right resources and interesting people and to discuss ideas with him. He also wanted to find peers who shared his passion so they could learn from each other. So he turned to social media and asked his community if anyone could help him in his quest. A friend recommended Socrates 2.0, a new platform that connected people with mentors in different fields.

At the time the platform was in beta but aimed to recruit thousands of mentors, former and current college professors and working professionals, to guide groups of mentees in their desired fields. The mentors would not only help students design courses of study individually tailored to meet their interests and learning styles but would also help them find learning resources wherever they might be: the Internet, community colleges, museums, meet-ups, and other places. Socrates 2.0 also provided lots of relevant resources and metrics for measuring learning progress. All Andy had to do was type in his zip code and area of interest, and profiles of potential mentors with reviews and backgrounds showed up.

There were five potential mentors Andy could choose from in his geographic area. He arranged meetings with each one, for the two to get to know each other and see if there was a fit. Socrates 2.0 provided suggestions for the kinds of questions the two might ask, and Andy found they really helped with the conversation.

Among the mentors Andy interviewed, Tom stood out. When Andy contacted him, Tom suggested that they have a "walking meeting." He'd take Andy around Santa Monica on foot and they would talk while looking at different buildings. This turned into a combination walking lecture and conversation, with Tom pointing out interesting architectural elements and at the same time engaging Andy in a conversation about his background, interests, and dreams. Andy was amazed at Tom's range of experiences and knowledge; Tom was teaching urban design theory a few hours a week at a prestigious architecture school but also had practical experience, having participated in strategic planning and inner-city revitalization projects. He was also involved in building villages in Panama and Senegal, and he had received various prestigious awards and published articles and books. They talked about the global water crisis, and Tom told Andy about the qanats (indigenous water systems) of Yazd, Iran, and the sacred water tanks of Varanasi, India.

Andy knew right then and there that he wanted Tom to be his mentor. He felt the excitement of learning coming back to him, something he had feared his first year of college had quashed forever. He applied to be in Tom's mentee group and was accepted along with four others. The five, who informally called themselves Tom's Squad, became the core of Andy's peer learning community. Three were college-age students, one a retired doctor who had always been interested in architecture, and one a midcareer professional who wanted to transition into architecture. Each paid $8,000 a year to be in the mentorship program. Socrates 2.0 kept 5 percent of this amount, and the rest went directly to the mentor.

After starting Socrates 2.0, Andy quit working at Burger Barn. He convinced his parents to pay for Socrates 2.0 in lieu of his college tuition, and they thought it was a good deal, although they did worry about the legitimacy of it. Now Andy's typical day starts with checking into Socrates 2.0, which keeps track of his learning progress: the levels of knowledge he has acquired, the books and articles he has read, and his contributions to various projects. Tom tracks Andy's progress on the site and often connects with him via video chat to give him suggestions or just to check in. He wants to make sure that Andy can get his architecture certificate in four years. (Luckily the new accreditation process grants accreditation to individuals rather than architecture schools.) The other day, for example, he told Andy to learn more about structural integrity. In addition to online check-ins, the mentee group gets together with Tom weekly for tutoring, to have conversations, and to work together on projects.

Andy and his peers also organize frequent architecture meet-ups that bring together students, professionals, and amateurs interested in architecture. These serve as learning spaces, places to meet other people, exchange ideas, and hear interesting people speak. In one of the meet-ups, Andy learned about the use of biomimicry in architecture. Leslie, who had been involved in the back-to-the-land movement and had lived in a yurt in her youth, told him about a building in Zimbabwe that was modeled on a termite mound, thus providing a natural way to air-condition the structure. She explained to Andy that Mother Nature is quite an architect and her works are a great source of learning. "Have you ever butchered an animal?" she asked. "Cut muscle tissue, sawed through the bone? You know, once you get through the fat and muscle, there's that sinewy stuff? The way that muscles and cartilage provide continuous pull and the bones discontinous push? That's architecture! That's the best way to build a bridge!"

It really got him thinking.

Museums and distinctive buildings are other resources Andy uses for learning. With an app called ArchGenius, he can point his augmented reality phone at any architecturally significant building and the phone will display information on the building's history and architectural details, sometimes even providing architectural drawings for the place. All of this information has been crowdsourced, that is, contributed and aggregated by others supplying links and annotations. Andy is not only the user of the app but also a contributor, since the app alerts him to "contribution opportunities," opportunities to add missing information such as blueprints, info on the architect's design intent, and site history. This way he accumulates currency on the platform that counts toward his architecture certification. These points are also tracked on Socrates 2.0.

Recently Andy was asked to come back to his high school as part of an alumni panel to share college experiences. He talked about Socrates 2.0 and how he is going about learning and pursuing his dream of becoming an architect. When the moderator asked him, "Would you recommend it to others?," he had to think hard. It was definitely working for him, but he was never cut out for institutional learning; it just deadened his desire to learn. "You have to be pretty self-motivated, self-directed, and organized for this to work" was his reply. "Socrates 2.0 is not for everyone. But if you can take on the burden of putting together all the necessary resources and making sure that you follow your path, it is the best learning I can think of."

The Trouble with Old School

Quick confession: while this scenario is based on an analysis of shifts that are beginning to reshape our education system, it is also a reflection of my own hopes for the future and a reaction to years of personal experience with the American education system. These experiences started in the mid-1990s when my son, Greg, entered Peninsula School, one of the last progressive schools in the San Francisco Bay Area. The school was founded in 1925 by Josephine Duveneck, an educator and environmentalist, and follows many principles of experiential learning pioneered by John Dewey, the early twentieth-century American educational reformer.

Defying decades of external pressures and changing mandates by state and federal regulators, Peninsula does not assign grades, its teachers give very little homework (and then only in the upper grades), and the school eschews participation in most organized athletics (although kids get plenty of game and exercise time outdoors). At Peninsula, students spend lots of time in unstructured play, social interactions, and reflection. Arts, shop, music, ceramics, and weaving are integrated into the curriculum along with academic disciplines. In the afternoon, kids can choose among different activities, thus experiencing firsthand self-directed learning. This allows those who are into science to spend all of their free time in the science room, those who are into music to play music for hours each day, and those who are into art or weaving or woodshop to engage in those activities to their heart's delight. Greg spent all his free time in the music room and is pursuing a music career today. Our neighbor Matt spent most of his free time in the science room, then went on to study at Cornell and is now getting his PhD in engineering at Stanford while working at NASA.

Instead of receiving report cards, parents are invited to meet with the teacher twice a year, mainly to talk about the child: how he or she is doing socially, emotionally, and physically, what he or she likes and dislikes. The teacher has a deep insight into the student and a deep connection with everything that goes on in the classroom. Academic performance is a minor part of such conversations. The assessment is about the child as a person.

Peninsula's radical departure from mainstream educational practices made my son's years there a real experiment for my husband and me, two overeducated adults schooled in the old system. For a lot of our time at Peninsula, we were nagged by doubt: yes, Peninsula is a great environment for kids; yes, Greg is turning out to be a creative, caring, thoughtful human being. But is he getting enough academics? Is he getting enough of the basics in math, writing, and science? Several times we seriously thought about taking him out of Peninsula and enrolling him in another, more academic school. Usually this happened after a conversation with a parent whose child was doing algebra in the third grade or writing ten-page essays in the fifth.

The experiment ended with Greg entering a highly regarded college prep high school because Peninsula ends after eighth grade. All three of us held our breath. Would he be able to function in an intense academic environment? Would he be able to adjust? Would he know how to take tests? Would he feel hopelessly behind his peers in math and science? When we came up for air after the first few months of adjusting to a new routine—new commute, new relationships, and everything else that goes along with the transition to high school—we realized that the magic of Peninsula School had worked for Greg. Like all those other Peninsula kids I was hearing from at yearly graduate forums, Greg was doing just fine compared to kids from "academically challenging" schools. The greatest adjustment was to be getting grades at all.

But a shift occurred sometime after his first year of high school and became fully apparent by the end of his high school career: during the four years of being in a highly academic environment, instead of becoming inspired to learn, Greg, year by year, had become turned off from learning and more and more cynical about teachers, the school's administration, and the whole education system. Learning had gone from being a joyful, often invisible part of the fabric of his daily life to being a chore, something he did because someone else was forcing him to, something he would be judged on and for which he would be either rewarded or punished. Upon graduating from Peninsula, Greg had said, "There wasn't a day I didn't look forward to going to school." Toward the end of his high school career, he told his advisor, "I hate school. Every morning when I wake up, I hate the thought of going to school." A sad transformation in less than four years!

To Greg education became a series of hoops you jump through: do this and you will get that. In other words, he adjusted well. This is exactly how most of his friends felt about school; in fact they couldn't fathom that there could be another system, a different way of learning. I've spent hours talking to students about the experience of institutionalized education killing the desire to learn. Too many have told me, "I used to love to read, but I don't read for pleasure anymore. I have too much assigned reading at school." These sentiments were echoed by the two hundred students in Michael Wesch's anthropology class at Kansas State University when he asked them to collaboratively create and then deliver a message online about their educational experiences. Here are some of the things they said:

Only 18 percent of my teachers know my name.

I am defined by numbers.

I complete 49 percent of the readings assigned to me. Only 26 percent seem relevant to my life.[1]

As we have done in other areas of our economy and society, we have created an education system optimized for massive scale, providing the same educational resources in essentially the same settings to masses of people whose educational attainment is measured and judged by narrow but universally applied metrics that have little to do with true mastery of content, long-term retention, or critical thinking. In this system, we measure achievement with scored tests such as the SAT, the GRE, the LSAT, the STAR, and countless others. The tests are rigorous but one-dimensional; the only creative thing about them is their acronyms. They may serve bureaucratic exigencies because they allow institutions to quickly sort people for acceptance or promotion to the next academic level, but they are poor reflections of individuals' abilities and capacity for long-term success.

This old system is slowly being dismantled, and not just by new technology and social platforms. Lack of government funding is pushing the quality of public education down and costs up. In fact, young people today are caught in the transition between these two worlds—the world of institutional production and the new world of learning that is coming to resemble Andy's. This world is characterized by four key elements, illustrated in Andy's scenario: easy, individualized, and highly contextual learning experiences; ubiquitous free content; community as a driver and enabler of learning; intrinsic rewards and meaningful learning currencies.

These forces are undermining the dominance of institutional education and are gaining traction today.

Microlearning: Easy, Individualized, and Highly Contextual

This probably sounds familiar: you are with a group of friends arguing about some piece of trivia or historical fact. Someone says, "Wait, let me look this up on Wikipedia," and proceeds to read the information out loud to the whole group, thus resolving the argument. Such an event is a genuine educational moment, or more precisely, a *microeducational* moment. Everyone is motivated to learn something at that particular moment; they are curious, they want the information, so they go ahead and get it in a quick, easy, and social way.

As I outlined in Chapter 1, one of the key characteristics of socialstructing is microcontributions by large numbers of people.

Microcontributions make difficult tasks virtually effortless as contributors work in bursts of inspired activity rather than an 8-to-5 shift under conditions mandated by employers or external demands. This doesn't necessarily mean working less; it means doing work on our own terms instead of someone else's. The equivalent of that in education is microlearning: learning that is effortless and done in context, when the person really wants or needs to learn. It is learning driven not by bureaucratic imperatives but by individual desires and needs.

Microlearning goes hand in hand with the notion of flow as described by Mihaly Csikszentmihalyi, a psychologist and an expert on creativity. He defined flow as "the state in which people are so involved in an activity that nothing else seems to matter; the experience itself is so enjoyable that people will do it even at a great cost, for the sheer sake of doing it."[2] We've all experienced such moments, and we've probably seen kids immersed in this state for extended periods of time. When a kid is in a flow state, she can spend hours doing something with complete abandon: studying books on dinosaurs, memorizing all their names and the fine distinctions among them. The same activity may be impossibly difficult if it is assigned when she really wants to play music. You can spend hours forcing a child to memorize the names, or she can do it on her own in a few minutes if she is interested. We all know this feeling of being totally involved in an activity so that whatever we are doing feels effortless. We long for such moments, whether we are engaged in writing, woodworking, reading, or running.

Most institutional settings, particularly educational ones, with their highly structured lesson times and sequences, go against the concept of flow. Kids who are interested in something are rarely allowed to spend as much time on the activity as they want to; they are often forced to spend time engaging in activities that don't interest them at all. This is one reason many schools place so much emphasis on discipline; discipline issues are often a direct result of boredom. When kids are truly engaged in something, they don't have time to be disruptive.

The more structured the school day is, the less free time students have, the less chance they have to achieve flow states and learn at their own pace. Instead of making learning easy for them, allowing them to pick up what they are passionate about at a particular time, we cram what *we* think is appropriate into *our* time schedule, not theirs.

For instance, most school schedules work directly against students' biological clock, their circadian rhythm. Research shows that the body clock of teenagers is naturally set to a schedule different from that of younger children or adults. This keeps adolescents from tiring until around 11 P.M., when they produce the sleep-inducing hormone melatonin, and it keeps them from waking up much before 8 A.M., which is when their body stops producing melatonin. Most high schools, however, require adolescents to wake up much earlier. The result is that the first class of the morning is often wasted, with over a quarter of students falling asleep in class once a week, according to a National Sleep Foundation poll.[3] Many of our adolescents therefore live in a state of permanent desynchronosis, which most of us know as jet lag, being out of sync with one's biological clock. Adjusting school start times just slightly could improve learning outcomes substantially. As the *New York Times* reported, when "high schools in Jessamine County, Kentucky, pushed back the first bell to 8:40 A.M. from 7:30 A.M.," attendance immediately went up, "as did scores on standardized tests, which have continued to rise each year."[4] Similar results have been achieved in school districts in Virginia and Connecticut. When several high schools in Minnesota moved start times closer to 9 A.M., "students' grades rose slightly and lateness, behavioral problems, and dropout rates decreased."[5]

This is one reason why Andy Rhimes' day using Socrates 2.0 feels easier. He may actually spend more time learning than he would in the classroom setting, but a lot of this learning occurs in context, in the real world, in places that are conducive to learning. Further, the learning happens according to his interests and needs, on terms that work for him. Online resources make it increasingly possible for people to create personalized learning, allowing them to learn at times and in contexts that are meaningful and convenient to them rather than to educational institutions.

The Whole World's a Classroom: Ubiquitous Free Content

Along with technologies and platforms that facilitate microlearning comes the democratization of content. As discussed earlier, a mass of information that was once the purview of a few credentialed teachers or locked in textbooks is being put online, for free. Take, for instance, the Khan Academy, the not-for-profit educational organization created in 2006 by Salman Khan, a former hedge fund analyst. With the mission of "providing a high-quality education to anyone, anywhere,"[6] the Khan Academy supplies free online microlectures in video tutorials stored on YouTube. Tutorials encompass subjects as diverse as mathematics, history, finance, physics, chemistry, biology, astronomy, and economics and are viewed by some two million users a month.[7]

Two years ago, a high school intern we hired at the Institute for the Future took it upon himself to watch all of the nearly seven hundred TED Talks videos available online at that time. The videos feature concise, provocative presentations delivered by leading thinkers in technology, entertainment, and design (TED). These categories are defined broadly so as to represent the best and the brightest from a wide array of fields, picked not only for their content but also for their ability to inspire. I would daresay the TED lectures beat 90 percent of lectures delivered in an average classroom in terms of quality, provocativeness, content, and entertainment value. So a summer spent immersed in TED lectures is not a bad learning experience! And today they are all available for free to anyone with a computer or a smartphone. With more and more courses and educational content becoming available online, Bill Gates predicted in 2010 that "five years from now on the web for free you'll be able to find the best lectures in the world. . . . It will be better than any single university."[8]

We are also able to query people with a broad range of expertise around the world to help us learn in real time. Platforms such as Fluther or Quora allow anyone to post a question for the community to answer. Posts vary from relatively trivial relationship questions like "How many days of silence mean that it is over?" to complex math questions. Dan Finkel, one of the founders of Fluther, asked for help in solving an algebraic question that came up in his work on the platform. He was pretty skeptical that anyone would be able to offer a solution, but to his surprise, twenty-seven comments later a fellow Flutherer who went by the name BonusQuestion did provide a solution and a proof. Here is an excerpt from their online exchange:

> Finkelitis: You're totally right, BonusQuestion. And you've incidentally answered another question that was on my mind (about the $d=0$ case). Thanks for the insight!
>
> BonusQuestion: You're welcome. Glad it helped. For those who are interested in the solution of Pell's equation, there is a rather elementary method for finding those solutions. For details check this pdf out.[9]

Not only do we have access to question-and-answer platforms that help us learn; increasingly we also have access to world-class experts who can provide personalized advice and mentorship. Expert Insight, founded by Brandon Adams, a PhD graduate of Harvard Business School, allows people to gain access to experts in multiple disciplines. Experts list their rates and availability, and those interested can select an hour or two from their chosen expert's schedule and pay online. They then receive the expert's proprietary email address for correspondence before the appointment. When the time comes, they log onto a Skype-type video chat system and ask away for the purchased hour. Some of the experts are academics who also teach in colleges and universities, including Jeffrey Miron, a senior lecturer and the director of undergraduate studies in the Department of Economics at Harvard University. For $4,000 you can even buy an hour with Gary Becker, a Nobel Prize–winning economist from the University of Chicago! Not everyone can afford to pay the price, but the same platform can be used for people to offer advice for free or at very low prices.

John Falk, who leads a project on free-choice science at Oregon State University, points out that we "spend less than 5 percent of our lives in classrooms, and an ever-growing body of evidence demonstrates that most science is learned outside of school."[10] The same is true for most other disciplines. For many subjects, in fact, the traditional classroom may be the least conducive environment for learning. The classroom is a sensory-poor place; it cannot compare to the vibrancy, colors, smells, and interactions of the world outside it. And when you are able to point your smartphone at what you are interested in and get the information you need or the answers to your questions, the world becomes an amazingly rich classroom.

We are living in an age in which technologies from smartphones to augmented reality and platforms such as Fluther and Expert Insight, combined with rich online content, make information increasingly cheap and widely available anytime and anywhere. The movement of information into the real world from restricted physical settings—classrooms and desktops—will greatly increase opportunities for learning. It will indeed become possible to embed learning into everyday experiences. We will be able to tap into this richness of information while walking, riding a bus, or sitting at home or in a park. The whole world can truly be a classroom and every moment can be a learning moment.

At Peninsula School, kids spend relatively little time receiving formal classroom instruction, but they learn just as much as or more than kids in conventional schools. This is because learning happens not just in the classroom in forty-five-minute chunks but anytime, anywhere: during school activities, at break time, and after school when kids are just hanging out together. At one graduates forum, where alums were asked to relate their experiences of transitioning into traditional high schools, a sophomore at an exclusive private school related how surprised she was to find out that at her new school "learning was something you did in the classroom," that kids didn't continue conversations started in the classroom when they went outside. Such separations do not exist at Peninsula. Barbie, the weaving teacher at Peninsula, once told me about a child asking her while weaving, "What is DNA?" Barbie's response was, "Do you want a ten-minute answer or a deeper one?" The question led to an impromptu discussion of the structure of DNA among about ten kids ranging in age from ten to fourteen. The same thing happens in woodshop, where, unbeknownst to them, kids are introduced to the basics of geometry while doing cool building projects.

While on the surface it appears that the Peninsula students are spending less time in academic instruction, in reality their days are filled with learning—learning that is meaningful to them and occurs on their terms. Conversations in the classroom about the Civil War continue in the gazebo at lunch or during activities, and because kids are not exhausted by, but are enthused about school, they bring those conversations home with them. With the new technology infrastructure, the experience of embedded, embodied, and highly contextual learning can indeed become pervasive, not just something one or a few unique schools practice, but something all of us can be a part of.

Socially Embedded Learning: Community as a Driver and Enabler of Learning

While easy access to unprecedented amounts of information is tremendously important, it is only one part of the education equation. Learning is social. This is something many schools have forgotten or decided to organize against, yet it is one of the key reasons Peninsula School excels at fostering learning. Peninsula's success rests on relationships. When you visit the school, you find small groups of teachers, students, and staff in the library, in the music room, in the gazebo eating lunch, in the classroom, or out on the Big Field playing games. Teachers and staff are students' friends, mentors, role models, and co-discoverers. They are teachers in the best Socratic tradition. Everything at the school is highly personalized and relationship-based. This is evident even in the names of the classes: there are no first, second, or third grades; instead there is Josie's class,

Gail's, and Rebecca's. Each class has a strong imprint of the teacher who leads it. At Peninsula, relationships—among teachers and students, among teachers who work together collaboratively, among parents, teachers, and staff—are at the core of everything. When graduates are asked "What do you value most about Peninsula?" one consistent answer is "Relationships." In his high school application, Greg wrote, "At Peninsula many of the teachers were my friends."

Relationships are important because they are a key driver of learning. Many proponents of distance learning miss the importance of relationships and social connections in education. I believe online learning and resources alone will not provide a solution to our educational needs. One needs mentors, someone to look up to and to guide the learning process, to help filter what one needs to know and to provide feedback. One also needs a community to discuss ideas with, to foster the desire to learn, and to receive recognition from. Once you have the inspiration, the mentorship, and the community, you can take advantage of the rich ecology of content described in the previous section.

This is exactly what the Socrates 2.0 scenario emphasizes. Andy has access to a mentor, and he is embedded in multiple communities that foster his learning, most of them outside of the traditional classroom setting. The meet-ups that he attends are learning communities; for example, he learns about biomimicry from Leslie, a participant who is quite a bit older and has a lot of experience. This is what is happening today in many meet-ups and hackathons organized around the country.

After all, learning is about participating in a conversation, and kids (and adults) want to participate in conversations with those who matter to them. If the conversation in their circle is about math or physics or Chaucer, they want to know enough to participate. It is amazing to what lengths we will go to acquire knowledge that can make us shine in our social circle or in front of people who matter to us. In too many classroom settings, the focus on academics misses this social aspect of learning. In fact, most of the time it is seen as a distraction or an impediment.

Eri Gentry, the founder of BioCurious, got excited about biology because she had friends who were doing fascinating research in the field. She decided she wanted to be part of a community that makes science accessible to the general public. BioCurious is a learning community of participants ranging from academics doing advanced biology research at universities to teenagers trying out basic but quirky experiments. Although Eri herself does not have formal training in biology, she is surrounded by people building science kits and other new products, and they are happy to explain to her, in intimate detail, how these work. She wants to take basic biology classes but says, "I am realizing that I have to provide these classes through BioCurious in order to make them affordable, do it around my schedule, make it fun, and around people who I like." BioCurious is a hacker space for biology, a place to access classes and equipment and meet collaborators. It is a place where "you don't have to be a scientist to learn science."

Eri keenly understands the need for mentors and teachers as an integral part of the learning experience. "I want someone to get in front of me with a list of things that I need to learn," she says. "Good teachers learned the right way to transfer information, the right order in which to present information."[11] So online learning does not spell the end of teaching; it calls for good mentors and teachers to operate in new ways, to work within communities of learners, realizing and taking advantage of how widely distributed information and resources are becoming, empowering students to learn on their own terms and in ways that fit them. In this environment, we need to reframe the role of instructors, lecturers, and professors and see them instead as social designers. In Chapter 1 I talked about the leaders of socialstructing efforts as community organizers rather than managers. This model holds for education. In the era of social-structed education, teachers need to be able to design and organize learning communities, whether in classroom settings, in meet-ups, or in other places.

Don Finkel, a former professor at Evergreen State College, wrote eloquently about this in his book *Teaching with Your Mouth*

Shut. There he argues that "a teacher's job is to shape [the edu-cational] environment in a manner conducive to learning"—that is, to create social and physical conditions that inspire students to learn.[12] He approaches learning as a designer, as a community or-ganizer. Every "learning design" that he offers in the book and that has worked in his classes aims to create an intellectual community that propels participants to want to figure things out for themselves rather than for a grade. Content is cheap; inspiration is priceless.

When learning is recognized as a social experience, the boundar-ies blur between teachers and students, between givers and takers of knowledge, between passive and active participants in the learn-ing process. Andy Rhimes learns about biomimicry from an older person in a meet-up. But he is not only a passive learner, he is also a contributor, giving something back to the community as he in-puts information on the building he is studying. Banking on the old adage that the best way to learn something really well is to teach it, socialstructed education turns everyone into an active learning con-tributor. Recognizing this, Howard Rheingold, a lecturer at Stanford and the author of numerous books on collaboration and technology, gives students in his online class Rheingold U the option of serving in different roles: as searchers (people who search for resources and upload them to the common site), note takers (those who take notes and share them with the group), summarizers, and so forth.[13] Rhein-gold U is a community learning space in which everyone is a learner and a teacher, a beneficiary and a contributor. Rheingold calls this approach to teaching peerology.

Another platform that fosters community learning and recognizes the blurry boundary between teachers and students is Skillshare, a community marketplace in which anyone can learn almost anything. "We believe that everyone has valuable skills and knowledge to teach and the curiosity to keep learning new things," the site proclaims. "This means our neighborhoods, communities, and cities are really the world's greatest universities. Our platform helps make the ex-change of knowledge easy, enriching, collaborative, and fun."[14] All of the classes offered by participants in Skillshare happen outside of a classroom, in the belief that learning is social and happens around shared interests and passions, and that "when you bring together a variety of voices and hands-on instruction, something truly spectacular happens. This magic just can't be replicated over a webcam and chatroom."[15]

Perhaps one of the most interesting experiments in socialstructed learning that occurs in microsegments and is highly community-driven is a project called 100 Days of Spring.[16] It was organized by Will Greene, a musician and videographer, and Sam Haynor, a chess champion and journalist, who worked together at a children's summer camp. 100 Days of Spring transformed a former boutique clothing shop neighboring an auto body shop at 1592 Market Street in San Francisco, into a community learning space. For a hundred days, people offered to teach something they were interested in and anyone could sign up to take their classes. Teachers ranged from programmers and mathematicians to graffiti artists, dancers, and musicians. The event spilled out into the street and served as a mass community celebration with music, dancing, and art. The motto of the organizers is "Teach something. Learn something. Create something."[17] After all, socially created learning not only enriches individuals, it also makes for a better community.

Beyond Grades: Intrinsic Rewards and Meaningful Learning Currencies

One of the hallmarks of socialstructing is reliance on intrinsic rewards and motivation, people doing things not for money but for myriad other social reasons: the desire to belong, be recognized, learn, accomplish something, or contribute to a community. So what is the equivalent of money in the educational economy? Grades and test scores (which are what most grades are based on), of course. Grades are something you can count like money, accumulate (think GPAs), and use to gain entry into the next level of the institutional ladder. However, just like money, grades replace intrinsic with extrinsic rewards, in most instances taking pleasure and self-direction out of the process of learning.

Shawn Cornally, a high school science and math teacher in rural Iowa, laments this situation in his essay in *Good* magazine entitled "'Will This Be on the Test?' An Overemphasis on Grades Might Be Killing the Desire to Learn." No matter how exciting the material is, or how hard he tries to engage his students, the specter of grading always creeps into his lessons. "This is fun and all; I'm learning and stuff," his students say, "but will this be on the test?" Or worse yet: "How many points is this worth?" "Why isn't the learning good enough?" asks Cornally. "Why are we so obsessed with ranking education? Does that even make sense? I would argue that it doesn't, and that our schools are the worse for it."[18]

Alfie Kohn, an educator and the author of a dozen books, including *No Contest: The Case against Competition* and *Punished by Rewards: The Trouble with Gold Stars, Incentive Plans, A's, Praise, and Other Bribes*, looked at a whole array of studies on educational achievement to come to this disturbing conclusion: "Students who are given grades, or for whom grades are made particularly salient, tend to display less interest in what they are doing, fare worse on meaningful measures of learning, and avoid more challenging tasks when given the opportunity—as compared with those in a non-graded comparison group."[19]

As I asserted earlier, grades and tests may provide an easy and convenient way of sorting people for potential employers, but they actually serve as a turn-off to authentic learning. They also prove to be poor predictors of longer-term performance and in-depth comprehension. Decades of research on various performance tests—SATs, grades, NFL scouting scores—all point out that there are huge differences between what researchers call maximum performance and typical performance. In a pioneering 1988 study, psychology professor Paul Sackett tested supermarket cashiers' item-scanning ability. Each cashier was given four carts to process and told he or she was being monitored for speed and accuracy.[20]

It was what the researchers called a "maximum performance" test, much like the SATS, GREs, or the kinds of tests they use to draft sports athletes. Researchers found that cashiers who were star performers under test conditions did no better than average when their performance was observed over a four-week period. Their typical performance was the same as that of the nonstar cashiers. Since then, research has found this same discrepency in performance in professional athletics, law, and education. People who perform well in high-stakes situations, that is, who do well on maximum performance tests, do not do well compared to others on measures of typical performance. People who know they're being tested are highly motivated and focused to do well. However, maximum performance measures have nothing to do with success outside of such test environments and over the long term. On the sort of test that measures typical performance, character traits that have nothing to do with maximum performance—grit, perseverance, social skills—influence the outcome. This is why a straight-A student in high school may not be successful in the workplace or in life, and why a C student may do quite well outside of the classroom setting.

It's easy to understand the allure of the maximum performance measures we subject young people to. They don't take very long, so we can quantify many people. They make assessment seem relatively straightforward, reducing the uncertainty of selecting a college applicant or a football player. In other words, many of these measures suit the needs of institutional production: efficiency, speed, and cost. But such high-stakes tests are often spectacularly bad at predicting performance in the real world.

There are many alternatives to assessing performance based on grades and tests. At Peninsula, teachers have a very good understanding of each student. This understanding comes from daily interactions inside and outside the classroom, many conversations, and knowledge of each student as a human being rather than just a student. The scenario reflects this; Andy's mentor, Tom, can assess how he is doing because he interacts frequently with Andy and can see how he has done on various tasks. In any work situation that requires group collaboration, participants can provide pretty good assessments of other team members—their skills, shortfalls, and capabilities. They learn about these not through tests but in the process of working and interacting with each other. Yes, such assessments require time and deeper levels of interaction. They may be less efficient, but ultimately they're more meaningful.

We can also learn about alternative assessments that motivate achievement from the realm of gaming, where players can fail many times but are motivated to improve in order to achieve a higher level in the game. As the game designer Jane McGonigal points out in *Reality Is Broken,* players are always operating at the edge of their abilities; if the task is too easy, the game is not interesting, but if it is too hard, they simply can't play. So they are constantly failing and working to get better, climbing to the next level. No B's, C's, or D's are needed; game players have to master one level in order to move on to the next.[21]

One of the attractions of the Khan Academy is that students are able to redo their work on tutorials as many times as they need to, thus achieving mastery at their own pace. This is in contrast to the traditional approach, whereby all students have to learn at the same pace and during the allotted time, creating what Salman Khan calls "Swiss cheese gaps."[22] Regardless of how fully a student has grasped a given concept—sixth-grade algebra, for instance—at the end of the semester that student either passes or fails. Students receiving a C go on to the next level of math, despite not having fully grasped all the necessary concepts to be successful there. Over time, gaps in a student's education start to reveal themselves, and these gaps expand exponentially as the years pass. All of a sudden, a good student starts failing calculus because he hasn't achieved mastery at earlier levels, and this erodes his confidence in ways that reinforce self-perceptions of inadequacy or even incompetence.

In contrast to this Swiss cheese model, some institutions, like the Quest to Learn charter school in New York City, are beginning to use the principles of gaming to organize the curriculum and assessment as a series of missions and quests. Each quest poses a problem students have to solve, either by gathering relevant resources, doing mathematical calculations, reading and analyzing texts, or doing a range of other activities. There are no grades. However, it is only when their mission is completed that students can move on to the next level.

Back to the Future

Socialstructed education may seem like a radical departure from current practices in most educational settings. Microlearning, an abundant ecology of online and real-world resources and tools, the leverage of intrinsic social motivation and gaming principles—these are all elements of the future. But the foundations of this kind of education lie far in the past. Leading philosophers of education, from Socrates to Plutarch, Rousseau, and Dewey, talked about many of these ideals centuries ago. It was Plutarch who famously said, "Education is the kindling of a flame, not the filling of a vessel."[23] And good teachers and mentors, with the help of peer communities, have the power to ignite and feed that passion. Young people are natural scientists, natural discoverers; all they need is someone to help them discover and to discover along with them. A Peninsula parent once told a story of his daughter coming home from a kindergarten field trip very excited. When he asked her, "So, what did they teach you on the field trip?," she looked at him quite bewildered. "Daddy," she said, "they don't teach us anything. They help us figure things out."

At the dawn of the twentieth century, the educator and philosopher John Dewey reimagined not just the way the learning process should take place but also the role the teacher should play in that process. According to Dewey, the teacher should not stand at the front of the room doling out bits of information to be absorbed by passive students. Instead the teacher's role should be that of facilitator and guide. As he wrote in 1897, "The teacher is not in the school to impose certain ideas or to form certain habits in the child, but is there as a member of the community to select the influences which shall affect the child and to assist him in properly responding to these influences."[24] The teacher is but one partner, one guide, a co-discoverer in the learning process.

Socialstructed education actually brings us back to a future envisioned by Socrates, Rousseau, and Dewey, but with a whole new set of tools—everything from the Khan Academy to smartphones and augmented reality to learning community meet-ups. These tools and platforms make it possible for us to pursue education that is individually paced and intrinsically motivated. We can use these tools to make the dream of Socrates, Rousseau, and Dewey a reality. We can create the kind of rich, meaningful, de-institutionalized education they envisioned.

Don Tapscott, a management consultant and the author of more than a dozen books on applications of technology in business and society, including *Wikinomics* and *Grown Up Digital: How the Net Generation Is Changing Your World*, wrote in an essay in *Edge* magazine in 2009, ominously titled "The Impending Demise of the University," "Universities are finally losing their monopoly on higher learning. . . . Specifically, there is a widening gap between the model of learning offered by many big universities and the natural way that young people who have grown up digital best learn. The old-style lecture, with the professor standing at the podium in front of a large group of students, is still a fixture of university life on many campuses. It's a model that is teacher-focused, one-way, one-size-fits-all and the student is isolated in the learning process."[25]

It is ironic that Tapscott echoes what Dewey was preaching more than a hundred years ago. It is not just "young people who have grown up digital" who don't learn well in lecture-style mass-produced educational settings. No one learns well in such settings. And an increasing number of experts are saying just that, criticizing the existing system and calling for its demise. Some, like Bill Gates, even question the need for schools at all. In a keynote address at Techonomy 2010, a major technology and society conference, Gates provocatively says, "There's no room for innovation in the standard system."[26]

But Gates and other techno-utopians are wrong to assume that online universities and schools can fully replace the face-to-face learning that has traditionally occurred in classrooms and lecture halls or in Socratic dialogues and interactions between mentors and students. What these proposals ignore is something Rousseau, Dewey, and other good educators understood so well: social interactions and physical experiences play a key role in the learning process. This is what teachers at Peninsula School know and practice on a daily basis. This is what Quest to Learn, 100 Days of Spring, Skillshare, and many other experiments are trying to leverage. They combine the best of technologies with the best of communities to enable learning that is meaningful and enriching to both the individual and the community. Their hard work and ingenuity are gradually turning Andy's scenario, and my dreams for the future, into reality.

5

Governance Beyond Government

The City is what it is because our citizens are what they are.

PLATO, *REPUBLIC*

Future Scenario 2021: The New Agora

Toothbrush. Toothpaste. Pens. Walking shoes. Calculator. Briefing book. . . . Briefing book? Where did I put it? Rosa frantically runs to the bedside table to find a book with the title *California Budget: History and Issues* stamped on the cover. Filled with highlighting, multicolored stickies, and notes in the margins, the dog-eared book is evidence of the hours she has spent poring over facts and figures.

For most of her life, Rosa had never paid much attention to politics; she had just worked hard, minded her own business, and cared for her family. That is, until she was called to the New Agora, California's citizen governance body that calls on private citizens to make key decisions for the state. It works like a jury system, except participation is determined by algorithm to select a group as representative as possible of the people living in the state in terms of ethnicity, gender, age, education, income, and other demographics. So many variables are taken into account that only with the help of software is it possible to compile the list of five hundred Agorans.

At first the New Agora had seemed like a radical idea. But after the impasse in the state legislature, the failure to pass the budget, the shaky economy, and the continuous string of high-profile government corruption scandals, not to mention the demise of several public colleges and universities, people were ready for a radical change. A group called Re-Imagine California put a proposition on the ballot to call a convention to rewrite the state constitution and put a new governance system in place. California was then widely considered ungovernable, so it was time for a transformation. Rosa did not sign the petition for the convention, but it passed anyway.

The convention lasted, on and off, for a year, from 2020 until early 2021, and it was streamed live by all the mainstream and alternative media channels. Opinion Space, an online platform for citizens to express their opinions and do instant polling, played a prominent role in getting ordinary Californians involved. There had probably never been such widespread citizen involvement in state issues since the original constitutional convention in 1849. Concurrent with the convention, the League of Women Voters in collaboration with the California General Assembly, a grassroots democracy movement, organized Deliberation Day, a state holiday dedicated to educating the populace on governance and policy issues facing the state. It was a day of teach-ins at local schools, Rotary Clubs, and other local organizations. Everyone was getting an ersatz education in citizenship and governance.

Rosa hadn't been paying much attention until her eighth-grade daughter, Aracely, came home one day and started talking excitedly about ancient Greece, the agora, the citizen assembly, and Plato. Rosa had never heard of the agora, so she looked it up on Wikipedia. She learned that the agora was a public space common in ancient Greek cities where free and equal citizens (these did not include slaves and women) discussed, debated, and shared information about public affairs in order to influence state policies. "Ha," thought Rosa, "that is what all those public squares in every town in Mexico are for. How come they are not being used for making decisions today? Why did we give up our power?" She had never thought much about it before. The idea of average citizens making decisions directly seemed like a faraway dream. Decisions were made by people who had money and political machinery behind them. On the other hand, why not? Most of the politicians didn't seem to know what they were doing any better than the average citizen, judging by the mess the state was in.

Aracely, in the meantime, was really getting into the whole ancient Greek thing, especially after the school decided to convert the school yard into an agora—they called it Rosemond Agora—and fifth- through eighth-graders were invited to reenact the ancient Greek assembly. The first thing up for debate was whether to start school thirty minutes later, at 9 rather than 8:30. "Well," thought Rosa, "that's a no-brainer. Of course the kids will want to start school later!" To her surprise, Aracely came home after the assembly had been going for three days to announce that the vote was to keep the current start time. Many speakers had shared their opinions on the benefits and challenges of each option, and there had been lots of discussion in smaller groups, facilitated by teachers. Aracely was disappointed, but the athletes in the school were pleased; later start times would have disqualified them from organized sports leagues. Lesson learned: you need to change the larger system, not just one school.

In 2021 the California Constitution was rewritten. The legislature was disbanded and a new system was put in place that called for rotating representation by five hundred citizens from the state. The chosen had to proportionately represent the state's demographics, but beyond that they were selected randomly. They were called upon to make major decisions confronting the state. Rosa's Agora session was dedicated to passing the new budget. The state would compensate the participants for their time, and employers were obligated to maintain Agorans' jobs. They would be aided in their deliberations by experts in relevant fields who would rely on data and simulations to review and analyze various options. In the process of setting up the new governance system, the best minds in the state and from abroad were consulted.

Aracely pokes her head in the door. "Mom, when can Dad and I come visit you?"

"Let's see, why don't you look at the schedule, see what deliberations you are interested in, and then we can arrange for you to sit in."

In preparation for her first session in the New Agora, Rosa had gotten an online orientation with clips from previous sessions and instructions from session facilitators. She also got background materials on the state budget. She had feared she wouldn't be able to comprehend all the data, but it was presented in a very intuitive and visual way, plus there was an online simulation that demonstrated the many complex effects of different budget decisions. Throughout the proceedings, New Agora members would have access to these online simulations that, facilitators explained, were created by the best scientific minds in the country. They allowed users to see the impacts of budget decisions on particular groups and regions, the environment, and so on. Facilitators also cautioned New Agorans not to overrely on models: "No model is perfect, so use them to understand patterns and connections between things, but don't forget to use your judgment when making decisions. Models are only as good as the assumptions on which they are based and the data that feed them." The good thing is, models are getting better every year because so much information is being accumulated. People are collecting data on everything: their health, the quality of their tap water, butterfly sightings, weather, and locations. On whatever topic you can think of, people are crowdsourcing and sharing massive amounts of data with each other. And there are so many garage data geeks and students eager to do research that the data is constantly being massaged, analyzed, and converted into easy-to-comprehend visuals. California has really taken the lead in citizen data collection, aggregation, and analytics—so much so that the *New York Times* recently called it the "quantified state, where data geeks are cool."

"John, don't forget to change the battery in the Water Canary,"

Rosa reminds her husband. A few years ago, concerned with the water quality in the area, several residents of Rosemond bought Water Canaries, inexpensive water-testing devices that make it possible to collect real-time water quality data. All you have to do is put your tap water in the device and push a button, and you can measure the water quality and share this information with the community. Last year her neighborhood used Water Canaries to identify unusually high levels of arsenic, which residents traced to a local chemical plant. Interesting how a device designed for the developing world is now commonly used by many residents in California!

Okay, back to packing for the New Agora. It's been a month since Rosa received her summons. At first she was scared. What did she know about the budget? How could she take on this responsibility? But she spent every free moment of the past month going over the numbers, reading expert opinions, talking to people. State budget and financial issues had become the subject of dinner conversations at home, lunch discussions at work, casual conversations in the store. She really felt the responsibility and the honor of being a citizen of California. For the next month Rosa, along with the other 499 members of the New Agora, would be meeting in plenary sessions and in small groups; they would be given briefings related to budget issues prepared by experts with differing views. They would be posing questions, drilling experts, running scenario simulations, debating and discussing. Several polls would be taken throughout the process, and then at the end of two weeks the budget would be voted on by the New Agora assembly and adopted by the state. All the meetings are open to the public and no lobbying of Agorans is allowed. (Lobbying had been outlawed in the new constitution.)

As Rosa turns the ignition key and waves goodbye to John and Aracely, tears roll down her face. Fear? Pride? Separation? "And don't turn off the computer! I signed us up to contribute spare computer cycles to the Quake-Catcher Network. It's just like SETI, but for earthquake monitoring," she yells as she waves to her family.

From Governance by Professionals to Governance by Citizens

To this day, whenever I enter a voting booth, I have to fight back tears. When I voted for the first time in the United States (Reagan vs. Mondale), I thought it would be the only time the simple act of voting would stir such deep emotions, a feeling of connection with all the other people in my precinct, a sense of pride at both being a citizen and having a voice. I guess the contrast with fake elections in the Soviet Union, where people with armbands came to our door to make sure that all the adults in my family went to the local school to cast their votes for the only candidate on the ballot (for most of my time in the Soviet Union it was the geriatric Leonid Brezhnev), has forever made real voting a precious right for me. Somehow it is an affirmation of the crazy choice I made to leave my family at the age of eighteen for an unknown future. And today more than ever I wonder what this country would be like if everyone thought of voting as a precious right. What would this society be like if citizens were truly governing the country, exercising this right not once every few years but all the time? What would our democracy look like? Is it possible to create a truly participatory governance system given the set of today's tools and technologies? I think we are at a unique time in our history when these tools will make this vision not only possible but inevitable. Let's explore why.

In ancient Greece it was the duty of every male citizen to take part in governance. Male citizens (not slaves or women) of Athens practiced direct democracy and were chosen randomly, just like Rosa and her fellow New Agorans, to participate on a rotating basis in a number of governing bodies, from citizen juries and assemblies to legislative commissions. Everyone had a right to speak and to vote in the assembly, which met about once every ten days on a hill called the Pnyx. For a small category of issues, a quorum of six thousand was required, and those who were not present for a vote were sometimes punished or fined, even exiled.

Representative democracies like those in the United States

and Europe trace their roots to this model. However, with low voter turnout and highly polarized public debate driven by political parties, these governments have become faint proxies of a truly participatory democracy. Political institutions are shaped by the social realities of their time and reflect the prevailing technological infrastructure, levels of knowledge, and citizen values. In ancient Athens, a small democratic state, it was possible to gather most citizens in an assembly or on a hill to practice a direct form of democracy, but in a country with millions of people this is nearly impossible.

The U.S. Constitution and governance structure emerged in the eighteenth century and were products of a Newtonian view of the universe. As Jim Dator, a futurist and political scientist at the University of Hawaii, explains, "Government and law were designed to run like a giant machine, leading to predictable, rational, and beneficial outcomes. People, as well, were expected to act by a rational calculus—that is, to determine 'what are the rewards and punishments for my actions?'"[1]

The architects of the U.S. Constitution, with their understanding of Newtonian mechanics, applied the latest technologies and scientific understandings of the eighteenth century to the design of governance, successfully addressing many of the problems of previous systems and eventually replacing the divine autocratic rule that had dominated the times. But while this framework of government and society as machines worked reasonably well for several centuries, it is increasingly out of sync with today's reality and level of knowledge. As Dator argues, "What happened in the 20th century is that a new cosmology called *quantum physics*—and the new technologies of the electronic information and communications revolution— became out of sync with many social institutions and practices, specifically with government systems, which are still very much locked into technologies of 200 years ago."[2]

According to my colleague, the political scientist Jake Dunagan, "While written constitutions have enabled an enormous range of human possibilities and techno-social evolution, their capacity to deal with global climate change, chaotic economic fluctuations, and a host of other emerging disruptions appears to be insufficient."[3] In other words, our political institutions are simply not up to the task of governance today. As we have become more globally connected and the issues we have to contend with at local, state, national, and global levels grow more complex—from coping with climate change to figuring out what to do about complicated financial systems—the ability of any one individual, whether a private citizen or a political representative, to make good decisions has diminished. Most of us are also subject to a widely known phenomenon in social science called rational ignorance: If my opinion is only one in a million and I'm just one vote of so many, what is the payoff of being truly informed about the issues, and why would I bother to vote? Thus we suffer a double whammy: we are not well informed, and we don't bother to participate.

Our response has been to outsource citizenship, that is, participation in major decisions of our state, to specialists—a professional class of politicians aided by professional opinion makers and enabled by big-money interests—and allow them to make decisions for us. Along with abdicating one of the most important of our responsibilities as members of a society, we have also squandered one of the best mechanisms for creating an educated citizenry. Being called to serve in the New Agora is an educational opportunity for Rosa and her fellow Agorans. It places the responsibility on them to think through and get educated about the complex intricacies of budget decisions. When they are called to serve, they rise to the occasion, just as most jurors rise to the occasion when faced with the responsibility of making decisions that affect people's lives.

"Democracy gives voice to 'we the people.' We think it should include 'all' the people. And we think it should provide a basis for 'the people' thinking about the issues they decide," writes James Fishkin, a professor of communications and the director of the Center for Deliberative Democracy at Stanford University, in his book *When the People Speak*.[4] With the help of today's technologies and tools, our institutions of governance can fulfill the promise of "we the people."

Experiments in new governance processes are underway in cities, nation-states, and global citizen movements. Just look around: the government of Iceland ran the process of creating a new constitution for the country as an open crowdsourced digital project, with citizens proposing new clauses, engaging in deliberation, and voting on them; citizens of Christchurch, New Zealand, used online engagement platforms to plan for the future of the city after a major earthquake in February 2011;[5] the U.S. Navy engaged crowds in thinking about strategies for combating piracy.[6]

Fishkin and his colleagues have developed a "deliberative polling" process that has allowed private citizens to make policy decisions in a range of domains and places as diverse as the United States, China, Australia, Bulgaria, and Northern Ireland. The process brings together groups that mirror the demographics of larger populations in their states, regions, or countries and puts them through a process of learning, discussing, and debating issues that affect them but that under normal circumstances are decided by power elites, either technocratic or political or both. Fishkin and his colleagues have found that average citizens are able to make good decisions in areas as complex as local budgets, regional integration, criminal justice, and tax policy. Studies have shown that in the process, participants greatly increased their understanding of the issues and often changed their minds on the best course of action; that is, they made better and more informed decisions as a result of deliberately thinking about the issues at stake and hearing different views on the subject.

If deliberative polling works for small samples, why not give every citizen a chance to engage in the same opportunity? Why not give a chance to every person to truly exercise the rights and responsibilities of citizenship and thus regain a voice in governance? The scenario in this chapter illustrates how this might be possible. Based on signals from today and underlining larger trends, it presents a vision of socialstructed governance—governance that involves average people, aided by experts and expert systems, making policy decisions that affect their communities.

We cannot all come together physically on a hill, but technologies are making it possible for us to come together virtually, express opinions, and even make collective decisions aided by online versions of the Pnyx, thus turning everyone into a real citizen, legally entitled and required to participate in the affairs of the community.

Socialstructed governance, as exemplified in the New Agora scenario, has four key elements: rich and open data for making informed decisions; sophisticated decision-support tools for exploring alternatives and uncovering complex interdependencies; engagement platforms for wide citizen involvement and deliberation; and microparticipation of regular citizens in government decisions and delivery of public services.

Open Data: Shifting Power from Elites to Citizens

Information is power, and today we are in the midst of a dramatic explosion in information. We are creating a world in which every object, every interaction is converted into a piece of data. Social media sites such as Facebook, Twitter, and Google+ give us accounts of who is in our social network. Amazon has a record of the books I buy and my purchasing preferences. Various portable devices, from simple pedometers to health watches, keep digital data records of the calories I burn or the number of steps I take. Cities instrumented with sensors are giving us the ability to see and measure previously invisible patterns, from the location of vehicles at a particular time to movements of trash throughout the urban landscape. We are enveloping every object, every interaction in a cloud of data, and in the process creating digital mirrors of ourselves and our world. Kevin Kelly, a writer and the founding editor of *Wired* magazine, in his blog called The Technium argues that "Information is accumulating faster than any material or artifact in this world, faster than any by-product of our activities."[7] In a study called "How Much Information?," Hal Varian and Peter Lyman, two Berkeley economists, estimated that total production of new information in 2000 reached 1.5 exabytes, or about 37,000 times as much information as is in the Library of Congress! Two years later the annual total was 5 exabytes, representing a 66 percent growth in information per year.[8]

This explosion of information is progressing hand in hand with a transformation in who creates information and who has access to it. No longer the purview of powerful institutions—government departments, corporate organizations, universities, and R&D labs—information is becoming accessible to individuals, with regular people increasingly becoming part of the information-collection process, often by choice but sometimes passively, without their awareness (think of a cell phone transmitting location information). Two developments are fueling this transformation: the opening up of substantial amounts of government data and the growth of data collection, aggregation, and sharing at the grassroots level. These processes are creating a new generation of empowered citizens able to create their own lenses on the world around them, often at a level of granularity never achieved before, instead of needing to rely on institutional sources for knowledge.

The Open Government Directive issued by President Obama in January 2009 spurred a virtual race to open up government data to the public, not just in the United States but also in the United Kingdom and many other countries.[9] The Big Society declaration published by the British government in the wake of the Obama administration's announcement included a key line: "We will create a new 'right to data' so that government-held data sets can be requested and used by the public, and then published on a regular basis."[10] More recently, in 2011, President Mwai Kibaki of Kenya launched the Kenya Open Data Initiative. Developed with support from Google, the World Bank's Mapping for Results platform, Ushahidi, and others, the initiative makes available a large number of data sets about population, poverty, education, energy, health, water, and sanitation. A user-friendly interface enables citizens to analyze the data, create maps and graphs, and—perhaps most importantly—see how their county or constituency fares in comparison with others.

By providing the users of services with this information, the Open Data Initiative empowers those users—who are also voters—to demand accountability from service providers and politicians.

As a result of these efforts, data on every aspect of our lives measured by the government, such as statistics on crime, health, education, and the economy, are becoming available to citizens in formats that can be put to use. And hacktivists—tech-savvy social activists—in collaboration with community organizations and ordinary citizens are using such data to create their own views of the world at levels both grand and small. The Sunlight Foundation, for example, combines data from multiple government and media sources in its Influence Explorer to track money flows within the political system: who is funding whom and in what amounts. Just type in the name of any state or federal elected official, and it reveals the money trail.

Release of government data in San Francisco heralded the creation of many useful local citizen apps, such as MuniApp,[11] which gives you real-time data on your smartphone on all the various Muni lines, including buses, trolleys, and street cars; NextBus, which helps you locate nearby stops and their respective bus routes based on your location; iBART, a real-time arrival feed that displays BART train arrivals; and SFScores, providing information on recent health violations by restaurants, including dates of the most recent citations and reasons for them. Outside of San Francisco, in one of the most sophisticated and easily accessible open data projects, LIVE Singapore! provides real-time visual information to citizens on everything from the location of taxis to traffic information and cell phone usage hubs.

On the other side of the spectrum there has been an unprecedented explosion of data collection by regular citizens, outside of any organizations or government agencies. People are collecting everything from environmental to health and crime information in their immediate locations and sharing and aggregating such data using Web tools. These DIY data collectors take a lightweight approach, using off-the-shelf devices such as phones, watches, and pedometers to record and share data. A thousand citizens in Paris, for example, wore "green watches" to produce an air-quality data set, rivaling the data produced by the city's official network of ten sensing stations.[12] In San Francisco, TenderNoise, a project created by many individuals collaborating on a pro-bono basis, placed professional decibel-monitoring equipment at intersections throughout the Tenderloin district and transformed the data into a Web-based interactive map that visualizes noise levels on various streets.

Beyond cities, citizens are getting involved in collecting environmental and ecological data. The Center for Embedded Networked Sensing at the University of California, Los Angeles, and the Santa Monica Mountains National Recreation Area have joined forces to create a mobile application to help locate and eradicate harmful nonnative plants found in environmentally sensitive public areas. The What's Invasive app for iPhone and Android handsets enables park visitors to snap photos, log locations, and automatically send files to the What's Invasive server. Using this data, park staff can revise maps in real time, providing a snapshot of where invasive weeds are popping up and where intervention is necessary.

Even earthquake researchers are increasingly relying on citizen data to advance discoveries. The Quake-Catcher Network, the one Rosa's household contributes to, is a distributed computing network linking together thousands of citizen computers to monitor motion and report big shakes to a central server. Although initially focused on the quake-prone San Francisco Bay and the Greater Los Angeles Basin areas, it can be extended to many other parts of the country and the world. In a similar project, more than eight thousand registered participants in the Citizen Weather Observer Program contribute weather-related data from their locations to improve the accuracy and timeliness of weather services.

Data is power because it provides reference points—the amount of crime in a particular neighborhood, levels of noise, environmental quality, plant and human ecosystems—for framing our reality.

These reference points enable us to tell stories about our world: this is a risky neighborhood, levels of stress are high here, this politician is in the pocket of oil companies, and so on. Think about maps, for example. Maps of all kinds (political, economic, ecological) aggregate data to create representations of reality. But these are top-down views, often representing political and power relations that determine what gets mapped and what gets left out as much as how things are mapped. Not surprisingly, maps of Australia show Australia as the center of the globe, which is hardly what U.S. maps show. U.S. World War II maps minimized distances between the United States and Europe. When average citizens are part of the process of creating reference points and constructing stories around them, they have the power to create *their* reality, to see the world from *their* perspective. As people get access to more and more data, they will increasingly be able to create their own narratives, their own maps of the terrain. When information is pushed down to the ground, linking to real people and real places, it will empower people to represent their views of reality and also to make decisions based on their representations.

Decision-Support Tools: Better Decisions with Help from Algorithms

Data and information are critical components for framing our reality and making decisions. But having great data and information, even at a fine-grain level, does not necessarily lead to better decisions. In her book *The Watchman's Rattle: Thinking Our Way Out of Extinction*, the sociobiologist Rebecca Costa argues that we have reached a point at which our cognitive tools are simply not capable of coping with the complexity of our civilization.[13] From looming water shortages to climate change, from massive degradation of our natural environment to gyrations of financial markets, we are faced with issues of enormous complexity but are equipped with cognitive tools that haven't changed substantially in millennia. Thanks to advances in neuroscience and behavioral economics, we are coming to terms with the reality that humans are not good at many elements of rational decision making, such as thinking through probabilities and risks and making choices based on those probabilities. A simple experiment in behavioral economics demonstrates this. If you are given $50 and are asked to choose to either keep $20 or lose $30, you are much more likely to choose to keep $20, although the outcome is exactly the same.[14] That is because when we are given a choice that involves risk of loss, our amygdala fires, generating feelings of fear and aversion. In other words, we humans are emotional, erratic, and situationally driven. In software-speak, this may not be a bug but a feature. We certainly don't want to use pure rationality when making moral or ethical decisions. As one writer puts it, "Pure reason is a disease."[15] It is something machines are good at, not humans.

Today we have an unprecedented opportunity to capitalize on the comparative advantages of both rational thinking and insight, bringing together the best of humans and smart machines. We can use machines to do rational analysis, accomplishing enormous feats of computation by crunching vast amounts of data, and we can rely on our human selves to formulate moral precepts, generate insight, respond spontaneously to the unique circumstances of the moment, and make decisions based on ethics, morals, and, yes, emotions. Thus we can enter into a new partnership with smart machines that amplifies our ability to deal with complexity and enhances the quality of our decisions.

To see glimpses of the potential of this new partnership, think back to the chess champion Garry Kasparov's defeat by the mighty IBM supercomputer in the 1990s. Many thought this spelled disaster for the human. Indeed today you can buy a $50 home PC chess program that will crush most grandmasters. But here is a twist: in 2005 the online chess-playing site Playchess.com hosted what it called a freestyle chess tournament in which anyone could compete in teams with other players or computers. Several groups of grandmasters working with several computers at the same time entered the competition. As Kasparov describes it, "The surprise came at the conclusion of the event. The winner was revealed to be not a grandmaster with a state-of-the-art PC but a pair of amateur American chess players using three computers at the same time. Their skill at manipulating and 'coaching' their computers to look very deeply into positions effectively counteracted the superior chess understanding of their grandmaster opponents and the greater computational power of other participants. Weak human + machine + better process was superior to a strong computer alone and, more remarkably, superior to a strong human + machine + inferior process."[16]

Amateurs armed with good strategies (thinking skills) and access to the computational power of machines turn out to be a winning combination. That's the best metaphor for the new kind of machine-human partnership we will see evolving in the future: with the help of smart machines as our partners, we can operate at the level of grandmasters not just in chess but in most other domains of our lives, from science and medicine to governance and policymaking. This powerful combination gives us hope for not only making better decisions today but also fulfilling what is, according to Jonas Salk, the discoverer of penicillin, our greatest responsibility: to be "good ancestors," people who maximize not only our individual well-being but also the well-being of a larger community today and of future generations.[17]

The ability to enlist the aid of smart machines in incorporating many different variables and playing out multitudes of different scenarios is what enables Rosa and her cohort of amateurs to make complex budget decisions. Using simulations and sophisticated data analysis tools, they are able to see complex interactions and interdependencies without being professional politicians or finance wizards. In fact we are already using such tools, some simple, some quite sophisticated, to help us make a whole host of decisions. We model climate change scenarios and impacts of financial market interventions; we use software to pick optimal places to drill for oil. On a personal level, we routinely check Amazon ratings before buying a product or scan Yelp reviews before deciding where to eat. Yelp, Amazon, and many other recommendation and rating sites are decision-support systems we have come to rely on in our daily lives. More and more of our choices, from which medical procedure to undergo to what food to eat, will be aided by decision-support systems.

As sophisticated tools for decision support become accessible to amateurs, we can improve our policymaking process. A prototype of how this might look was recently created by a group of hackers, artists, and social activists during San Francisco's Summer of Smart, an effort to create new models of governance in the city. A simulation game called YAY TAXES! invited participants to visualize connections between beneficial public services and tax dollars. "Do you enjoy watching a holiday fireworks display? You betcha! Glad your toilet flushes when you want it to? Of course!" proclaimed the game. "Let's visualize the connection between beneficial public services and tax dollars. Participate in allocating California income taxes. Decide how much tax money to collect and how to allocate your budget, then see what sort of neighborhood you've created. Listen in as residents tweet about how your decisions affect their health and safety."[18] Later versions of the simulation promise participants the ability to compare their choices with their neighbors', highlighting differences in priorities between neighborhoods and also indicating which politicians have a voting record that reflects these priorities. A similar but more developed version of citizen participation in budget decisions is Budget Hero, a game-like platform that educates players about the federal budget and engages them in the process of making decisions and trade-offs for allocating federal money. It's just a game today, but why not make it into a real decision-making platform?

In a different domain, a simulation developed by the Brookings Institution called FamilyScape analyzes factors influencing unintended pregnancy such as sexual activity, contraceptive use, and fertility levels and their impacts on rates of abortion and children's chances of being born into poverty.[19] This simulation can be used to estimate and compare the cost-effectiveness of different policies that affect family formation and child poverty rates. FamilyScape is part of a more ambitious simulation project called the Social Genome Project, whose aim is to create a simulation model of social mobility over the life cycle—from the prenatal stage to age forty—in the United States in order to help policymakers, practitioners, and researchers assess the cost-effectiveness of various strategies for improving children's life prospects. The model could be used to assess a variety of policies designed to increase the proportion of children who are "middle class by middle age." Creators of the tool envision that "the Social Genome Project will produce a powerful and unique new tool for policy analysis—a tool that would, for the first time, make it possible to use rigorous logic and good data and evidence to discipline and improve the efforts of all those interested in the goal of advancing opportunity."[20]

In an even more ambitious project, a consortium of European researchers led by a Swiss scientist, Dirk Helbing, is working to develop the Living Earth Simulator, which would be capable of considering interactions between up to 10 billion individuals to facilitate the modeling and analysis of "techno-commercial-sociological-ecological systems."[21] The aim of this ambitious platform is to understand how the world works so that imminent crises can be predicted and ameliorated or even prevented. Integral to the initiative's success is a platform that can record and analyze massive amounts of data, transfer it to computer models, and make it universally usable. New data-mining methods and real-time data set collection will enable what is called reality mining, analyzing real-time data streams and making forecasts based on them. The project is interdisciplinary, bringing together computer scientists, information and communications technology specialists, complexity scientists, economists, sociologists, and sustainability and systemic risk experts. Think of it as a kind of Google Earth for society. And while claims that we will have the ability to predict financial and other crises may never be realized (because the process of gathering such information is likely to change the outcomes), the ability to unearth patterns and interconnections between events through such simulations is promising.

When relying on tools such as modeling and simulations, it is important to keep in mind that models are not reality. The map is not the territory. This is the warning and admonition that Rosa and her fellow Agorans hear from facilitators. Models are only as good as the data that feed them. Models are also based on algorithms and assumptions about how things work, and these assumptions sometimes turn out to be wrong. However, with more and more data pouring in, the quality of our modeling tools is improving daily. In the end, basing decisions on solid models and bringing the best science into the policy and governance process may be far preferable to the way too many policy decisions are made today: on the basis of rhetoric, demagoguery, political exigencies, and self-interest.

If we use these tools well, understanding their promise and their limitations, we will achieve a powerful combination of the thinking skills of humans and the computational power of machines that will enable us to engage in policymaking and governance far more in line with the complexities of the issues facing us today.

Engagement Platforms: From Rational Ignorance to Public Deliberation

In April 2010 the U.S. State Department launched an innovative experiment in public engagement. Called Opinion Space, it is a game-like platform that combines elements of deliberative polling, collaborative filtering, and data visualization to ask average individuals what policy priorities Secretary of State Hillary Clinton should pursue. New visitors to the site were asked to what degree they agreed or disagreed with five baseline statements, such as "Climate change poses a threat to political stability around the world." The responses were combined to display each new participant as a unique point on a map, showing to what degree her or his opinions concurred with those of others. Participants could also express their own ideas and rate those of others on levels of insightfulness and degrees of agreement. Thousands of people from around the world expressed their views over a period of months, and the results could be easily seen on an intuitive graphical map displaying patterns, trends, and insights. Opinion Space is an easy-to-comprehend intuitive snapshot of what people think should be U.S. policy priorities.[22]

Opinion Space and many other platforms like it (creators of Opinion Space have now introduced a new participatory platform called Hybrid Wisdom) are part of what the publisher Tim O'Reilly calls the "architecture of participation," design of the Web that enables and facilitates participation and contributions by the masses.[23] Ken Goldberg, an engineering professor at University of California, Berkeley and the lead creator of Opinion Space, argues that we are moving from the age of information to the age of opinions. And the architecture of participation—multitudes of platforms built for people to express opinions, share views, and review products and services—is what is enabling this move.[24]

Technologies of participation call for new political structures and new political processes. They level the playing field: everyone can express their opinions directly, undermining the need for proxy representation that is built into the government structure in the United States and many other countries. Today's technologies, for the first time in world history, may enable a true democracy of the kind we have not seen since ancient Greece. The challenge is to improve the quality of our opinions—that is, make them more grounded in solid data and information—in order to improve the quality of our decisions. There is a big difference between creating the Twitter hashtag "f---youwashington,"[25] with thousands of people streaming 140-character frustrations over government gridlock (an important way to take the pulse of the nation, no doubt), and the kind of positive engagement based on thoughtful debate and discussion envisioned by James Fishkin and his colleagues.

Early experiments such as Opinion Space integrate elements of deliberation and thoughtful debate into engagement platforms, but more work remains to be done. At the Institute for the Future our platform Foresight Engine is specifically geared to exploring potential future scenarios and engaging both experts and nonexperts in generating insights and potential solutions to complex issues. The platform presents a future scenario and calls on participants to think through possible outcomes—the best and the worst thing that could happen. Participants are asked to play a positive or a negative imagination card. They can then play additional cards to add to other people's ideas or disagree and offer a different opinion. The process of engagement is moderated by game masters who guide online conversations, highlighting interesting ideas and redirecting conversations that have been exhausted.

Since 2006 Foresight Engine has been used in both public venues and large multinational corporations to generate ideas and come up with solutions to various challenges. The Myelin Repair Foundation, as mentioned in Chapter 2, used it in an exercise called Breakthroughs to Cures to generate new ideas for how to change the medical research system to develop treatments and cures for patients faster. The engineering society IEEE used the Foresight Engine platform to explore the technologies, policies, and resources needed to create the best possible future for the smart grid. During the Magnetic South exercise using the Foresight Engine run by Landcare Research and the city council of Christchurch, New Zealand, more than 850 people around the world took part in an online discussion about the long-term future of Christchurch.[26] Almost nine thousand ideas were generated on how the city might recover from the February 2011 earthquakes.[27] All the data from the exercise was released under a Creative Commons Attribution 3.0 New Zealand license in order to enable people to create their own visualizations and analyses. As one of the participants summed it up, Magnetic South is "about the power of social wisdom."[28] Landcare Research, together with the Christchurch Earthquake Recovery Authority, plan to conduct more of these crowdsourcing events around specific policy issues.

In one of the most interesting and perhaps most ambitious public engagement experiments, the Institute for the Future in collaboration with the Naval Postgraduate School in Monterey, California, used a platform called MMOWGLI (Massive Multiplayer Online War Game Leveraging the Internet) for a project conducted for the U.S. Office of Naval Research.[29] The purpose of the platform was to engage participants in finding solutions to sea piracy. Participants visiting the website viewed a video scenario of three pirate ships holding the world hostage. In the scenario, Chinese-U.S. relations are strained to the limit; both countries have naval ships in the area; humanitarian aid for rig workers is blocked; and the world is blaming the United States for plundering African resources. Those who signed up to play the game were asked, "What do you do?" Two text boxes popped onto the screen: one, labeled *Innovate*, asked, "What new resources could turn the tide in the Somali pirate situation?" and the other, labeled *Defend*, asked, "What new risks could arise that would transform the Somali pirate situation?"

TenderVoice is another project that harnesses the power of engagement platforms. It takes stock of the needs of a population and engages citizens in thinking about what change is necessary for their city or a neighborhood. Created in less than forty-eight hours at the Great Urban Hack held at San Francisco's Gray Area Foundation for the Arts in 2010, the project blended microblogging and location-based storytelling to paint a compelling picture of the most urgent human needs and desires in the city's Tenderloin neighborhood.[30] Members of the project team ventured out across the neighborhood to ask people two simple questions: What do you need? and What do you think? The questions demanded just a few seconds of time to answer and were left open to interpretation. The resulting online audio map captured the essence of one of the most diverse and historically troubled neighborhoods in the city. The team hopes to use this approach to complement formal City Community Needs Assessments.

These early experiments in public engagement in policymaking reveal how the diffusion of engagement platforms can turn every citizen into an opinion maker and participant in the governance process. The trick is to ensure that these opinions are informed—that is, to use the flood of data and the power of simulation and modeling to enable everyone to increase their levels of knowledge about issues and to make the process of governance more deliberative.

Microparticipation:
Citizen Engagement in Governance and Provision of Services

For five weeks during the spring of 2009, my colleagues at the Institute for the Future ran a simulation game called Ruby's Bequest. The game turned participants into citizens of a fictional town called Deepwell, a typical town strapped for resources and coping with financial problems and low levels of community engagement. One of the wealthiest citizens of Deepwell has passed away and left a large sum of money to be given to the town under one condition: the town has to increase its level of caring. The wealthy patron did not specify what that meant other than to make it apparent that the current level of caring within the community is low and has to be increased significantly. Over five weeks, participants shared their stories, frustrations, advice, hopes, and ideas for how to increase the level of caring in Deepwell.

The alternative reality of Deepwell, for better and worse, has and will increasingly become the reality of many communities forced into a process of civic soul searching. They will need to make hard decisions about how to provide public services and how to govern in the new circumstances of budget cuts and slow growth. So the responses that participants in Ruby's Bequest provided and the strategies they came up with can be viewed as blueprints for the future of governance in many communities. The most important and widespread strategy we saw in the game was to increase levels of engagement by average citizens in the provision of services in a net-worked, collaborative, and ad hoc fashion, breaking down many big professional tasks and services into microcontributions provided by many individuals.

This is not new. In fact for most of urban history, the role of government was limited. What few public services existed were typically delivered by religious or community-based organizations. Over the coming years, as cities everywhere struggle to maintain services, we will see a renaissance of citizen-provided services. These initiatives will utilize rich data ecologies and engagement platforms to replace and sometimes enrich existing services with loosely coordinated citizen efforts. These efforts will transform how services are delivered and funded in every area, from caregiving to education and emergency services.

This is already beginning to happen around the country. In San Ramon, California, for example, if you have a heart attack, chances are someone around you will send an alert on a smart-phone that will locate people in the immediate vicinity who are trained in CPR. More than 300,000 people in the United States require CPR annually, yet only 26 percent of them actually receive this lifesaving procedure! However, this percentage may increase dramatically if the app developed by the San Ramon Valley Fire Protection District is widely adopted by other municipalities.[31] The app is a location-aware service available on smartphones that alerts users who are trained in CPR if someone nearby is having a cardiac emergency. It directs citizen rescuers to the location of the emergency and the location of the closest public access AED (automated external defibrillator). It gives average citizens who are trained in CPR a chance to provide a valuable public service and in return receive a sense of accomplishment and satisfaction that goes along with it. And it gives those suffering a cardiac arrest a greater chance of surviving. Since the announcement of the service, demand for CPR training has increased dramatically in the San Ramon area. People want to serve when the service is meaningful and when they are called upon. Just as Rosa became an expert on budgets, rising to the occasion when called to serve in the New Agora, many people when given responsibility to serve—be it providing CPR or contributing data for the community's welfare—want to excel at the task.

This desire of people to contribute in the service of a larger good is the premise on which Groundcrew (later called Citizen Logistics) was built.[32] A social tool for coordinating local action networks to complete real-world missions, Groundcrew utilized geolocation and messaging to help average citizens rally community members around a particular issue, mobilize teams in real time, and reuse, manage, and share resources during and after emergencies. The inspiration for the platform was cofounder Joe Edelman's experience as a relief worker in post-Katrina New Orleans, where he was appalled to see the slow coordination and mobilization of relief efforts. Groundcrew was successfully deployed in the Boston area after a severe blizzard to assemble and coordinate the work of SnowCrew, volunteers who were ready and willing to shovel snow for their neighbors. The uses of this service are potentially endless—from oil rig evacuations to the provision of emergency medical care and management of traffic flows. Traditionally only large organizations with multimillion-dollar budgets have had access to real-time planning and mobilization software, but today we're seeing a host of small projects and initiatives like Groundcrew entering the domain.

The growing accessibility and capability of tools for networked collaboration will allow us to unbundle many large tasks, adopting the model of open-source systems to distribute ad hoc smaller tasks across a community. In some cases, such efforts will be filling gaps left by cutbacks in government services; in others, they will be enhancing existing services, making them more efficient and far-reaching. An example of how this might look comes from Hawaii, where residents tapped into their collective skills and resources to repair a flooded-out section of a road when the state's transportation budget lacked the funding for repairs. Updating the tradition of a community barn raising, this group repurposed online collaborative tools to identify needed skill sets, coordinate participation, and manage the overall process. While there will certainly always be tasks too critical or specialized to be left to self-organized networks, many public services could be improved by citizen microcontributions.

Restoring Democracy to "We the People"

In 1961 Buckminster Fuller proposed the creation of a World Game for the purpose of "making the world work for 100 percent of humanity in the shortest possible time through spontaneous cooperation without ecological damage or disadvantage to anyone."[33] The World Game he imagined was a collaborative process in which players came together to propose solutions to large-scale world problems within a specific time frame. The team that could demonstrate a solution using the fastest known technologies and available resources would win the first round. Subsequent rounds would be won by teams that could improve upon earlier solutions. Today the World Game continues to be played across universities and is currently being further developed by o.s.Earth. John Hunter, a public school teacher in Virginia, carries the torch lit by Fuller by engaging his grade-school students in playing the World Peace Game, which he describes in a TED Talk.[34] In a similar but more far-reaching proposal aimed at even broader citizen engagement in governance, Stanford's James Fishkin has proposed the establishment of a new national holiday, Deliberation Day, during which all voters would be invited and incentivized to participate in local, randomly assigned discussion groups as preparation for the voting process later.[35]

Both Fuller's and Fishkin's proposals aim to restore the democratic process to "we the people," to make the policy process more deliberative, more democratic, and more transparent. Our technology infrastructure, the new levels of data and information at our disposal, and our urgent need to create new patterns of governance in line with today's level of scientific knowledge make it possible for us to turn these two interrelated ideas into reality. These and other experiments outlined in this chapter are blueprints pointing us in the direction of not only creating a better governance system but also reinventing our patterns of living and our roles in our communities. In the New Agora, we take back our citizenship—the right and the privilege to decide how we govern ourselves. These fundamental rights and privileges are not outsourced to elites but are the purview of every citizen. By taking back our citizenship, we once again become "we the people."

Everyone's a Scientist

All human beings by nature desire to know.
ARISTOTLE, *METAPHYSICS*

Future Scenario 2021: Open-Source Biology

guess I just don't get it," Deepa Jeffery's father tells her, shaking his head. "People should be excited about science, not about getting a T-shirt."

"Well, Dad, maybe a T-shirt is exactly what people need to get really excited about science," Deepa laughs. "Or at least excited enough to open their wallets."

In truth, Deepa was still getting used to the idea herself. Asking the public to contribute directly to research—and plying them with thank-you gifts—had become pretty much a requirement for most funding agencies, government and foundations alike. Even the National Institutes of Health (NIH) and the National Science Foundation had turned over 50 percent of their budgets to the public to decide what projects to fund. Increasing numbers of researchers were bypassing agency funding altogether and soliciting money from the public directly through crowdfunding platforms such as SciFund. Of course, it was easy to get the public to donate if you were doing research on photogenic animals—just post an appeal to help save the whales or owls or even frogs, add a couple of cute photos, and the money poured in. Thousands of donors even wanted to participate themselves, doing observations from their locations, tagging photographs, contributing computing resources, sometimes doing statistical analysis. But how do you get people interested in the pneumococcus bacterium? It isn't cute at all. Photos of tiny maggot-looking lumps growing on a blood-agar plate don't quite have the appeal of an endangered baby fox snuggling up to its mother in the snow.

That was why, at the last meet-up held at BioSci, a community lab where Deepa was conducting her research and teaching a class in synthetic biology, she and her team brainstormed ways to get the public interested.

"Why should people care about this bacterium?" was the first question the group had, and Deepa was eager to answer it.

"The pneumococcus bacterium is responsible for 1.1 million deaths globally each year, and in the United States it's one of the top ten causes of death," she responded. "It has real economic consequences too. The economic burden resulting from associated diseases and deaths exceeds $5 billion annually."

She noticed a couple of yawns. One team member was checking her phone. It's time, she thought, to pull out the big guns.

"Look, it's the most common cause of bacterial meningitis, community-acquired pneumonia, and bacteremia in the world!"

There was silence. These horrifying facts were not being received with the stunned gasps she hoped they would evoke. Deepa sighed.

"So, uh, those things you listed," a twenty-something with spiky hair and thick-rimmed glasses said, lazily raising his hand. "Those are all bad, right?"

"Absolutely," Deepa said, wondering if it was a sincere question or if she was being mocked. "Those things I listed, they're infections of the brain and spinal cord, lung infections, bacteria in the blood, all sorts of infections. Pediatric ear infections . . ."

"Ear infections?!" exclaimed Angela Dane, herself a new mom. "Man, I hate those things! I can't tell you how many times we've been to the doctor for an ear infection in the last six months. Now you've got my interest."

"Yeah, I guess '1.1 million deaths globally' was a bit of a snooze," Deepa thought. "All these people dying, and what really gets people's interest is ear infections!" But she didn't voice her sarcasm. After all, this was exactly the kind of input she was looking for to help her BioSci team craft an appeal for funding.

In the span of a few days, the group came up with a plan for framing the appeal for money, decided on sponsorship levels, and made a list of rewards for contributions, including a T-shirt with a cute crying baby created by a member who was a design school student. They also developed plans for spreading the word about the project to different communities. The agreement was that appeals for funds would be posted on multiple websites so the money could be pooled. In fact, having funding from another community, such as Kickstarter, often helped projects get funding from the NIH. For each of these sites, the appeal would be framed differently. When talking to the NIH, Deepa was firmly in her wheelhouse; she would include a lot of scientific data on mortality and morbidity, cite other research, and explain her methodology in depth. But to get attention from the public she would talk about the research in lay terms, appealing to parents and anyone else who would love to help conquer pneumonia and earaches.

Everyone on the team would activate their networks and appeal for contributions. Angela would use her mom networks to spread the word. Mike Bright worked with a network of nursing homes, so he would be spreading the word through that community. "And don't forget moms and dads, relatives, friends, neighbors, anyone . . . We want to raise $100,000, not a small amount of money. But just think, it's only two thousand people at $50 each. We can do this," said Peter Milovich. He knew what he was talking about, having raised $1 million the previous year to build a super-cheap laser cutter that was currently being produced at a manufacturing facility nearby.

Deepa felt lucky to be part of the BioSci community. There

was no way she could undertake the project without their support. She thought of everyone who would be working on her team as her "amplifiers." Within this larger community, some knew how to take dense scientific language and convert it into something average people could get excited about; others knew how to activate networks, how to program, where to get the cheapest equipment; and, yes, some even knew the best places to produce cheap T-shirts and keychains.

When Deepa was an undergraduate, she had gotten only glimpses of this new, more collaborative way of doing science. In 2010 her postdoc team at Berkeley won the award for Best Health Project at the International Genetically Engineered Machine (iGEM) competition, the premiere student synthetic biology competition. As part of the competition, each team received a kit of biological parts at the beginning of the summer from the Registry of Standard Biological Parts. Over the years iGEM teams had been amassing a centralized, open-source genetic library of thousands of these biological parts, called BioBricks. Teams used these pieces of DNA to build their projects and also to contribute new BioBricks to the registry. Bio-Bricks ranged from those that killed cells to ones that made cells smell like bananas. The composition and function of each DNA fragment was catalogued in an online wiki, and copies of the actual DNA were stored in a freezer at MIT. Deepa vividly remembered getting the envelope with the BioBricks; they looked like red smudges or stains. Over the summer, her team used these to modify DNA from E. coli to diagnose and treat environmentally accelerated asthma in children. The team was ecstatic; the power to create new organisms was something they had never dreamed they could have. She still remembered how stunned they were to accomplish this feat.

As excited as she was by the promise of synthetic biology and the ability to create biological systems from standard parts, what Deepa had loved most about the project was the spirit of teamwork. She wanted to continue working with a diverse mix of people. The team at Berkeley, which included computer scientists, electronics engineers, and molecular biologists, went on to start a new company that partnered with the CureTogether asthma patient community to help develop a research agenda and populate clinical trials. They licensed the final technology to a pharmaceutical company in India. By then BioSci was up and running, so instead of building her own lab, Deepa and a few of her colleagues started using BioSci as a base for their research. BioSci had more equipment than they could afford on their own, and the lab had been certified by the government. But perhaps the most important thing BioSci provided was access to a community. It was like having an army of volunteers working with you.

Deepa's hope was that once the pneumococcal genome had been sequenced and the genes responsible for severe disease had been isolated, they would be able to produce biological agents that would target them, thus helping prevent, diagnose, and treat various pneumococcal diseases. She was not sure whether, when that day came, she would turn the process over to another company or she and her team would continue to try to do it on their own. After all, there were now several communities doing independent clinical trials and it was becoming increasingly possible to manufacture drugs in outsourced facilities that were reputable and certified. The whole field had been turned upside down in the past ten years thanks to advances in synthetic biology. There were so many more options for how and where to do research and how and where to produce and distribute products.

Deepa frequently talked about all the changes in biology with her dad, who was her biggest booster. While he didn't get the T-shirt thing, he did get open-source biology, and it excited him. He himself liked to spend his free time tinkering with electronic components in the garage and was responsible for introducing Deepa to the idea of open-source software at a young age. So he was excited and eager to advise her. He had hoped Deepa would become an engineer like him, but alas, she chose biology. "Well, biology seems more and more like engineering," he told her, "so you followed in my footsteps after all."

A New Ecology of Science: From Small to Big Science and Back

In his famous lecture and later book titled *The Two Cultures,* the British scientist and novelist C. P. Snow lamented the growing gap between the intellectuals (mostly literary intellectuals) and the scientists. Between the two, he saw a "gulf of mutual incomprehension—sometimes (particularly among the young), hostility and dislike, but most of all lack of understanding."[1] Interestingly, the gap Snow lamented was a gap between two elites, two otherwise very similar groups, "comparable in intelligence, identical in race, not grossly different in social origin, earning about the same incomes, who had almost ceased to communicate at all."[2]

As important as the gap between the two elites may have been, the larger gap that Snow (and most other observers until recently) did not consider is the one between average people and scientists. In fact we have become used to treating science as a priestly profession open to a few highly degreed experts, a world of its own, accessible only to those with the right credentials. Yet developmental psychologists such as Alison Gopnik at UC Berkeley argue that all human beings possess an innate "explanatory drive," motivating us to actively test hypotheses concerning causal relations in the natural world. In this sense, we are all scientists by nature. Gopnik argues that this explanatory drive is "like our drive for food or sex. When we're presented with a puzzle, a mystery, a hint of a pattern, something that doesn't quite make sense, we work until we find a solution."[3] We feel pleasure at the "Aha!" or "Eureka!" moments, when we're satisfied that we have solved some cognitively irksome problem. Explanatory instinct is particularly evident in babies as they discover the rules of the world around them and test theories of how things work.

Testing hypotheses, trying out different solutions, and discovering patterns are a natural part of who we are. We have done this for centuries, in caves, in fields, in alchemists' labs, kitchens, and garages. In fact one of the most impactful scientific inventions of our time, the long-lasting electric lightbulb, was the creation of a school dropout without any formal degree whose elementary school teacher thought the hyperactive youngster's brain was addled. Thomas Edison held many jobs before the age of thirty, from selling newspapers to being a telegraph operator, but he worked his whole life to satisfy the explanatory drive. He was the ultimate tinkerer, one of the most prolific inventors in history, holding 1,093 patents in the United States as well as many in the United Kingdom, France, and Germany.[4]

Early in his life, Edison conducted research in self-built labs and developed a hearty dislike for the obtuse language of much of science. (He thought the aristocratic terms in which Newton wrote his theories were unnecessarily confusing to the average person.) Then, ironically, he created the first industrial research lab in Menlo Park, New Jersey, the opening of which in 1876 heralded the beginning of "big science."[5] For a hundred years after the establishment of Edison's lab, "serious scientists" displaced tinkerers in the discovery business. Production of science became highly organized and turned into a huge enterprise practiced almost exclusively within the confines of large institutions, mostly university, corporate, and government R&D labs with access to large budgets and expensive equipment.

Just as the creation of large hierarchical corporations was a necessity and an outgrowth of existing technologies and the level of scientific knowledge at the time, the creation of large R&D labs was a great innovation, leading to efficiencies and enabling us to do such amazing things as send humans into outer space, create a supercomputer, and conquer polio. In the period starting with World War II and lasting through the Cold War, the federal government viewed science as a strategic imperative, building new laboratories to conduct military research at MIT, UC Berkeley, CalTech, and dozens of state universities, and creating a network of government-owned facilities for atomic physics, aerodynamics, and other specialized sciences. In the 1980s the passage of the Bayh-Dole Act allowed universities to privatize research done with public funds, resulting in closer ties between universities and industry, with many professors and students pursuing academic research and commercial applications simultaneously.

Thus industry, government, and universities have been the key drivers of science for more than a hundred years.[6] But just as in every other domain of human activity, the foundations of this model are changing, and the outlines of a new ecology of science are emerging. As exemplified by Deepa and her BioSci community, this new ecology rests on several key elements. With the help of new lightweight tools for conducting research, a growing army of amateur scientists and tinkerers can begin participating in the discovery process. Amplified by crowdfunding platforms for science and for sharing data, they create new kinds of online and physical communities for science, expanding the ranks of who does science and blurring the boundaries between credentialed scientists, hobbyists, and passionate amateurs.

Lightweight Research Tools: Empowering Amateurs

A polymerase chain reaction (PCR) machine has become an indispensable tool for molecular biology research. PCR is a method for replicating DNA that makes it possible to take a small amount, or even a single molecule, and copy it an almost infinite number of times. This is important because DNA of interest often exists in quantities too small to detect or may be mixed in with other DNA. The process has been used for everything from exploring personal genomes to detecting diseases such as HIV and H1N1 virus.

In a famous case, two New York high school students used PCR machines in a school science project to expose fraud in sushi restaurants in New York. Kate Stoeckle and Louisa Strauss, students at Trinity School in Manhattan, checked sixty samples of seafood from New York restaurants and found that one-fourth of the samples with identifiable DNA were mislabeled: "A piece of sushi sold as the luxury treat white tuna turned out to be Mozambique tilapia, a much cheaper fish that is often raised by farming. Roe supposedly from flying fish was actually from smelt. Seven of nine samples that were called red snapper were mislabeled, and they turned out to be anything from Atlantic cod to Acadian redfish, an endangered species."[7] So much for paying for expensive sushi!

The PCR process for DNA analysis was developed by Kary Banks Mullis, an American biochemist who subsequently won the Nobel Prize in Chemistry for perfecting the process while working for Cetus Corporation, which sold the patent to Roche Molecular Systems.[8] As mentioned in Chapter 1, until recently PCR machines were selling at around $10,000, hardly affordable for average citizens. Then two biohackers, Josh Perfetto and Tito Jankowski, created the OpenPCR machine, which you can purchase online for about $600. At that price, the machine has become affordable to many, including high school and college teachers as well as individuals for their home and community spaces.

Many other kinds of scientific instruments and tools are increasingly moving from R&D labs into homes, garages, and shared community spaces. In a December 2010 article, the *New York Times* reporter Peter Wayner noted the growth of home labs, which feature telescopes, infrared thermometers, wearable cameras, microscopes connected to computers and smartphones, and many other lightweight and portable scientific tools and devices that can be converted for use in science.[9] Some people who set up home laboratories are serious hobbyists; others are home-schooling parents educating their children, or just tinkerers.

Numerous websites have sprung up where people can purchase lab tools for their homes. Sites such as ThinkGeek.com and Carolina Biological Supply offer, among other things, three models of microscopes, telescopes, cameras with motion-activated sensors, and kits for testing your genes. The citizen science these tools enable is often serious but is also often imbued with a sense of whimsy and discovery. Many members of the BioCurious community, for example, have used a kit from Carolina Biological Supply to test themselves for a gene that causes them not to taste the bitterness in brussels sprouts. Turns out that only a few people have this gene, and you can find out if you are one of them for about $200, the price of the home test kit.

Even without the tools at home, people can get access to expensive scientific resources and databases online. Today anyone with a computer and a connection can join forces with owners of large scientific telescopes to observe galaxies, see pictures from the Moon's surface, track comets, and explore faraway stars. Ariel Waldman's Spacehack is a directory of ways to participate in this kind of space exploration from the comfort of your home, interact with the space community, and get access to equipment and data. For example, participants in the Galaxy Zoo project get access to data from NASA's Hubble Space Telescope. The purpose of the project is to understand different types of galaxies and how galaxies form. If you decide to participate, you will be given a short tutorial on how to classify galaxies according to shape (elliptical, spiral, or irregular) and rotation (clockwise or anticlockwise), and you will get images taken by the robotic telescope as part of the Sloan Digital Sky Survey. The original Galaxy Zoo was launched in July 2007, with a data set made up of a million galaxy images.

Another project, the PlanetQuest Collaboratory, will turn your computer into a virtual astronomical observatory that you can use to make and share real scientific discoveries. The telescopes involved in the project are focused on extremely dense star regions, such as the center of the galaxy in Sagittarius. When an observing run ends and thousands of images have been collected, data will be downloaded to your computer. Then special Collaboratory software will begin analyzing it. You can classify stars no one has catalogued before and maybe even find a new planet. Consider the discovery by the amateur astronomer Nick Howes on March 18 and 19, 2010. While working from his desktop computer in the United Kingdom using a remotely controlled telescope located in Hawaii and operated by the Faulkes Telescope Project, he dialed up the coordinates of a comet he had been observing and shot a set of six photos showing an object moving away from the icy nucleus of the comet. What he captured was the breakup of comet C2007 C3, an observation hailed by the International Astronomical Union as a "major astronomical discovery."[10]

If instead of buying or accessing a remote telescope, you want to build your own, you can join the Telescope Makers' Workshop, an all-volunteer group. Bring your materials and they will provide you with knowledge, enthusiasm, and advice to help you make your own telescope. No experience necessary. You can have a complete eight-inch telescope for less than $300.[11]

If you want to be involved in exploration here on Earth rather than in space, you can join projects such as National Geographic's Field Expedition: Mongolia.[12] As part of the project team, you can examine real-time satellite photos from the Valley of the Khans—a remote region that was once Genghis Khan's homeland—and help flag irregularities for scientists on the ground to investigate. Dr. Albert Yu-Min Lin, a research scientist at the University of California, San Diego, and a National Geographic Emerging Explorer, and his team are conducting a first-of-its-kind noninvasive archaeological survey using state-of-the art equipment: unmanned aerial vehicles, ground-penetrating radar, remote sensors, satellite imagery, and even a 3-D virtual reality chamber. But all the technology in the world doesn't compare to the human eye, which is needed to go through the thousands of images these technologies generate to spot irregularities and potentially interesting sites for further investigation. Lin is hoping to recruit a citizen science expedition team of between a thousand and ten thousand people to do the work.

In his book *What Technology Wants,* Kevin Kelly, a writer, futurist, and founding editor of *Wired* magazine, explores the notion of what he calls the technium, the globalized, interconnected system of technological development of which we humans are a part.[13] Arguing that the processes of creating the technium are akin to those of biological evolution, Kelly writes that the technium exhibits a similar tendency toward self-organizing complexity, following several laws in the process. In answering the question in the book's title, he argues that technology wants, among other things, to increase diversity, maximize freedom and choices, expand the space of the possible, reach ubiquity and free-ness, and increase social codependency.[14]

Whether or not you agree with Kelly's laws of technology, we are clearly seeing scientific tools following the path he outlines. Our tools for scientific discovery are becoming less expensive, smaller, and more ubiquitous, and in the process they're increasing the diversity of people involved in doing science and the interdependencies between professionals and amateur scientists and nonscientists.

Democratizing Discovery: A Growing Army of Professional Hobbyists

John Falk, the Oregon State professor and specialist in free-choice learning mentioned in Chapter 4, points out an interesting statistic: "For more than a decade, performance by U.S. school aged children on international tests such as the quadrennial Trends in International Mathematics and Science Study (TIMSS) and the Programme for International Student Assessment (PISA) has followed a consistent pattern. Elementary-school-aged U.S. children perform as well as or better than most children in the world, but the performance of older U.S. children has been mediocre at best. Interestingly, however, for more than twenty years, U.S. adults have consistently outperformed their international counterparts on science literacy measures, including adults from South Korea and Japan, as well as Western European countries such as Germany and the United Kingdom."[15]

Explanation: the public learns science in settings and situations outside of school. American adults live in a science-rich environment, surrounded by museums, technologies at home and at work, parks, science centers, and science programs on television. Our environment and media channels are saturated with scientific information and opportunities to learn science. A 2009 report by the National Research Council cited by Falk, *Learning Science in Informal Environments: People, Places, and Pursuits,* describes a range of evidence demonstrating that even everyday experiences such as a walk in the park contribute to people's knowledge and interest in science and the environment.[16] People also become deeply engaged in science once they have a pressing personal need to know. This is exactly what happens when someone is diagnosed with leukemia or diabetes; the individual and often family members and friends become experts on the disease. And with more and more information available online, they can acquire a lot of relevant knowledge. This is precisely what motivated an MIT grad student, Kay Aull, to build her own genetic testing kit in her closet. Her father was diagnosed with the hereditary disease hemochromatosis, a serious condition in which too much iron builds up in the body, leading to fatigue and joint pain. This motivated her to find out if she had the same genetic mutation.

Even without the threat of serious disease, dedicated hobbyists often have a very impressive level of knowledge. Research conducted by Marni Berendsen, an education researcher and the project director of the NASA Night Sky Network, showed that amateur astronomy club members lacking college-level astronomy training often knew more general astronomy than did undergraduate astronomy majors.[17] Research by others has also shown that hobbyists, many with little formal training, exhibit high levels of knowledge and depth of understanding. Such hobbyists often have collegial relationships with experts in the field, and some, like Nick Howes, having put themselves in the right place at the right time, have contributed scientific discoveries and investigations. A series of studies by the Canadian science education researcher Wolff-Michael Roth and his colleagues found that members of an environmental activist group working on the revitalization of a local creek and its watershed used knowledge derived from a wide variety of resources, virtually none of which required or drew from school-based sources, to inform their work.[18]

These professional hobbyists are blurring the lines between amateur and professional in science. With knowledge available on the Web, inexpensive tools, and new ways of connecting with other amateurs and professionals, their ranks are growing and they are changing the landscape of science. Empowered with these tools and knowledge, many more people are turning into inventors, makers, and tinkerers, doing science in garages and community lab spaces, or contributing to scientific projects led by professional scientists. They are part of a larger maker movement, a growing population of do-it-yourself and do-it-ourselves enthusiasts who are eager to create, design, modify, and build things on their own, from robots to biological organisms.

Tapping into this growing interest, O'Reilly Media launched *Make* magazine in February 2005 as a celebration of the DIY mind-set and as a means to encourage the sharing of ideas, tools, and experiences. In 2007 the magazine reportedly had a circulation of 90,000;[19] by 2009 the number was more than 125,000.[20] The editor of *Make*, Dale Dougherty, has also created Maker Faire, a two-day event that celebrates arts, crafts, engineering, and science projects and the DIY mind-set. Described variously as a Grateful Dead concert for geeks and a Burning Man for families, Maker Faire puts the explanatory drive on display. It is an inspiration for kids and adults, where everyone can find something that fires imagination, from a turkey baster that converts into a flute to a giant talking giraffe or rocket launchers showcased by the venture capitalist Steve Jurvetson. First held in the San Francisco Bay Area in 2006, Maker Faire has now spread to other urban centers, including New York, Detroit, and Kansas City. Attendance at the Bay Area Maker Faire increased almost eightfold in its first four years.[21]

In the same DIY or maker spirit, Ariel Waldman's Science Hack Days bring together designers, developers, scientists, and other enthusiasts in the same physical space for brief but intense periods of collaboration. More than a hundred people took part in a Science Hack Day hosted by the Institute for the Future in the spring of 2011. In forty-eight hours they produced thirteen different hardware and software "hacks," or projects, among them Fancy Pigeons, a prototype of a game aimed at teaching players about genetics; Android Participatory Exploration, a device combining a low-cost spectrograph with an Android-based robot; and Grassroots Aerial Mapping, a project that explored the outdoors by strapping cameras to high-altitude balloons to create unique, stitched-together aerial maps. The Particle Physics Wind Chime won both the Best Use of Data and People's Choice awards. The project took particle collision data from accelerator laboratories around the world and mapped it across various sounds. The idea for the project came from Matt Bellis, a Stanford physicist interested in finding new ways to share scientific results with the public. A trained musician, Bellis thought it would be interesting to "sonify" the data, in other words render it as sounds. He brought the idea to Science Hack Day, where he rounded up an interested group of attendees, among them programmers, Web designers, and science fans, many of whom did not have a background in science, and laid his idea before them. That weekend they developed the kernel of the Particle Physics Wind Chime. They not only got swept up in the physics of colliding particles, but they also amplified Bellis, providing the needed skills to convert the idea into a working prototype.

Nowhere is the DIY movement more evident than in biology. The emerging field of synthetic biology has transformed biology into an engineering science in which standardized biological parts can be snapped together to produce more complex systems. Because engineered systems are prime for hacking, modification, and creativity, it's no wonder synthetic biology is attracting a new generation of enthusiasts into the ranks of biology research. Shared synthetic biology tools and parts are enabling this. Such tools include a catalogue of several thousand public domain BioBrick parts at the Registry of Standard Biological Parts. The annual iGEM competition, in which Deepa and her cohorts took part in the opening scenario, promotes the concept by involving undergraduate and graduate students in the creation and use of biological parts. Various DIY bio groups such as BioCurious and Genspace in New York City, a community biotech lab, are using open-source BioBricks and cheap DNA sequencing equipment to program new organisms or modify existing ones.

In his book *Biopunk,* the journalist Marcus Wohlsen documents the rise of this biohacker movement. Wohlsen sees biohackers, like the open-source programmers and software hackers who came before them, as being united by a profound idealism. They believe in the power of individuals as opposed to institutions, in the wisdom of crowds as opposed to experts, and in the incentive to do good for the world as opposed to the need to turn a profit.[22] Suspicious of scientific elitism and inspired by the success of open-source computing, the DIYers believe that individuals have a fundamental right to biological information, that spreading the tools of biotech to the masses will accelerate the pace of progress, and that the fruits of the biosciences should be delivered into the hands of the people who need them the most. Meredith Patterson, one of the leaders of the DIY biology movement, whose background is in linguistics and computer science, summed up the ethos of the DIY bio community in "A Biopunk Manifesto," delivered at a symposium at UCLA:

> Scientific literacy is necessary for a functioning society in the modern age. Scientific literacy is not science education. A person educated in science can understand science; a scientifically literate person can *do* science. Scientific literacy empowers everyone who possesses it to be active contributors to their own health care, the quality of their food, water, and air, their very interactions with their own bodies and the complex world around them.
>
> Research requires tools, and free inquiry requires that access to tools be unfettered. As engineers, we are developing low-cost laboratory equipment and off-the-shelf protocols that are accessible to the average citizen. As political actors, we support open journals, open collaboration, and free access to publicly funded research, and we oppose laws that would criminalize the possession of research equipment or the private pursuit of inquiry.
>
> . . . As biohackers it is our responsibility to act as emissaries of science, creating new scientists out of everyone we meet. We must communicate not only the value of our research, but the

value of our methodology and motivation, if we are to drive ignorance and fear back into the darkness once and for all.[23]

DIY biologists and other citizen scientists are trying to take science back from large bureaucracies and re-create the kind of science environment in which people like Thomas Edison, Marie Curie, and Benjamin Franklin invented and experimented before science became its own separate culture.

Crowdfunding Platforms for Science: Alternative Funding Sources

When Eri Gentry founded BioCurious, at first only a few people came to her garage lab to socialize, learn from each other, and do biology research together. Within a year the community had grown to a size far exceeding the capacity of the garage. They needed more space, but space in Silicon Valley is expensive. So what do you do when you need funding for a cool project? Today many people are turning to crowdfunding sites like Kickstarter. This is exactly what Eri and her friends did. They asked for contributions in amounts from $3 to $2,500. The appeal for a Coffee Pledge level of sponsorship ($3) simply asked, "Can you live without Starbucks for a day? Forgo that skinny pumpkin soy latte for A DAY, and pledge toward the advancement of Citizen Science!" For a contribution of $500, the BioCurious team offered to analyze the cancer-killing ability of the contributor's blood—that is, how well the contributor's immune system could fend off cancer. The call was answered by 239 backers who contributed a total of around $35,000.[24]

Why did they do this? When one reads BioCurious' appeal to the community, the answer becomes clear: supporters wanted to be part of something "epic," a chance to get in on the ground floor of a revolution: "The 20th century saw an unprecedented centralization of science around an industrial model. The plummeting costs of enabling technologies has brought meaningful biological research back within reach of the independent citizen scientist. From Bio-Art to BioFuels, the wave of next generation biotech applications is set to transform our culture and economy. BioCurious will be Ground 0 for this revolution."[25] Just think, for only $3 you can be part of a revolution in science. A bargain even at $2,500!

The money BioCurious was asking for was needed to pay for a basic starter kit for a synthetic biology lab, to provide a security deposit on warehouse space, and to cover liability insurance for all lab users. In the summer of 2011, with the money raised on Kickstarter (more than the group was originally asking for), BioCurious moved into a 2,400-square-foot facility in Sunnyvale and became the world's first hacker space for biology. The plan is to sustain operations as a nonprofit with monthly membership fees and by offering classes.

The same desire to be part of something great also motivated backers of the OpenPCR project submitted to Kickstarter by Tito Jankowski and Josh Perfetto, members of the BioCurious community. Their appeal for funding to create a functioning open-source PCR machine—"Explore your own genome, hack together DNA code, build your own biofuel, or prove that the trees in your backyard really are Truffula trees"—brought them $6,000 in only ten days.[26] Encouraged by the response, they promised to use additional funding to improve their design, making the heated lid more sturdy and effective, adding Wi-Fi and a REST control interface, and developing more integration to further reduce the component cost. Within thirty days they had raised twice the requisite amount, and today you can order OpenPCR online. Like BioCurious, the Open-PCR team had to be creative in structuring their appeal to potential sponsors. They offered everything from T-shirts and stickers to a DNA origami model printed on colorful card stock as rewards for donations. For a pledge of $256, contributors could even get their own 3-D-printed radiolarian protozoan E. coli model with flagella. With these enticements, how could anyone resist the opportunity to become a patron of the first open-source PCR machine?

Kickstarter is just one of the platforms making it possible for scientists and professional amateurs to raise money for research or for dream science projects. These platforms are important not only because they are enabling people to raise money, but also because they are enabling professional and DIY scientists to bypass traditional institutional funding sources (governments, foundations, and corporate R&D labs), in the process undermining existing hierarchies that make it particularly difficult for younger researchers or those without approved credentials to be engaged in the enterprise of science. This is precisely what drove Andrea Gaggioli, a psychology and technology researcher at the Catholic University of Milan, to start Open Genius Project, a crowdfunding initiative aimed at providing seed money for breakthrough research. He himself wanted to conduct research on virtual reality and neural rehabilitation, but in Italy, as in many other countries, it is almost impossible to get funding if you are under thirty. As part of the Open Genius platform, he plans to set up a peer-review process to "separate garbage from good science."[27] His hope is that this process will be a lot more open than institutional reviews and will allow people to invest in projects to be carried out by young people.

This is also the ambition of FundScience, which hopes to enable funding of small pilot research projects up to $50,000. In a statement detailing their hopes and dreams, the founders write, "We hope that we can make science more understandable and accessible to everyone and that we can foster an environment where people get together to solve the tough challenges our society faces in terms of a brain drain and technological advancement. If we can shift some of the decision making to the public and away from the NIH and other large corporations, who knows, maybe in a few years with the help of the public we can fund our own drug trials, create our own research institute and spin off our own technologically advanced socially responsible biotech companies."[28] FundScience also hopes to encourage a new relationship between researchers and donors. It aims for full transparency in terms of how funds are spent both for FundScience and for donor-funded projects and will use social networking tools to bring donors and researchers together to spread the message through grassroots efforts.

These new models of funding science are gaining the attention of traditional funding agencies, and some are incorporating elements of crowdfunding into how they allocate money. Cancer Research UK, a London-based charity, took the idea to heart and started its MyProjects initiative in September 2008.[29] MyProjects allows people to choose which cancer research projects they want to support. On the MyProjects site, unlike on Kickstarter or other purely public platforms, all the projects are vetted by scientists and already receive financing from Cancer Research UK. Funds are guaranteed regardless of whether the MyProjects goal is reached. In this sense, public contributions serve to substitute for or add to existing funds.

In 2008, in another effort to both obtain funding and open up the black box of contemporary scientific research, three neuroscientists, Priyan Weerappuli, Parakrama Weerappuli, and Sarath Joshua, founded the Open Source Science Project, a platform for academic researchers seeking to develop, finance, and conduct basic research projects. Crowdfunding of scientific projects is just one of the goals of this platform. Its broader goal is to create a more scientifically literate populace, eliminating some of the barriers and divisions between scientists and nonscientists. The founders believe that a scientifically literate citizenry will be far more likely to contribute constructively toward furthering the efforts of researchers. They want governmental officials, who are entrusted to make decisions regarding which research projects (or fields of research) are funded and which are not, to be held accountable for their decisions by the citizens who elect them, and they believe a scientifically literate public is more likely to support government officials making wise funding choices. To accomplish these goals, the site encourages interactions between scientists and nonscientists. Academic researchers (and later possibly citizen scientists) are encouraged to create publicly accessible profiles on the site, interact and exchange ideas with peers and colleagues, manage scholarly publications, and secure research funding in the form of microgrants from the broader nonresearch community. Simultaneously nonresearchers can register as investors on the site, which enables them to read through cutting-edge (peer-reviewed) research proposals, interact with academic researchers, exchange ideas, and provide funding for academic research projects.

Deepa's concern that scientists have to offer T-shirts to solicit contributions may not be far off. Government budgets in many Western countries are shrinking, and many existing funding institutions want to engage the public in funding research directly. Being able to enlist the support of the larger nonscience community, whether with T-shirts, compelling photos, or other persuasive means, may indeed become a necessary skill for scientists and explorers alike.

Science Information:
From Closed and Expensive to Open and Widely Accessible

"Publish or perish" is a familiar refrain among scientists. Jobs, status, and promotions in most academic settings are tied to a researcher's ability to get his or her work published in peer-reviewed journals, and the more select and prestigious, the better. The scientific, technical, and medical journal industry, however, is dominated by five commercial publishers, who collectively take in almost 50 percent of industry revenue. The other 50 percent is split among ten thousand publishers.[30]

The model for academic research journals is somewhat peculiar: the content for such publications is provided for free by researchers and scientists, for whom publication is a requirement for career advancement, and by peer reviewers. Academic journal publishing companies, in the meantime, operate at considerable profit margins, without seeming to add much value to the process.[31] In an investment analysis report on one of the publishers, Reed Elsevier, a Deutsche Bank analyst, argues that the value added to the publication process by academic publishers is not high enough to explain the margins earned: "We believe the publisher adds relatively little value to the publishing process. We are not attempting to dismiss what 7,000 people at [Reed Elsevier] do for a living. We are simply observing that if the process really were as complex, costly and value-added as the publishers protest that it is, 40 percent margins wouldn't be available."[32]

High profit margins are not the only problem with the existing academic publishing model. In many ways the model slows down the scientific discovery process and makes many of the results unavailable to the public due to the high cost of access (despite the fact that much of the research supporting publication is funded with public money through government grants). In the current model much of the experimental data, including lab notes and data on failed experiments, remains unpublished and thus unavailable to other researchers, leading to potential duplication of efforts and making it difficult to improve on existing experiments. The process of publication is slow, and recently the quality of the peer-review process (which often justifies the slowness) has also come under fire.[33]

New platforms for sharing scientific data and research results are emerging. Some scientists themselves are becoming publishers, writing blogs and curating scientific information. In a series of posts on his blog, the mathematician Terence Tao, for example, shares his proof of the Poincaré conjecture.[34] In his blog, Gödel's Lost Letter and P=NP, Richard Lipton, a professor of computer science at Georgia Tech, explores his ideas for solving a major problem in computer science: how to find a fast algorithm for factoring large numbers.[35] Timothy Gowers, a British mathematician, posed the question "Is massively collaborative mathematics possible?" in a 2009 post to his blog and subsequently created the Polymath Project, which uses the comment functionality of his blog to produce math collaboratively.[36]

As an alternative to the closed academic publishing model, the Public Library of Science (PLoS) was launched in 2001 with a petition by Patrick O. Brown, a biochemist at Stanford University, and Michael Eisen, a computational biologist at the University of California, Berkeley, and the Lawrence Berkeley National Laboratory. The petition called for all scientists to pledge that from September 2001 forward they would stop submitting papers to journals that did not make the full text of their papers available to all, free and unfettered, either immediately or after a delay of no more than a few months. Some scientists now make their papers available right away in open-access journals, such as *BioMed Central,* or after a six-month period from publication in what are known as delayed open-access journals. PLoS itself began full operation on October 13, 2003, with the publication of a peer-reviewed print and online scientific journal titled *PLoS Biology* and has since launched seven more peer-reviewed journals. *PLoS ONE* started the PLoS Hub for Clinical Trials to collect journal articles related to clinical trials.

Other platforms such as Mendeley and SciVee enable researchers to crowdsource results in text and visual formats. The Mendeley software platform extracts research and aggregates information that users put into their Mendeley libraries in the form of PDFs, Word documents, Excel or Photoshop files, or links to websites of academic journals and research papers. It has become the world's largest open-access research database,[37] with over 143 million documents as of December 2011.[38] In addition to a documents database, the platform offers a layer of social information that allows users to leverage all the information generated, such as trends in research, so that they can discover not only where their field is heading but also how each individual's interests have changed over time. When users share papers or load their bibliographies, Mendeley points them to papers they may have missed as well as a list of people who have written, read, or collected them. It fills the potential knowledge gaps that can occur with crowdsourced citations by recognizing papers that a researcher may not be aware of.

SciVee, a collaboration between PLoS, the National Science Foundation, and the San Diego Supercomputer Center, is a platform that allows researchers to upload, view, and share science video clips, connecting them to scientific publications, posters, and slides. While other researchers are the primary audience for the site, students, educators, and the general public are also frequent visitors, and content ranges from complex technical explanations of scientific publications to science presented at the elementary school level. Registration is free and gives users access to social networking services that allow them to interact with other members through messaging, blogging, and community forums.

These are just some of the examples of the flourishing ecosystem of open platforms and resources that make scientific information and the latest research findings increasingly available to peers and the public.

Alternative Science Communities:
Meet-ups, Hack Days, and Community Labs, Oh My!

Hobbyists and lay enthusiasts have been contributing to science for many decades, if not centuries. In fact the longest-running citizen science project currently active is the Audubon Society's Christmas Bird Count, started in 1900 by the ornithologist Frank Chapman, an officer in the then recently formed National Audubon Society.[39] Instead of killing as many birds as one could, as was the tradition at Christmastime in the nineteenth century, he proposed counting the numbers of live birds as a Christmas pastime. In 1900 twenty-seven observers took part in the first count in twenty-five sites in the United States and Canada. Today tens of thousands of people are involved at some two thousand sites in twenty countries.[40]

With the growth of connective technologies, the number of projects in which citizens can contribute to science and that could not exist without citizen engagement has grown exponentially. They include many older projects, such as the Citizen Weather Observer Program, which collects weather observations from thousands of privately operated weather stations into databases operated by the National Oceanic and Atmospheric Administration in order to improve weather forecasting. And there are newer ones, such as the previously mentioned Foldit, a game developed as a collaboration between the University of Washington's Computer Science and Engineering Department and its Biochemistry Department in which players, as a side effect of playing, help scientists understand the workings of protein structures and how molecules fold into a functioning three-dimensional structure.

People are donating their computers to ventures such as SETI@ home in order to help search for intelligent life in the universe. World Water Monitoring Day (WWMD) engages citizens in conducting basic monitoring of their local water bodies. Using simple water-testing kits, children and adults sample local bodies of water for parameters such as temperature, acidity (pH), clarity, and oxygen levels. Results are then shared with participating communities around the globe. In 2011, 340,000 people participated in data collection around the world, and the coordinators of WWMD, the Water Environment Federation and the International Water Association, plan to expand participation to one million people in one hundred countries.[41]

As part of the eBird project run by the Cornell Laboratory of Ornithology, volunteers are sharing observations of birds and thus contributing to growing databases used to monitor population trends, nesting phenology, and the behavior of birds across the country. Citizens are contributing photos of sharks with sighting information to the ECOCEAN Whale Shark Photo-Identification Library, used by marine biologists to collect and analyze whale shark encounter data to learn more about these amazing creatures. Today, citizen scientists are key contributors to virtually every area of research that requires substantial data collection or that can benefit from the sort of tagging and large-scale data-patterning skills that humans are uniquely good at. Many such projects, as John Falk and his colleagues point out, improve scientific literacy and generate increased interest in science. You can learn a lot about water quality by sampling it continuously or about birds by monitoring their nesting behaviors.

In many of the projects mentioned above, however, average citizens are somewhat passive participants, contributing data or equipment, but ultimately it is the scientists who use the data to advance the state of the art in their respective fields. We are only in the early stages of turning citizens from more passive collectors of data and analyzers of patterns into primary discoverers, either as part of collaborative teams with scientists or on their own. The Yale astrophysicist and Galaxy Zoo founder Kevin Schawinski, for example, distinguishes citizen science projects such as Galaxy Zoo as qualitatively different from crowdsourcing projects; in the former, citizens are actually doing science and are real collaborators. "Galaxy Zoo volunteers do real work," he says. "They're not just passively running something on their computer and hoping that they'll be the first person to find aliens. They have a stake in science that comes out of it, which means that they are now interested in what we do with it, and what we find."[42]

New efforts to connect hobbyists, amateurs, and credentialed scientists in communities, online and in physical spaces, are paving the way for new kinds of collaborations and new ways to conduct research. BioCurious is just one of the growing number of community labs and meet-ups where communities are beginning to do serious scientific research. Similar to BioCurious, Genspace is a nonprofit organization based in the New York City area dedicated to promoting citizen science and access to biotechnology. Founded by a group of science enthusiasts from different backgrounds—artists, engineers, writers, and biologists—Genspace sees the diversity of its members as a distinct strength and a source of innovation often absent from traditional institutions. Since 2009 it has provided educational outreach, cultural events, and a platform for science innovation at the grassroots level. In December 2010 it opened the first-ever community biotechnology laboratory, offering members opportunities to work on their own projects—commercial, artistic, or just fun.

Daniel Grushkin, a science journalist and one of the founders of Genspace, says in an interview in *Volume* magazine, "We're not averse to working with institutions; in fact, many of our members work in universities by day. But corporate institutions are beholden to profits and university labs are beholden to grants. DIYers are beholden to neither, and that allows us to work on projects that are a little more speculative."[43] He and another cofounder of Genspace, Ellen Jorgensen, a molecular biologist, recently coauthored a paper for the journal *Nature Medicine* titled "Engage with, Don't Fear, Community Labs," in which they point out that the DIY biology movement has exploded in recent years, and professional biomedical researchers stand to benefit from partnering with the legions of garage biotechnology enthusiasts.[44]

Today DIY bio meet-ups are being held in many parts of the country, including Boston, Los Angeles, and San Francisco. Participants learn to extract DNA from everyday food products, get lessons in synthetic biology, create microbial maps of cities, and share lab notes from experiments they are conducting. In a nonbiology arena, Ariel Waldman has held Science Hack Days several times in the San Francisco Bay Area; with the help of a grant from the Sloane Foundation she is training others to organize Science Hack Days in other locations in the United States and globally. The growth of Maker Faires in the United States and overseas is bringing together DIY science and technology enthusiasts in many parts of the world. FIRST (For Inspiration and Recognition of Science and Technology), a brainchild of the inventor Dean Kamen, has engaged a million students in robotics and science contests. According to a study by Brandeis University, kids involved in FIRST teams are more likely to pursue science and engineering careers and to develop a lifelong interest in these disciplines.[45]

Two Cultures No More

The world of two cultures, the scientists' and everyone else's, is on the way out. The diffusion of lightweight scientific tools, the emergence of new platforms for funding research, and the development of new online and physical communities bringing together people from different disciplines are increasingly blurring the boundaries between professional scientists and amateurs, hobbyists, and tinkerers passionate about science. In the socialstructed world of science, credentialed scientists may well need to know how to design T-shirts to engage the public in their research, while amateurs empowered by access to scientific information and inexpensive tools will increasingly find themselves doing research alongside scientists and other nonscientists. The ivory towers may soon empty out, as scientists come out to play with the rest of the world.

The Era of the Amplified Patient

It is more important to know what sort of person has a disease than to know what sort of disease a person has.

HIPPOCRATES

Future Scenario 2021: Partnership of Experts

Well, Vlad, what have you got for me today?" Dr. Michaels asks as Vlad takes a chair in her office. She knows he will have updates for her. He always does.

"You know, Dr. Michaels, I've been tracking all the research on H. pylori that's out there."

"Yes, I remember, Vlad," she replies, trying not to sound dismissive. Vlad shares all his findings as they come, and she doesn't need a recap. "Your genome analysis turned up a predisposition to gastric cancer. It's a good thing you did that test."

"Yep, good to find out now," Vlad says with a smile.

"It is," Dr. Michaels replies. "And you're handling the news okay?"

"To be honest, I just feel lucky to not have that CHD1 mutation. Otherwise I probably wouldn't have a stomach by now. Not a pleasant prospect." Vlad is referring to a genetic mutation associated with a deadly form of stomach cancer, which has afflicted his mother and for which the best preventative measure is removal of the patient's stomach.

"No, it certainly isn't," she says. "So you're mostly feeling lucky, then?"

"I am," he says. And she can tell he really means it.

"That's great," she replies. "The feeling of gratitude is supposed to be really good medicine. That's what a lot of research is saying."

It would be easy for Vlad to feel sorry for himself. After all, he has H. pylori in his blood, a particularly nasty bacterium that not only causes ulcers but can lead to stomach cancer. And what's more, Vlad has done nothing to deserve it. It was just his bad luck—at least in terms of his stomach health—that he happened to be born in Russia, where rates of H. pylori infection are high. As one might expect, rates of stomach cancer are higher there as well.

Given the bacterium's malevolence, stamping it out would seem to be an obvious course of action. But there has been some controversy around the treatment of H. pylori. It's found in two-thirds of the population globally, with much higher rates in developing countries, and some researchers have begun arguing that when you eliminate it from a person's body, you throw his or her internal microbial environment out of balance, potentially causing unintended long-term consequences. Ever since discoveries on the importance of microbes were made ten years ago, there has been a backlash against the use of antibiotics and antibacterial soaps and medications. This presents Vlad with something of a dilemma.

"You know, Dr. Michaels," he says, "I've had some reservations about antibiotics."

"What is your research suggesting?" she asks. Dr. Michaels never has to point Vlad toward informational resources or remind him to track data.

"I've been using my.microbe," Vlad explains. He meticulously collects data on his gut bacteria and shares it on the site. Through that platform he has identified a group of people with similar genetic profiles and the same susceptibility to gastric cancer who track their symptoms, changes in their bacterial makeup, and treatment results.

They also compare their data to data from populations without a predisposition toward gastric cancer.

"One of the people in the group is a statistician," Vlad continues. "She translates all the complicated data into easily understandable language. So far, we've found that along with higher rates of infection with H. pylori, members of the cancer-prone group also have higher levels of other bacteria and lactoferrin, a protein that binds to the bacterial wall." He opens up a display on his laptop and shows Dr. Michaels the group's findings.

"So, should I be treated for H. pylori or other bacteria?" he asks. "Looks to me like people with a predisposition toward gastric cancer do have these higher levels of multiple bacteria, including H. pylori. I guess I should try to get rid of these. Seems like a course of antibiotics is in store."

This is a familiar process. Vlad often essentially knows what treatment he wants but consults with Dr. Michaels for confirmation. Ultimately, though, if she recommends something else, he usually defers to her judgment.

"Let me consult Watson," says Dr. Michaels. She turns to her computer and says, "Find the best treatment for H. pylori."

"The best treatment for H. pylori," replies Watson, "according to PatientsLikeMe, is a daily dose of Ciptium at 500 mg for a week. Do you want to order a prescription?"

"Not yet. What does the American Medical Association think?"

"The AMA recommends 500 mg of Cipro daily for two weeks."

Dr. Michaels thinks for a moment. "Let's go with PatientsLikeMe. Oftentimes they have the latest data. And Cipro is a very old medication. I would put my trust in the later ones. Let's just make sure that it is the best one for you." She turns back to the computer. "Watson, what would be the best medication for H. pylori for Mr. Basov?"

"He's allergic to the quinolone family of drugs. I would recommend Ciptium."

"Well, there you go. Seems like Ciptium is the right one for you, Vlad. Watson, send the prescription to Mr. Basov's regular phar-

macy." She turns to Vlad. "You'll be tracking your treatment results, I assume?"

"Of course."

"So what else is happening, Vlad?" Dr. Michaels asks. "Besides
the my.microbe communities and all the online ones, how's your
social life? Are you going out with people? Do you have social support? Are you dating?"

"Oh, yeah, my kayaking friends, my neighbors, and all the people
from work have been just great. It's at times like these that you realize the value of human contact."

"For sure—having extensive social networks is one of the primary factors in positive health outcomes."

She suddenly remembers a statement Vlad made earlier, about
being lucky not to have CDH1. "By the way, Vlad, how's Ben
doing?" Ben is Vlad's nephew.

Vlad's face replies before any words leave his mouth. Dr. Michaels cares for the whole family, so she knows exactly how Ben is
doing. All his latest data are available to her at the touch of a button. But she wants to know how Vlad feels about it. Two years ago,
Vlad's mother was diagnosed with HDGC, hereditary diffused gastric cancer, which meant not only that her prognosis was dire but
also that, since it's a genetic condition, the whole family was at risk.
The gene associated with HDGC is called CHD1, and anyone in the
family could have had it.

For years Vlad had resisted doing any kind of genetic testing.
Why worry unnecessarily when the data was still not clear? After
all, he was an engineer; he liked clean, elegant solutions, not may-
bes and possiblys. It's why he had transferred from economics to
engineering in college; economists could never give you a straight
answer, and the ones who did usually turned out to be wrong.

But within a few weeks, the whole family—Vlad, his brother,
Yuriy, his sister, Lyudmila, and her children, sixteen-year-old Scott
and eighteen-year-old Ben, who was just getting ready for his first
year of college—had gotten their cheeks swabbed and sent the
samples to a lab. Everyone had been on pins and needles. Vlad had

immersed himself in researching treatment options, including the latest clinical trials, as much for his mom as for himself. HDGC is a lethal cancer, and having the gene made getting the disease more a question of when than if. What was particularly scary was that besides living a healthy lifestyle, the only real preventative measure those affected could take was having their stomach removed. Those who chose to do so had stunningly better chances of survival than those who did not.

Since their results were to be posted at the same time, the family had gathered together to wait. They had tried to make a little party of it, but the laughter had been forced, the food had remained largely uneaten, and eyes had frequently darted to the clock. When it was time to read the results, no one needed a reminder. They had silently pulled out their computers and learned their fates. One by one, family members had heaved a sigh of relief and then turned their attention to reading the reactions of others in the room. Soon everyone but Ben was looking up; Ben's eyes were still fixed on his computer.

"Ben?" Lyudmila had asked.

Ben swallowed hard, looked up at his mom, and forced a smile. "At least I won't have to worry about getting fat."

After that day it wasn't just Vlad doing the research. On Dr. Michaels's advice, the whole family had joined CHD1.org, an online community of researchers and people with the CHD1 gene alteration, to keep up on all the latest advances in HDGC research and clinical trials. They had contacted researchers through the site and gotten in touch with centers specializing in understanding and treating the disease globally. Ben, along with hundreds of others, had shared all his genetic and other health and behavior data on the site. By comparing his data to that of others, Ben learned that his likelihood of developing cancer in the next ten years was pretty low. The most common onset of the disease is after thirty. However, living without a stomach is not easy, especially if you're in your twenties. Many people on CDH1.org shared their everyday struggles with maintaining their weight, getting necessary nutrients through highly reduced caloric intake, and various food intolerances.

The family had gathered all the data from various sources and consulted with Dr. Michaels. Together they had decided that it was better for Ben to proceed with college and not disrupt his life just yet by having the surgery. They felt that he had at least ten years before he needed to make a decision on whether to have his stomach removed, and new preventative treatments or cures could come along in the meantime.

"I know that the decision not to do anything for now was the right one, but, you know, I'm still a bit concerned. And Lyudmila is too, so we talk about it a lot," Vlad tells Dr. Michaels. "It's not like Ben's life hasn't been disrupted already. He doesn't get to have the same kind of fun his classmates do. Every time he makes a choice about what to eat or drink or how late to stay out, he's thinking about how it will affect his chances. And recently, that girl, the one he's been seeing for almost a year now . . ."

"Yes?"

"He finally told her about his condition, which we had all told him to do up front when they started dating."

"And?"

"And at first she was fine, but then a couple days later, she asked for some space. She says it has nothing to do with the CDH1, but he doesn't believe it."

"That's too bad," Dr. Michaels says. "But it's hard to know what's really going on. She may just be processing. I know how much you care for your nephew, but have you had time for yourself recently?"

Part of Dr. Michaels's job is to keep the whole family network strong. She knows that if any one member burns out, it could have ripple effects.

"Well, we brought Mom home, and Lyudmila and I are taking turns driving her to appointments, cooking, and just spending time with her. We are lucky to have each other, but I haven't been sleeping well and don't have time for my regular exercise."

"That's normal, of course, and it's okay for a short period of time, but if this continues, we'll probably need to do something. I'll have Lisa come and visit you and your mom in two weeks to see how you are all doing. And of course, please do call or send messages anytime in the meantime."

"I will."

"Watson is tracking the data you share, so he'll alert me if he sees anything out of the ordinary."

"That sounds good," Vlad says. "It was great seeing you, Dr. Michaels."

"You as well, Vlad."

The door behind Vlad closes and the room is silent for a moment.

Dr. Michael turns to Watson: "Watson, please note that Vlad seems a bit down today. Extended social network is strong, but Ben's condition is emotionally upsetting. Vlad is also spending a lot of time caring for his mother and is neglecting exercise. Put in the calendar to send Lisa to visit the home in two weeks and remind me to call him in a week to check in."

A New Health Model: From Paternalism to Partnership

The science fiction writer William Gibson is often quoted as saying, "The future is here; it is just not evenly distributed." Indeed there are people among us today who are already living in the future described in the scenario in this chapter, or similar to it. Empowered with personal genetic information, using new tools for self-tracking and a growing range of platforms and data sources where people share health information, they are transforming health and medicine. These people are practicing socialstructed health.

One of them is Larry Smarr, a physicist, supercomputing pioneer, and founder and director of the California Institute for Telecommunications and Information Technologies in San Diego. The opening scenario incorporates many elements of his current practices and tools.[1] For more than ten years, Smarr has been "quantifying" his body—tracking aspects of his biology, from simple metrics like weight to more challenging measures like the bacterial composition of his gut. Among the items he is measuring on an ongoing basis are the following:

- Weight (daily for eleven years)
- Caloric intake
- Caloric expenditure
- Sleep patterns
- Chemicals in his blood, sixty of them, as markers of internal organ health
- Genomic data, indicating his predisposition toward various conditions
- Microbes in his colon and intestine[2]

By constantly tracking indicators of the conditions of various interconnected systems in his body—genetics, microbes, blood chemicals, behavior, and environment—Smarr was able to diagnose a serious medical condition, Crohn's disease, before he had any symptoms. In fact the specialist he turned to when indicators he was tracking began to show something was wrong did not know what to do when confronted with years of detailed data showing deviations from the norm and no clinical symptoms. Smarr was more of an expert on his body than the clinician was!

This way of understanding his physical well-being has become second nature to Smarr, a lifelong scientist. What he has learned about himself in the process, he writes, "illustrates and foreshadows the ongoing digital transformation of medicine. As our technological ability to 'read out' the state of our body's main subsystems improves, keeping track of changes in our key biochemical markers over time will become routine, and deviations from norms will more easily reveal early signals of disease development. In this new world, we become personally responsible for monitoring our bodies, noticing deviations from trends, and making appropriate changes. Use of this paradigm will allow us to avoid many of today's chronic disease states. In coming decades, the new model will be maintenance of wellness rather than treatment of chronic illness."[3]

In health, as in other domains, we are seeing the early signs of how the rise of participatory platforms, sophisticated expert systems, personalized tools for tracking and monitoring information, and amplified individuals—empowered with knowledge and tools to make decisions and acquire resources outside of institutions— will socialstruct the health landscape. It was only a few years ago that doctors began to see (many with horror) patients come into their offices with stacks of articles they had found on the Internet. In the not too distant future patients like Larry Smarr and Vlad Basov will come in with reams of detailed personalized health data and comparisons of their data to that of thousands of others they are sharing information with.

This new type of socialstructed health care, which I will explore in this chapter, takes a systems approach to understanding the body and health outcomes. It relies on distributed collection and aggregation of vast amounts of data—genetic, environmental, behavioral, and other. It involves democratization of medical research and expertise, blurring boundaries between health professionals and biocitizens, regular people empowered with health information and connections to others like them. They become powerful participants in health research, treatments, and health-related social movements.

The Body as a Complex System:
Collaborating to Decode the Mysteries

The genomic revolution has generated much excitement. We thought decoding the human genome would allow us to gain control of our bodies and health outcomes. We saw genetics as a kind of central code for our bodies that could be manipulated to produce desired outcomes and to facilitate a new era of personalized medicine. But despite great hopes and much hype, truly personalized medicine—that is, medicine that is able to predict with precision the likelihood of an individual's developing a particular disease, and then prevent it or treat it with tools suited to that specific person rather than a larger population cohort—remains a distant dream. This is because the body and mind turn out to be much more complex than we had imagined. Health outcomes are products of the interactions among multiple systems, each operating at its own level of complexity and interfacing with others in ways that will take us decades to fully understand. As soon as we develop an understanding of one part of the system, new puzzles emerge.

While the individual genome gives us some understanding of our predispositions, we're less like a computer program and more like a complex ecosystem—of genes, proteins, and even bacteria. Understanding the whole body ecosystem, with all its intricate parts and interconnections, is the project of the century, and it will not be completed by one or two researchers. The enterprise of creating truly personalized medicine will require heroic efforts that will bring researchers and average citizens together in collaborations on a scale we haven't seen before.

One such collaboration is George Church's Personal Genome Project at Harvard, which calls on people to share their genome sequences and other health information. Asking people to share their genomic, environmental, and trait data as an open resource is a step toward unlocking the causes of various diseases and developing treatments, even cures, for them. However, this is just one step. For most diseases, genomic profile information provides only knowledge of one's general predispositions. To get a more precise reading of a particular body, we need to decode the workings of protein structures and their interactions in a given cell, tissue, or organism. So, on the heels of the genomics revolution, we have begun another revolution in proteomics, the decoding of protein structures. Proteomics promises a transformation of biological and medical research even more radical than genomics. Encoded proteins carry out most biological functions, and to understand how cells work, one must study what proteins are present, how they interact with each other, and what they do. They are key to determining which genes are expressed. In the language of computers, the genome is the code or program; before it can be used, it needs to be compiled into a proteome. Proteomics is the study of the entire protein complement in a given cell, tissue, or organism.

Compared to genomics, proteomics is a much harder system to decode. This is because while humans have relatively few genes (thirty thousand, fewer than some "lower" organisms), there are eight different regulatory mechanisms functioning at four different times that can influence which proteins will be created from these genes. Think of the amount of data, computation, and analysis this involves! To help speed up the process of understanding the workings of proteins, a lot of people and machines need to participate in the analysis of such data. The sheer scale of proteomics research makes it a community endeavor.

This is why researchers in the University of Washington's Computer Science and Engineering Department and Biochemistry Department created a game called Foldit, referred to earlier. Foldit is an experimental puzzle video game about protein folding in which players fold the structures of selected proteins to the best of their ability using various tools provided in the game. The best solutions are analyzed by researchers, who determine whether the suggested configuration can be applied in the real world to target and eradicate diseases. For instance, in 2011 Foldit players helped model the structure of an AIDS-related enzyme that the scientific establishment had been trying to unlock for a decade. And they did it in three weeks for no pay! Unlocking this enzyme will help researchers treat retroviral conditions like HIV.[4]

Genomics and proteomics are just two systems we need to understand in order to deliver highly personalized health treatments. To add to the complexity, we have only recently begun to see our bodies as part of a platform for another complex system, the microbiome, a term coined by the molecular biologist Joshua Lederberg to refer to the totality of microbes, their genomes, and their environmental interactions. The Princeton scientist Bonnie Bassler compared our thirty thousand genes to the three billion bacterial genes inhabiting our skin and gut and demonstrated that we are only 1 percent human, at least genetically.[5] It has long been known that the number of bacterial cells on our skin and in our gut is ten times greater than the number of cells that belong to us. But with this discovery, a new vision is emerging of humans serving the role of complex transport and maintenance hosts for bacteria. Thus to fully understand the workings of our bodies and minds, we need to map the human microbiome—genetic elements of bacteria and their interactions in our bodies and in the environment around us.

Although it is still early in the process, researchers are beginning to show that bacteria play a key role in how we feel, both physically and mentally. And it looks like gut bacteria affect our immune tolerance and may have an influence on autoimmune diseases and even how we use vitamin B6, with resultant effects on the health of nerve and muscle cells.[6] Sven Pettersson and his colleagues at the Karolinska Institute in Sweden and the Genome Institute of Singapore were the first to demonstrate that gut bacteria affect the biochemistry and development of the brain.[7] Mice lacking normal gut microbes were more active and less anxious than those with normal gut bacteria levels. In one experiment where mice were given the choice of staying in the safety of a dark box or venturing into a lighted box, mice without gut bacteria spent significantly more time in the lighted box than their littermates with normal gut bacteria levels. When the mice were given the choice of venturing out on an elevated and unprotected bar or remaining on a bar protected by enclosing walls, the bacteria-free mice were once again bolder than their "normal" littermates.

Pettersson's team found roughly forty genes affected by the presence of gut bacteria, and they demonstrated the amazing ability of gut bacteria to influence whether brain cells turn specific genes on or off. How they accomplish this feat is still unclear; actually controlling chemical signals released from the gut into the bloodstream that then go to the brain is one of several possibilities. Scientists like Michael Gershon, professor of pathology and cell biology at Columbia University Medical Center, an expert in the nascent field of neurogastroenterology, call the gut our "second brain."[8]

As if genomics, proteomics, and microbiomics were not complex enough systems to understand, we are now beginning to see, at a much finer-grained level, the impacts of interactions between our bodies and the environment. Of course, we've known for a long time that the environment plays a key role in health and disease outcomes. We have seen the results of living close to nuclear waste dumps, long-term impacts of radioactive fallout, and increased rates of asthma in areas with high concentrations of CO_2. However, we are only beginning to understand how such interactions between our bodies and the environment may manifest at the genetic level and may even be genetically transmitted across generations. The study of such interactions is called epigenetics. The field looks at heritable changes in gene activity that are not due to changes in underlying DNA sequence. Some of this research is showing that stress, for example, may change genetic expression.

One such research project was a longitudinal study of thirty-eight pregnant women who were either at or near the World Trade Center at the time of the 9/11 attacks, some of whom went on to develop post-traumatic stress disorder (PTSD). The researchers, led by Rachel Yehuda, a professor of psychiatry and neuroscience at Mt. Sinai Medical Center in New York, found that the hormone cortisol, which is released in response to stress and acts to restore homeostasis, was present at significantly lower levels in the saliva of those women who had developed PTSD than in the saliva of those who were similarly exposed but did not develop PTSD.[9] A year later measurement of cortisol levels in the children born to these women showed that those born to the women who had developed PTSD had lower levels of the hormone than the others. Yehuda and her colleagues also found that the children of women traumatized by 9/11 subsequently showed an increased distress response when presented with novel stimuli. Research from the past decade or so suggests that epigenetic mechanisms that alter expression of the glucocorticoid receptor, which plays a key role in the body's response to stress, are probably responsible for these effects.[10] More recent research at the University of Pennsylvania found that epigenetic markers can be transmitted through two generations of mice; this suggests that children who inherited the stress imprint of the World Trade Center attacks from their mothers while in the womb may in turn pass altered gene expression patterns on to their own children.[11]

The more we learn about ourselves, the more complexity we encounter. We will need a lot more data to get to the level of personalized health and prevention that we have been promised in the past ten years. And we will need the engagement of more people to collect, share, tag, and analyze all this data. To succeed, we need to make health information gathering and sharing a collective—social—endeavor.

Collection and Aggregation of Health Data: Quantifying the Self

In a seminal 1945 article in the *Atlantic* titled "As We May Think," Vannevar Bush, President Roosevelt's science advisor and the brains behind the Manhattan Project, outlined a vision for a device in which "an individual stores all his books, records, and communications, and which is mechanized so that it may be consulted with exceeding speed and flexibility. It is an enlarged intimate supplement to his memory."[12] He named the device "memex," combining the words *memory* and *index*. The concept of the device and the vision outlined in the article influenced the development of the Internet, the PC, and many of today's other technologies. The idea of individuals storing and accessing vast amounts of information about themselves, as outlined by Bush, is becoming reality. Such information includes not just books, communications, and records but increasingly vast amounts of personal data—including health data.

To see where this is leading us, we have only to look at the work of Gordon Bell, a computing pioneer and researcher at Microsoft. As part of the project he and his colleagues developed called MyLifeBits, Bell has been digitizing all his personal possessions—creating online digital archives of coffee mugs, old T-shirts, photographs, everything he encounters as he goes about his daily activities. He collects the daily minutiae of his life so comprehensively that he owns the most extensive personal archive of its kind in the world. In addition to scanning, archiving, and storing all his possessions and everything that he comes across, Bell wears around his neck a camera (SenseCam) that ambiently takes photographs and indexes them whenever the internal sensor is triggered by a change in temperature, movement, or lighting. The resulting photos represent almost every experience of Bell's day. In addition, more recently the data collection in MyLifeBits is being expanded to include psychological and health data obtained through wearable devices such as BodyMedia, which measures heart rate, energy use, and sleep patterns.

If we conceive of the body as a system, as outlined earlier, then clearly individuals are beginning to capture and archive increasing amounts of information about their individual systems. They are converting many aspects of this system into data, which they can collect, store, aggregate with that of others, and analyze. Gordon Bell and Larry Smarr may be extreme data hogs, but the ranks of data gatherers are swelling rapidly as devices such as the SenseCam are becoming cheaper and more and more people are doing genetic testing using various platforms, such as 23andMe and Navigenics, and a whole array of new measuring devices and platforms are coming online daily. Already many of us have daily accounts of our thoughts, feelings, and photographs on various social media platforms such as Facebook, Twitter, and Google+ and in various blogs and photo and video archives. A growing movement of self-trackers and self-quantifiers is thinking creatively about uses for this data, from finding treatments for various health conditions to self-improvement.

In early 2010 we at the Institute for the Future hosted the first meet-up of a group called the Quantified Self (QS), a term coined by the writers Kevin Kelly and Gary Wolf. The QS community is made up of people who continuously monitor aspects of their lives, often focusing on health, and then share this information with others. You can think of QS members as researchers on the self. They are doing such research by carefully monitoring their lives and trying to find cause-and-effect relationships behind conditions and states of mind. In the process, self-quantifiers are creating rich data streams that when aggregated help unearth previously invisible patterns, such as correlations between diet and feelings, energy levels, sleep patterns, and so on. With all this tracking, a tremendous amount of health-related data is being produced. When that data is analyzed, you learn things that would be much harder to learn using the traditional methods of a clinical trial or a population study.

Only a few people showed up at the first QS meeting to share their experiences and tools for self-quantification. By 2011 the movement had hundreds of members in the Bay Area and twenty-seven groups worldwide, where people gather and learn from each other and collaborate on self-tracking projects. Some five hundred people participated in the first QS conference in Silicon Valley in 2011. IFTF is no longer able to accommodate the meetings of the group because it has grown so substantially. With a grant from the Robert Wood Johnson Foundation, Alex Carmichael and Gary Wolf, two of the core organizers of the network, produced the Quantified Self Guide to Self-Tracking Tools, where one can find tools, apps, and projects to help guide self-measurement. These are tagged, rated, and reviewed by the global QS community. The goal is "to gather and organize the world's collective self-tracking resources in one place, in a way that is useful and encourages collaboration between self-tracking experts and beginners who are just starting out."

As is evident from the guide, the Quantified Self movement is empowered by a growing portfolio of tools. These include sleep-tracking devices such as Zeo, designed to help you analyze your sleep patterns and improve your sleep. The tool includes a lightweight wireless headband, a bedside display, a set of online analytical tools, and an email-based personalized coaching program. Another self-tracking tool, Moodscope, is a Web-based application for measuring, tracking, and sharing your moods. You rate your mood daily using an online card game and share it by email with friends; the idea is that these activities can improve your mood in and of themselves. The mood log can also be charted to see progressions and to identify events that may have influenced your mood. Digifit is a full suite of Apple apps that record your heart rate and the pace, speed, cadence, and power of your running, cycling, and other athletic endeavors. Data can be uploaded to well-established training sites to help you improve your outcomes.

BodyMedia, mentioned earlier, is a system that gives highly accurate information on your activity levels, calories expended, and sleep patterns. The system consists of the BodyMedia armband monitor, an online Activity Manager, and an optional display watch and iPhone and Android apps. The armband automatically tracks the calories you burn and the quality of your sleep. The tracked information is synchronized with the Activity Manager, where you can explore your physical activity and sleep quality. You can also record your food consumption, which, along with your physical activity data, can help you lose weight. Jawbone manufactures a wearable tracking device in the form of a band called UP, which is infused with sensors and is connected to a smartphone, allowing you to track your eating, sleeping, and activity patterns. UP's sensors collect data about how much you've been sleeping and how much you've been moving. The data is then fed into a smartphone app, which also takes in information about your meals—you enter meal data manually, in part by taking pictures of your meals. Based on all that information, the smartphone program provides "nudges" meant to help you live healthier each day. For example, the app might suggest a high-protein breakfast and an extra glass of water if you haven't slept much the night before.

New data and quantification tools and platforms for the body are created daily. Developments in "epidermal electronics," a term coined by researchers at the University of Illinois at Urbana-Champaign (UIUC), may enable constant medical monitoring anywhere without wires or device synching.[13] John Rogers from UIUC cofounded mc10, an electronics company in Cambridge, Massachusetts, which aims to turn the epidermal monitor prototype into a commercial product. The technology can theoretically be used both inside the body and on the skin. Right now the patches are to be used under a doctor's supervision to monitor patients, but, as with most technologies and devices, one can foresee these moving into the general population once the cost of manufacturing goes down and the technology diffuses into everyday commercial applications. The day is not far off when people interested in collecting data on themselves will wear these as tattoos on their skin.

Aggregations of rich data about ourselves and our bodies have become gold mines for research and analytics, some of it done by ourselves, some in collaboration with others. All we need now is distributed tools and platforms for conducting such research.

The Democratization of Medical Research:
Experimenting on Ourselves

Over the centuries, many of the most important medical advances have come from scientists who experimented on themselves. In 1847 the Scottish obstetrician Sir James Young Simpson was the first to test chloroform on himself and two assistants. All three were discovered unconscious under a table.[14] After dramatic successes on patients, the anesthetic won royal approval when Queen Victoria enjoyed a pain-free childbirth with its aid in 1853. The first use of spinal anesthesia, at the end of the nineteenth century, was similarly pioneered by two German doctors, August Bier and August Hildebrandt, who tested it on each other.[15] More recently, in 1984, an Australian gastroenterologist, Barry J. Marshall, proved his theory that most stomach ulcers are caused by the common bacteria *Helicobacter pylori* by drinking a mixture containing the bug. The familiar symptoms of gastritis appeared within days. Marshall and his colleague Robin Warren won the Nobel Prize for Medicine in recognition of their discovery, which transformed a chronic condition, previously thought to be caused by stress and treated with surgery or lifelong medication, into an easily treatable condition that can be eradicated with a short course of antibiotics.[16]

Although the stringent regulatory system governing medical research would normally preclude doctors from taking part in their own trials, this has not stopped many researchers from becoming their own guinea pigs in recent years. With tools and platforms for people to come together and aggregate data becoming easily available, we may witness a new wave of medical and health research conducted by both experts and amateur self-experimenters. We may soon find ourselves saying, "If you aren't prepared to undergo this experiment on yourself, how dare you expect others to do so!"

This is precisely what a collection of citizen scientists are doing with parasitic worms called helminths, a group that includes hookworms, pig whipworms, and human whipworms. Why helminths? If you were to draw a world map of severe immune disorders and superimpose it on a map of infections caused by these parasitic worms, you would see a very clear pattern—but not the one you would expect. Where immune disorders are common, helminthic infections are rare, and vice versa. In the 1990s some experts hypothesized that this is because living in an ultraclean environment deprives the immune system of necessary exposure to pathogens and parasites, throwing it out of whack. If that's true, then reconciling people with their long-lost worms could help to reset malfunctioning immune systems. Indeed in 2004 a twenty-nine-year-old man with ulcerative colitis, an immune disorder that ravages the intestines, flew from the United States to Thailand to swallow five hundred eggs of the human whipworm (*Trichuris trichiura*), provided by a parasitologist. A few years later, virtually symptom-free, the man asked Ping Loke, then a professor at the University of California, San Francisco, to study his gut and look at what, if anything, the worms had done. Repeated colonoscopies revealed that wherever worms had colonized the colon, the inflammation and bleeding that characterize colitis were significantly reduced or nonexistent. The findings were published as a case study in *Science Translational Medicine*.[17]

But helminthic therapy has not gotten very far. There has never been a full-scale clinical trial, and most published studies have recruited only a handful of people. Pig whipworm (*Trichuris suis*) has been granted the status of Investigational New Drug in the United States, but given that it usually takes hundreds of millions of dollars and more than ten years to get a drug to market, worm therapy is still a distant prospect. This is not deterring some people from taking matters into their own hands: breeding the worms at home, swallowing eggs isolated from feces, or buying worms from companies that have sprung up to meet the demand.[18] In a case study of one such self-experiment profiled in *New Scientist,* a longtime Crohn's disease sufferer who had undergone multiple operations and had tried a slew of drugs without much relief decided to try helminthic therapy. He ordered a batch of pig whipworm eggs from the German company Ovamed (it is illegal to sell or breed helminths in the United States) and drank them every two weeks for three months. His symptoms began to disappear. In April 2010 he allowed thirty-five hookworm larvae to burrow into his skin and says that his Crohn's disease has been in remission ever since. When Moshe Rubin of New York Hospital Queens examined the man's intestine in early 2011, he found that his "small bowel looked almost completely normal."[19]

To facilitate sharing of data and self-discovery in this new arena of bacterial research, a new social network called my.microbes has sprung up.[20] The site connects people based entirely on similarities in their gut bacteria. According to a report in *Nature* magazine, one of the site's cofounders, the biochemist Peer Bork, who specializes in digestive chemistry, says he got the idea for my.microbes after receiving nearly a hundred emails from people concerned about their gastrointestinal problems. He believes the social network will help those with similar digestive profiles share and gather information about their digestive health. In the process researchers also hope to gather a wealth of data about the bacteria living in people's guts.[21]

Individuals as Biocitizens: Taking Action on Biological Data

What do you do when you notice that your young daughter has unusual health symptoms and misses many developmental milestones, but her doctors are unable to come up with a diagnosis? Well, if you are Hugh Rienhoff, a physician and scientist, you do a lot of research, you analyze your daughter's DNA on your own equipment, and then you create a site called My Daughter's DNA that becomes an online forum for those searching for answers and help in cases that defy medical explanations.[22] Very quickly, a father from Bulgaria shares information on his daughter's unusual symptoms, and Rienhoff and others start chiming in with suggestions of various avenues for investigation, comparing test results and symptoms. More parents join in, sharing pictures, clinical data, treatment protocols, and other relevant health information about their children. In addition to Rienhoff, other parents, doctors, and scientists dispense advice, information, and support.

Empowered with technologies for self-tracking, personal genetic information, and rich data, people like Hugh Rienhoff and many others are turning into what IFTF calls "biocitizens," people who use biological information to create online communities, do research outside of traditional institutional boundaries, and create movements around specific diseases or genetic conditions.[23] From AIDS activists to migraine sufferers and people fighting for access to particular drugs, individuals amplified with data and connected to each other are not waiting for doctors and experts to come up with solutions but are increasingly taking matters into their own hands.

Initially biocitizens may seem like a distinct group of early adopters, like those participating in the Quantified Self movement or those doing personalized genome analysis and sharing data with others. But as all of us gain more access to our own biological information, such information will become a lens through which we will view ourselves and our interactions with others. We are all slowly becoming biocitizens, and as biocitizens we will reshape the terrain of health on several levels.

First, as discussed in the previous section, average citizens will increasingly participate in creating the health information they use and rely on. Health information will no longer be exclusively packaged and created from the top down by doctors, insurance, and health care companies. Instead it will come from patients themselves, whether they are recently diagnosed with cancer and sharing their experiences with treatments on sites such as CureTogether or PatientsLikeMe or are conducting citizen clinical trials through platforms such as Genomera. Biocitizens will actively participate in creating content from the bottom up in whatever form and on whatever scale suits them. Sometimes it will challenge and sometimes it will complement traditional health information authorities.

Take a serious disease such as amyotrophic lateral sclerosis (ALS, or Lou Gehrig's disease). Patients and their families are desperate to find remedies to cure or at least slow down the progression of this deadly disease. When in 2009 a small study suggested that lithium could alter the disease's rapid decline, a number of desperate patients immediately put themselves on a lithium regimen. Many shared their treatment data and results on PatientsLikeMe, which combined their reports at virtually no cost. Results were disappointing; lithium didn't seem to offer relief. Eighteen months later a professional medical journal, the *Lancet Neurology,* published a study also showing that the generic drug lithium did nothing to slow the course of ALS.[24] These findings were the result of a large, expensive, and lengthy clinical study, yet those with access to data from PatientsLikeMe knew the outcome almost two years earlier.

The advantage of sites such as PatientsLikeMe is the number of people eager to contribute personal information. Around 120,000 people share their symptoms and treatment information in several disease categories on the site, ALS being prominent among them. It's as if PatientsLikeMe is running a continuous clinical trial but without the costs and time required by pharmaceutical companies. In an interesting reversal of roles, today many pharmaceutical companies are buying patient and clinical data from PatientsLikeMe. Similarly, CureTogether, another platform for sharing health information, created by Alex Carmichael and her husband, Daniel Redda, found that antidepressants are not particularly useful for treating depression when compared to exercise, meditation, and getting adequate sleep. This finding was based on data from a thousand depression sufferers self-reporting their symptoms and treatment regimens on the site. These CureTogether findings were recently confirmed by a study published in the *Journal of the American Medical Association* that found that antidepressant medications work no better than a placebo in people with mild or even moderate symptoms of depression.[25] CureTogether came to the conclusion much earlier—again, at virtually no cost.

Not only will biocitizens participate in creating health information, but they will also, like Vlad Basov in our fictional scenario, increasingly interact and engage with each other—contributing data to a wiki, starting a blog, or opening a Google group—to find, filter, and make sense of health and health care information. They will talk about symptoms and about service experiences with health care providers, and they will organize groups to initiate clinical trials or advocate for regulatory changes or access to certain drugs. Biocitizens will not fill out a comment card; they'll open a site like Hugh Rienhoff did when he couldn't find information on his daughter's condition from traditional sources. And as media platforms for health sharing grow, more professionals like Rienhoff—and the biostatistician who participates in CNG1.org, helping the group analyze data and translating it into lay language—will engage in biocitizen communities to expand and deepen their own research or out of a desire to share expertise.

As their ranks expand, biocitizens will leverage and trust what the group knows rather than rely only on experts. The world in which health knowledge resides only with individual authorities is giving way to a collective intelligence that emerges from the collaboration of many individuals creating and sharing information. Some will be formal experts, most will be engaged citizens. This is not surprising because trusted health information sources are few and far between. We are bombarded with health information on television, in print, online, on packaging and billboards, and even in grocery stores, and filtering and making sense of health information is no easy task. And increasingly, biocitizens will be turning to others like them for advice and guidance.

Biocitizens (and doctors alike) will also turn to expert systems such as IBM's Watson to help them access information and make complex decisions. Watson can process 200 million pages of content in less than three seconds. It has been successfully used to diagnose patients. At the National Press Club in Washington, D.C., in September 2011, an IBM team fed the computer hypothetical patients' symptoms, and Watson correctly identified Lyme disease as the illness.[26] With medical evidence and medical content doubling every five years, it is virtually impossible for a single health care practitioner to keep up with the latest discoveries. Smart machines and AI platforms such as Watson will come to the rescue of lay people and doctors alike.

Finally, biocitizens will increasingly drive research agendas and action in the health arena. Consuming information not simply out of interest but to inform collective action, biocitizens are using new media tools to reveal new patterns in data and are using that knowledge to advocate for new research funding (for helminth therapy, for example) or changes in existing conditions (removing lead from children's toys). While consumers demand choice, biocitizens will demand rights to the conditions that enhance health.

Partnering for Health

In a provocative essay, Farhad Manjoo, a writer for *Slate,* argues that the doctors who should be most concerned about their jobs being taken over by smart machines are specialists who focus on narrow slices of medicine: "They spend their days worrying over a single region of the body, and the most specialized doctors will dedicate themselves to just one or two types of procedures. Robots, too, are great specialists. They excel at doing one thing repeatedly, and when they focus, they can achieve near perfection. At some point—and probably faster than we expect—they won't need any human supervision at all."[27]

Indeed in an era when new medical knowledge is accumulating rapidly, when such information is easily accessible and shareable, when we have smart AI systems that can filter such information and deliver customized results, and when people are habitually and continuously tracking their own health information and data, effectively becoming experts on their own bodies, we have to rethink the role of medical practitioners. Dr. Michaels in our scenario is less a specialist and more an old-fashioned family doctor, albeit amplified with the intelligence of Watson and relying on information from her patient, who through his own research and participation in communities of interest is up on the latest advances in gastric cancer.

The unique skill Dr. Michaels offers—what machines cannot do—is conversation. After all, we humans are complex. We are more than a collection of symptoms, biological markers, and well-tabulated graphs. It is in conversation that we reveal what no numbers and no machines can indicate: whether we are lonely, isolated, stressed, depressed, or just need time to share our concerns and get another opinion or have someone check our thinking. And it is in conversation that a doctor brings to bear her ability to read a patient's body language, to gauge his emotional state, to determine how sophisticated an explanation he can handle, and to figure out if there are other factors in his life that may affect the treatment. In a socialstructed health care system, the doctor is not an omniscient God but a great conversationalist, astute observer, and insightful partner; that is, she is less a robot and more a real human being.

8

The Socialstructed Future:
A World of Unthinkable Possibilities

The process of socialstructing has begun. In fields as diverse as education, governance, science, and health amplified individuals are boldly engaged in de-institutionalizing production, taking value out of traditional ways of organizing, and actively building alternative platforms and tools. While the future in these domains may not proceed exactly as in the scenarios in the previous chapters, the directions of transformation are clear: the future lies in micro-contributions by large networks of people creating value on a scale previously unthinkable, bringing sociality and social connectivity back into our economic transactions, in the process redefining notions of rewards, incentives, growth, and currencies. So, where does socialstructing lead long term? Let's look with our immigrant eyes at the new socialstructed landscape unfolding before us.

Here again I want to turn to scenarios as a way to outline some of the key features of the emerging future. When it comes to big social and economic shifts, no one can predict the future; the level of complexity is just too great. Scenarios let us construct plausible, internally consistent visions that help us frame the range of possibilities and the kinds of issues we are likely to confront along the way. I want to specifically focus on three scenarios for us to consider. The first involves simply rebalancing the scales, pointing to an environment in which more of our creativity shifts to socialstructs, but the two parallel economies of money and non-money exist side by side in a kind of symbiosis. The second involves a more radical transformation, in which the current money economy is replaced by a social currencies economy. The third envisions a large-scale transformation to a new kind of gift society that decommodifies our society and radically redefines what constitutes value and wealth. To me these three scenarios best span the range of possibilities and challenges we are likely to encounter as we socialstruct our system of production.

Scenario 1: Rebalancing— A New Symbiosis of Money and Socialstructs

Imagine two economies, one driven by money and populated by traditional types of profit-optimizing business organizations, and the other dominated by socialstructs that soak up what Clay Shirky calls our "cognitive surplus" or free time we all have, existing side by side, one feeding the other in a kind of symbiosis. New mechanisms for creation of value destroy some existing businesses, reshape others, and create a whole host of new projects and value-creating opportunities, of the type described throughout this book. Whereas in the current economy most of the things we rely on in the course of our daily lives—products, services, innovation, entertainment—are created by institutions, with socialstructs appearing on the margins, in this scenario a lot of our time and effort would be spent on socialstructing, with a relative decline in the importance and contribution of industrial or traditional market-based production.

What we will see is significant growth in organizations and projects such as PatientsLikeMe, CureTogether, Wikipedia, and YouTube—socialstructs that rely on microcontributions by large networks of people. But ultimately the socialstructed economy in this scenario still depends on the existence of a money economy. Wikipedia depends on the financial contributions of its sponsors (many of whom operate in the traditional money economy) to sustain its operations even though the budget is relatively small. PatientsLikeMe sells health data, gathered from member profiles, to drug makers and others for scientific and marketing purposes. YouTube's revenues come from selling ads on the site. Think of this as a scenario in which fewer numbers of institutions and people engaged in institutional value creation are supporting the work of a growing number of socialstructs.

Socialstructs themselves might take a variety of forms, from non-profits to slow-growth businesses and those monetizing social production efforts that enable them. Let's look at these alternative forms of socialstructs and how they might coexist and intertwine with the traditional market economy.

An Explosion of Nonprofit Socialstructs

In this model, which is already familiar to us, socialstructed efforts are supported by individuals and for-profit organizations through multiple means: contributions, grants, subscriptions, endowments, and so on. What distinguishes nonprofits is that they do not have shareholders demanding returns on their investments; most of the money is used to support ongoing operations or, in the case of foundations and charities, distributed to the grantees.

With the help of technology, the new generation of nonprofits is able to operate on very small budgets with relatively few staff while at the same time reaching vast numbers of constituents or users of the service. Khan Academy, the nonprofit online school described in Chapter 4, is a good example. It is run largely by one man, Salman Khan, but, as of December 2011, offered over 2,700 tutorials in subjects ranging from arithmetic to art history,[1] viewed by two million users a month.[2] Wikipedia is another shining example. In a 2005 TED Talk, Wikpedia's founder, Jimmy Wales, said that it had (at the time) one employee, Brian, a former volunteer eventually hired as the lead software developer so that he could quit his other job and "get a life and go to the movies sometimes."[3] Everything else was done by volunteers; ninety servers in three locations were managed by volunteer system administrators; the content was, of course, contributed primarily by volunteers. With this small staff and virtually no budget, Wikipedia was getting 1.4 billion page views monthly at that time. Today it is the unsurpassed global resource for knowledge—still with fewer than a hundred staff members.

In the latter part of his career, the visionary management guru Peter Drucker took note of the tremendous potential of nonprofit organizations. In his 1989 *Harvard Business Review* article "What Business Can Learn from Nonprofits," Drucker wrote, "The nonprofit sector is by far America's largest employer. Every other adult—a total of 80 million plus people—works as a volunteer, giving on average nearly five hours each week to one or several nonprofit organizations. This is equal to 10 million full-time jobs. Were volunteers paid, their wages, even at a minimum rate, would amount to some $150 billion, or 5% of GNP."[4] When Drucker asked people why they volunteered, many gave the same answer: paying jobs didn't offer enough challenge, enough opportunity for achievement, or enough responsibility, and they didn't promote a mission people could get excited about. As if foreseeing the attractiveness of the socialstructed organizational model and its likely growth in the future, Drucker sounded a warning to businesses to study how successful nonprofits operate and manage their vast staffs by giving them the sense that they are working on something meaningful, something that matters to them personally, something that gives them a sense of community and intrinsic rewards.

So, working in the nonprofit sector is already part of the DNA of American society. With new technologies and platforms in place, we are likely to see tremendous growth in this sector.

The Growth of a Slow Business or Sustainable Lifestyle Model

The popular blog site Boing Boing is a for-profit company run by a small, eclectic, irreverent group of cofounders who curate it as a "directory of wonderful things," writing about what interests them: technology, futurism, music, culture, and various curiosities.[5] Unlike many other blogs that have tried to become major media outlets by professionalizing, studying their demographics, taking on investors, and trying to attract more and more advertising money and staff, Boing Boing isn't interested in growth. It has no physical offices, no clear management structure, no strategic plan. It continues to be a group of friends and colleagues doing what they love to do: writing about things that interest them and that they are passionate about. They may rant about digital rights management (copyright protection software) or point readers to a YouTube video of an adorable six-year-old narrating pictures of kittens in a book titled *Kittens*. In addition to their work on Boing Boing, each of the cofounders is doing other things—writing books, managing a magazine, doing research, producing videos. The site supports itself through advertising, but because the staff is small and expenses are limited, it can be choosy about the kinds of advertising and the amount of money it takes in. It accepts advertising only from organizations whose activities are not in direct violation of the core beliefs and messages of its founders, either individually or collectively.

An article about Boing Boing in *Fast Company* magazine in November 2010 put it this way: "They continued to treat their site as a side project, even as it became a business with revenue comfortably in the seven figures. Basically, they declined to professionalize. You could say they refused to grow up. . . . Yet boingboing.net remains among the most popular 10 or 20 blogs around. According to Quantcast data, it gets about 2.5 million unique visitors a month, racking up 9.8 million page views, a traffic increase of around 20% over 2009."[6] While Boing Boing does take in money to support its ongoing operation, Mark Frauenfelder, one of the cofounders, sums up the ethos of the platform best when he says, "This is the kind of thing I would do for free anyway—and that we all were doing for free, for years."[7]

Boing Boing's approach exemplifies the model of slow business, wherein founders and employees seek to earn enough money to support and enable what they are doing but do not aim to grow the organization for the purpose of maximizing financial returns. In fact in the slow business model, the organization serves to support what the key people involved like to do, and they eschew doing things that place management or other organizational burdens on them. Personal interests and passions come first. The organization, which can take the form of a nonprofit or a for-profit company, is an after-thought.

Of course, you might say, not many people would refuse the potential of huge financial rewards. However, in the socialstructed world it takes only a few Boing Boings to disrupt a publishing industry, a few Wikipedias to reshape the knowledge industry as we know it, and a few Khan Academies to remake the educational landscape. The socialstructed world is a world in which a few amplified individuals can remake the world.

Several U.S. states are beginning to realize the possibilities and some of the advantages of this slow business model. In 2008 Vermont became the first U.S. state to allow registration of a new type of business called an L3C, a "low-profit" limited liability company that operates for profit but has as its primary focus achievement of socially beneficial goals, with profit making as a secondary goal. As of December 2011, Vermont had been joined by Michigan, Illinois, Wyoming, Utah, Louisiana, North Carolina, Rhode Island, and Maine, as well as the Crow Indian Nation and the Oglala Sioux Tribe. Once formed in any of these states, an L3C can operate legally in all fifty states.[8]

Another attempt at providing a framework for businesses whose aim is not just shareholder profit but also social good is the B (for "benefit") Corporation. A certified B Corporation "uses the power of business to solve social and environmental problems."[9] In order to receive B Corporation certification, a business must meet comprehensive and transparent social and environmental performance standards, comply with higher legal accountability standards, and build a business constituency for good business.

There is a bit of "back to the future" irony in these attempts to rethink the charter and meaning of the corporation. We forget (or perhaps simply don't know) that after proclaiming independence from England, the founding fathers remained quite fearful of corporate power and put severe limits on corporate operations. Specifically corporations were forbidden to attempt to influence elections, public policy, and other realms of civic society. Corporate charters were granted for a limited time and could be revoked promptly for violating laws. Initially the privilege of incorporation was granted selectively and only to enable activities that "benefited the public," such as construction of roads and canals. Enabling shareholders to profit was seen as a means to that end. Let's not forget that the first chartered corporation in the United States was Harvard University, an educational institution.[10] Some of the initial conditions imposed on corporations would be seen as quite radical and left-wing today.

We've strayed a long way from the dreams of the founding fathers, but we might be finding our way back with new kinds of slow business enterprises. These could look like L3Cs or simply be products of individuals who choose not to scale up their organization in search of higher and higher profits. But while such slow growth or sustainable lifestyle businesses may eschew financial growth, today's technologies enable them to reach millions of users and have huge impacts on our society. They can achieve scale without being big, without acquiring debt, and without losing control of their organization to the stock market and the shareholders.

Monetized Social Production

The online community PatientsLikeMe, referenced in Chapter 7, was inspired by its cofounder James Heywood's brother, who developed Lou Gehrig's disease. Heywood, his other brother Benjamin, and longtime friend Jeff Cole set out with the goal of building a community for people with similar conditions to share treatment information and get knowledge and support from peers. Since its founding, the platform has been extremely successful, with over 120,000 members sharing information on over a thousand conditions and treatment regimens as of December 2011.[11] But as the community grew and the scale of operations increased, turning the community into a business—monetizing the community— became increasingly attractive. The data aggregated by PatientsLikeMe benefit both patients and pharmaceutical companies trying to develop new treatments. But to earn profits, today the data is also being used to create more effective drug marketing campaigns, something that may actually harm community members, betraying the platform's original goal.

PatientsLikeMe's need to sell its community's personal data is an example of the kind of conflicts inherent in monetizing social-creation efforts (discussed in greater detail later in this chapter). Organizations pursuing this model usually start with a high and lofty social goal or stumble onto a project as a fun or geeky venture, but under pressure to reward founders and investors with high returns, they often come to see the endeavor less as a social enterprise and more as a platform for making money. In many cases they have to sacrifice the interests of the larger community in order to be financially sustainable or reap high monetary returns.

Facebook, Twitter, YouTube, and many others started out as fun projects meant to connect groups of friends, create a communal resource, or just share information. But in the quest to scale up operations and make a profit, they turned to monetizing their communities—the very people whose contributions make these sites successful in the first place. Each one has attempted to do this in a different way, inflicting varying degrees of damage on its community of coproducers. Facebook's unilateral decisions regarding changes in privacy terms for members are but one example. The company operates without the transparency of information that is at the core of the social network it enables. No one outside of Facebook knows exactly what information it is collecting on its subscribers, how such information is being aggregated, who it is being sold to, and many other aspects of the company's operations.[12]

Platforms such as PatientsLikeMe, Facebook, and Twitter exemplify a growing clash between the promise of commons-based technology platforms and the imperatives of the larger market economy in which they exist. In fact, the two operate in two different realms. Our technology tools and platforms are highly participatory and social. They take advantage of intrinsic human motivations to contribute in order to be noticed, to share opinions, to be a part of something greater than ourselves. They do offer people rewards and compensation but these are social in nature. Our business models, by contrast, are based primarily on market, i.e., monetary rewards. They take contributions provided freely by thousands of people and turn them into commodities to be sold for profit to marketers, advertisers, and promoters. Such conflicts are likely to grow simply because the number of such endeavors is growing exponentially.

Scenario 2: The Social Currencies Economy— Turning Social into a Commodity

In our second scenario, the present money economy is replaced by a social currencies economy. This is a much more radical departure from the status quo than the first scenario. It requires an entirely new economic model and a new infrastructure for value creation and value exchange.

As I mentioned in Chapter 3, the past few years have seen impressive growth in alternative, often virtual currencies created by different social and gaming communities, from World of Warcraft gold to Facebook credits, currencies created within certain communities and given for certain types of activities: contributing to a site, climbing to a new level in the game, completing a mission. These alternative social currencies are bringing sociality back into our transactions. They facilitate a new kind of barter system—

think of it as Barter 3.0—that brings people together across geographies and many other boundaries thanks to our social technologies. These technologies enable us to scale up the traditional barter system by making socially embedded transactions possible on a much larger geographic scale—across places, times, affinities, and many other boundaries—and with much greater levels of efficiency.

In this sense, the exchange systems many social currencies facilitate are distinct from pure market exchanges. Traditional market-based incentive mechanisms are built upon the idea of a commodity economy in which "rational" human behavior is driven by price. In Chapter 3 I pointed out that research has shown that such market-based exchanges can actually reduce the sense of community, an important aspect of social production platforms such as MITBBS.[13] Efficiency and maximization of economic rewards are not the drivers of such online platforms. What drives them is social rewards, social connections, recognition, and community reputation, i.e., social currencies. Unlike money, therefore, social currencies promote community creation driven by social relations. As anthropologists who have studied the MITBBS platform point out, "MITBBS supports direct exchanges of MBs among individual users, creating an interesting gift economy and enabling a wide range of 'user generated' rather than system-imposed incentive practices that are valuable in sustaining the online community." This study found that these user-generated practices "help sustain and enrich the community by supporting emotional needs (i.e., not always rational) and community culture."[14]

While the system of social or alternative currencies being created today by individual platforms seems small and marginal compared to the well-established monetary system, it is worth remembering that it took centuries for the global financial system as we know it today to emerge. On the way there, communities used many types of currencies, from shells to grain to paper. With today's suite of technologies and the explosion of socialstructs, the process of building institutions and infrastructure to support and enable new types of exchanges is likely to evolve faster but may still be a project of several generations. We will need to create:

- Platforms for valuing individual contributions to social-structed efforts

- Platforms for exchanging social currencies produced in different platforms (equivalent to foreign exchange markets)

- Systems for monitoring and oversight of online currency transactions

- Mechanisms for insurance and enforcement of community currency rules

It is a big undertaking that will require a new set of institutional arrangements, tools, and processes. In fact, if we are serious about it, it may require a new architecture for the Internet itself. We will need to integrate a new layer of social measurement and flow-monitoring capability into the Internet's architecture so that these new values are captured seamlessly and consistently.

Today most alternative and community or social currencies are proprietary and limited. Credits are either limited to use within a platform or can be exchanged for money or goods outside of it in specific venues or for specific purposes, but can rarely be traded between platforms. Early experiments, however, are underway to make exchanges across platforms and communities possible. The Community Exchange System (CES) provides the means for users to exchange their goods and services, both locally and remotely. It acts as a global complementary trading network that operates without money. There are many similar trading systems around the world, commonly known as local exchange trading systems, mutual credit trading systems, or time banks.

The CES takes this a step further by providing the means for intercommunity trading, right up to the global level. CES exchanges compile and distribute a directory of goods and services offered by the users registered with them, as well as a list of their wants and requirements. When a user wants something advertised in the directory, the seller is contacted and the trade takes place. The buyer pays the seller by signing a trading sheet provided by the seller or by handing over a check-like trading slip that records how much the buyer agrees to be debited by the seller for the goods or services delivered. The slip is either handed by the seller to a group administrator, who will enter the amount into the computerized system, or the information is entered directly by the seller. Sales are recorded as credits for sellers and as debits for buyers. The central bookkeeping system records the relative trading positions of each. Those in credit can claim goods and services from the community to the value of their credit, and those in debit owe the community goods and services to the value of their debit. Traders receive a regular statement of account that lists their trades and gives their balance at the end of the period. Information about the trading position of others prevents unscrupulous buyers from exploiting the system. Newsletters assist in building links and enhancing the sense of community.

The MetaCurrency Project is attempting to build technology platforms and protocols to support the flow and interactions of multiple currencies seamlessly. The project recognizes that money is just one type of currency (other types are frequent-flyer miles, college degrees, grades, five-star ratings, Olympic medals, etc.), a small part of a much larger ecology of value flows. Flows of trust, reputation, knowledge, information, value, goods, services, resources, gifts, and admiration are some of the things that can be activated with these currencies. And while examples such as MIT-BBS and Bunchball Nitro show that many platforms can generate value, only a few institutions—federal reserve and central banks around the globe—are able to create money today. The goal of the MetaCurrency Project is to enable any community to create currencies—to decide what they value and how this value will be measured and acknowledged—and create an infrastructure that will allow for the exchange of such values across communities, in the process strengthening such communities and the social ties within them.

Scenario 3: Return of the Gift Society—
Reintegrating Economics into Life

When I think of gift societies, the case of Grisha Perelman, a Russian mathematician who declined the Fields Medal in mathematics, comes to mind. This act made many, including me, question his sanity. After all, who in his right mind would turn down the fame and riches (and in Russia, $500,000 is definitely riches) that go along with winning the Fields? Is he a nut—a familiar caricature of a quirky mathematics professor, riven by social anxiety, unable to hold a conversation or tie his shoelaces? I wondered. A Russian version of Bobby Fischer or John Nash?

Grisha Perelman may be all that, but the more I read about him, the more I found myself feeling nostalgic for people like him, people I used to know in the Soviet Union in the 1970s—writers, poets, artists, musicians, physicists. They lived in the rarefied world of ideas, completely removed from cares for success defined by money and fame. They gathered in tiny kitchens around cramped tables to drink tea, smoke cigarettes, argue, exchange the latest news of travails with the Soviet bureaucracy, recite poetry, sing underground songs, and talk about big ideas. Troubles with the bureaucracy, being denied publication, or having their movie premiere canceled by the censors was their badge of honor, their status symbol. They lived in the world of certain intellectual and spiritual freedom that seemed possible only in a totalitarian state where ideas are the only escape and the only reward. People like Perelman built their own worlds. They created, invented, and wrote for the pure pleasure of it. What did that gain them? Besides the pleasure of creation, the ability to be a part of a circle of the best of the Russian intelligentsia. Succeeding in any traditional sense—by being published, getting high-level jobs, being rewarded with trips overseas—meant selling out. Often it led to exclusion from the circle. Despite their lack of recognition and often persecution by the state, intellectuals like Anna Akhmatova, Boris Pasternak, and Andrei Sakharov served as beacons for the rest of the progressive Russian society. They set the moral tone and were a model to aspire to. They were heroes of my youth. My high school friends and I fashioned ourselves after them—we were intellectuals, reading, debating, and in many cases imitating their lives. They, rather than Bill Gates or Paris Hilton, were our paragons of success.

In the absence of commodities, these people lived in a kind of gift economy not dissimilar to the gift economy found by Malinowski in Melanesia. But instead of exchanging valuable shells, the Russian intellectuals exchanged poetry, stories, conversations, ideas, and discoveries. Their contributions were not measured in any tangible way; they were not converted into a currency. Perelman likely saw receiving $500,000 and being given a medal as a distraction from what was giving him real pleasure: being able to create elegant solutions to math problems. And this cannot be measured in money.

Robert P. Crease, a professor of philosophy at Stony Brook University and the author of *World in the Balance: The Historic Quest for an Absolute System of Measurement,* distinguishes between two kinds of measurements: ontic, which involves measurement of existing objects or properties (foot, pound, inch), and ontological, which describes how something exists as an act, an experience, and can be felt but not measured by ontic means. We sense that things do or don't "measure up" to what they could be. Aristotle, for instance, called the truly moral person a "measure," because our encounters with such a person show us our shortcomings. Crease argues that "the distinction between the two ways of measuring is often overlooked, sometimes with disastrous results. . . . Confusing the two ways of measuring seems to be a characteristic of modern life. As the modern world has perfected its ontic measures, our ability to measure ourselves ontologically seems to have diminished. We look away from what we are measuring, and why we are measuring, and fixate on the measuring itself. We are tempted to seek all meaning in ontic measuring—and it's no surprise that this ultimately leaves us disappointed and frustrated, drowned in carefully calibrated details."[15] Reading Crease helped me understand that those awarding the Fields Medal to Perelman were using ontic measures to value an ontological experience.

The gift society scenario represents perhaps the most radical transformation in how we think about economics and wealth and in how we organize our society. It involves large-scale decommodification of production and refocusing on the unmeasurable or ontological. Gift economies, whether in Melanesia, among intellectuals in the Soviet Union, or among open-source programmers, focus on acts and experiences instead of relying on alternative commodity structures such as game points or social currency. Interactions in such circles are based on implicit and intrinsic rewards—giving, creating, being—rather than openly utilitarian trade in commodities. While this third scenario may seem idealistic and impossible to achieve, it is good to remember that we have lived in gift-based societies before and that there are pockets of gift economies around us today.

Remember that economics as a separate discipline did not exist until a few centuries ago and that Adam Smith, the father of modern economics, was a Scottish social philosopher. His two pivotal books, *The Theory of Moral Sentiments* and *An Inquiry into the Nature and Causes of the Wealth of Nations,* examined moral, economic, and social aspects of wealth and consumption. To him and many other figures of the Scottish Enlightment who greatly influenced our economic thinking, economic man did not exist in isolation from social, moral, and philosophical considerations. The gift society scenario will require us to rethink the status of economics as a separate discipline that views everything through the lens of commodities that can be measured and traded. It will call on us to bring back morality, philosophy, and psychology into how we think about wealth and production. It will call on us to rethink our economy from the focus on production efficiency to a focus on social efficiency. It is a tall order, but the rewards might be substantial: more poetry, more music, more art, more stories, and more connectedness. In a world in which smart machines will replace us in many rote, repetitive operations and will enable us to do things we previously could not, in a world where we can produce with very little human effort at scales previously unimaginable, it may well be that we humans will increasingly be dedicating our time and our minds and skills to things that are unique expressions of us: art, poetry, music, discovery, storytelling, and myriad other creative and novel endeavors. Not a bad future.

Beyond Scenarios: Directions of Transformation

Scenarios are useful tools for uncovering underlying trends and forcing us to ask important questions as we speed toward the future. But it is usually not the case that a particular scenario we create becomes reality in the way it was envisioned. If it does, it is probably as much a matter of luck as of the uncanny ability to foresee the future. To construct a perfect scenario would require having answers to all the uncertainties—and if we had those answers, we wouldn't need to create scenarios! That is why, when developing scenarios, it is helpful to focus on larger transformations that underlie them and that are irrefutable, the ones we truly believe will inevitably come about. These larger transformations point to a direction rather than pinpoint a final destination. How they manifest and in what time frame, however, are where the uncertainties lie. The more we can foresee the directions and shapes of such transformations, the better we can prepare for the future.

So what are the larger transformations that the three scenarios just outlined point to? What are the larger underlying shifts that are certain to shape how we live, create value, and work in the future? First, it is clear that *much new value and innovation will move from commodity- or market-based production to socialstructed creation.* We are already seeing an explosion of socialstructs, from Wikipedia to Patients-LikeMe to BioCurious. The number is likely to grow considerably as the tools and practices diffuse throughout society. Socialstructed creation may in fact overshadow market-based production in terms of the amount of time people spend on such activities, the value they create, and the types of innovations they spur. Money and social economies have coexisted for a while—hence my mother's ability to use social currency and social capital to gain access to tangible goods. What is different in the new symbiosis is that the socialstructs will be producing things that were previously produced in the money economy, draining value out of existing institutions and becoming dominant models of value creation. The symbiosis is likely to create much social tension and division as two modes of production—social and market—inreasingly collide. The key question and the key unknown is whether the blended economy, with its inherent dangers, is the end point or a transition phase.

Another part of the transition to socialstructed creation we are likely to see is an *explosion of new currencies, including social currencies,* that will increasingly provide incentives and drive social creation. In modern market-based societies, money is the fundamental informational tool used to coordinate flows of goods and services. However, as a society, we create many kinds of flows, particularly social flows that are not reflected in our financial exchanges. Money is but one instance of a broader category of flows that make societies work. New currencies will allow us to quantify and capitalize on these other kinds of flows. They will also be used to create incentives for us to engage in production that is not market-based—that is, production aimed not at financial profit maximization but at maximization of other desired outcomes, such as solving large-scale problems or creating happiness and community vitality. If money is the grammar and syntax of the functioning market economy, in the next several decades we will be building the grammar and syntax of the socialstructed economy.

Most importantly, we are moving to a *new point of equilibrium between market and gift economies.* In his book *The Gift* the writer and MacArthur Fellow Lewis Hyde argues that the tensions between accumulation-based (market- or capital-driven) and gift economies is an ever-present part of our social existence, an "essential polarity between the part and the whole, the one and the many. . . . Every age must find its balance between the two, and in every age the domination of either one will bring with it the call for its opposite."[16] For where, on the one hand, there is no way to assert identity against the mass, and no opportunity for private gain, we lose the well-advertised benefits of a market society—its particular freedoms, its particular kind of innovation, its individuals and material variety, and so on. But where, on the other hand, the market alone rules, and particularly where its benefits derive from the conversion of gift property to commodities, the fruits of gift exchange are lost. At that point, commerce becomes correctly associated with the fragmentation of community and the suppression of liveliness, fertility, and "social feeling." In the end socialstructing may be about rebalancing the scales, finding a new point of equilibrium between market- and gift-based forms of value generation.

Caution: The Potential Dark Side of Socialstructed Economies

In his January 2011 essay "Life after Capitalism," Robert Skidelsky—the author of the widely regarded book *Life after Communism*—asks what happens to capitalism when scarcity has been turned to plenty: "Does it just go on producing more of the same, stimulating jaded appetites with new gadgets, thrills, and excitements? How much longer can this continue? Do we spend the next century wallowing in triviality?"[17]

Skidelsky does not deny the value of the market economy. He just views it as a system that has outlived its purpose, at least in the developed world. He sees it as a superb system for overcoming scarcity, a system that by organizing production efficiently and directing it to the pursuit of welfare rather than power has lifted a large part of the world out of poverty. But he adds, "Capitalism may be close to exhausting its potential to create a better life—at least in the world's rich countries. By 'better,' I mean better ethically, not materially. Material gains may continue, though evidence shows that they no longer make people happier."[18]

We have an unprecedented opportunity to answer Skidelsky's call and to transition into a new way of creating value, of coming together, of enriching our lives with social connections and reengaging with each other in ways that bring us not only material satisfaction but also happier and healthier lifestyles. But the new system we are building will not be a utopia. Along with opening up exciting opportunities to create new kinds of social organizations—systems for producing not merely goods but also meaning, purpose, and greater good—there is a possibility that it will bring new challenges, new inequities, and new opportunities for abuse. We need to understand these potential disadvantages of socialstructing in order to minimize their potential. So with a note of caution I want to address two challenges of the system that we need to be particularly aware of.

Digital Manor Economies

The blended economy of socialstructed and monetary production has the potential to resemble the manor economies of the Middle Ages. The manorialism of feudal society in medieval Europe contained many elements of commons production. In most manors, peasants and tenants were assigned rights to use the commons—pastures, forests, fisheries, lands—within the manor's boundaries. Inhabitants had to agree on rules for cultivation, grazing, and fishing.

The dark side of manor economics lay in the fact that it perpetuated huge inherited disparities in incomes. While most of the population in these medieval pastoral settings survived at subsistence levels, the lord of the manor was able to live lavishly off the rent, taxes, and free labor the tenants were obligated to supply him with, as well as various fees tenants had to pay for the use of resources such as mills, bakeries, and wine presses.

And here the similarities emerge. Socialstructing is driven by technologies that at their core are commons-creating. They define a new path for creating value that is different from institutional production, which relies on paid employees. Digital manor economies rely on "production" by the many nonemployees, and they promote the ethos of the commons: openness, transparency, speaking out of turn, making microcontributions, adding to others' content. However, the ethos of the commons is undermined when the commons are traded as commodities, which occurs when these platforms go public or are sold, with huge financial payoffs accruing to the few founders and investors and none at all to the volunteers who contributed their labor and attention to making such platforms successful. Then the dark side of manor economics comes to the fore. The results of social production come to resemble digital manor economies, with the founders and some of the early investors functioning as the lord and his family. We, the armies of digital peasants, scramble for subsistence in digital manor economies, lucky to receive scraps of ad dollars here and there but mostly getting by, sometimes happily, on social rewards: fun, social connections, online reputations. But when the commons are sold or traded on Wall Street, the vast disparities between us, the peasants, and them, the lords, become more obvious and more objectionable.

The clash is evident in the lawsuit by bloggers against the *Huffington Post* and its parent, AOL, which acquired the publication in March 2011 for $315 million.[19] The same writers who were happy to contribute for free before the sale accused the publication of turning them into "modern-day slaves on Arianna Huffington's plantation."[20] The suit claimed that about nine thousand people wrote for the *Huffington Post* on an unpaid basis and that their writings helped contribute about a third of the sale value of the site. These bloggers weren't paid a single penny in the sale; the money went mostly to Huffington and a few investors.

The suit highlights the tensions inherent in social production as large networks of microcontributors receive payment in *social (reputation, recognition, audience)* rather than *monetary* currencies. The *Huffington Post* case brings us face-to-face with the reality that we, as social producers, are all becoming digital peasants. We are the heroic commoners feeding revolutions in the Middle East and, at the same time, modern serfs working on Mark Zuckerberg's and others' digital plantations.

The lawsuit against the *Huffington Post* is not just about an army of disgruntled bloggers. It is about how we build the new socialstructed economy. It is our way of beginning to scrape together a new regulatory structure and a new set of norms for the new way we work and create wealth. Let's hope that in the process we don't repeat the past. We can do better than to reconstruct the Middle Ages in the digital economy.

Commoditization of Social Connections

In his novel *Dead Souls,* originally published in 1842, the celebrated Russian writer Nikolai Gogol paints the exploits of Chichikov, a man on the lower rungs of Russian society. Driven by a desire to enhance his social standing, Chichikov develops an ingenious scheme: he travels to Russian villages and buys the records of dead serfs. It's a brilliant idea that capitalizes on a unique and grotesque feature of feudal Russian society: ownership by landlords of the people who live and work on their land.[21]

The number of serfs, or "souls," one owns is a measure of one's economic and social status. Landowners, in fact, pay taxes based on that number. The government keeps count of owned souls based on census numbers. Unfortunately the census takes place only infrequently, and many landowners end up paying taxes on their dead serfs. Grasping an opportune moment between the two censuses, Chichikov buys records of these dead souls from landowners eager to lighten their tax burden. Papers certifying Chichikov's ownership of four hundred souls rapidly elevate his status: landed gentry open their homes to him, try to give away their daughters in marriage, and celebrate him at town functions. And all it took was a record of ownership of hundreds of souls.

With social connections, social standing, and social influence becoming new standards of value and something that we increasingly measure, we may end up creating many more Chichikovs. But instead of collecting records of dead souls, the modern day Chichikovs may be driven to acquire more followers on Twitter or friends on Facebook or otherwise hoard social connections for money, fame, or reputation.

As we embark on the large-scale enterprise of creating a new infrastructure for social currencies, it is important to remember that social currencies operate quite differently than money. Their purpose is to facilitate social flows that often operate not on market principles but on intrinsic motivations to belong, to be respected, or to gain emotional support. Once we start measuring such connections or such flows we may purposefully or inadvertently take intrinsic value out of them, creating perverse motives and incentives. In fact instead of turning market transactions into social flows, we might be turning social interactions into market commodities. In the words of sociologist Chase, we would be applying ontic measurements to ontological phenomena.

It is this possibility that we envisioned at IFTF in 2004, when my colleague Jason Tester created the "Reputation Statement of Account," an "artifact from the future," a plausible but imagined future object.[22] At IFTF we often create such artifacts not as prototypes for building new products or services but as a way of converting abstract, high-level trends and future visions into tangible objects that help people internalize our forecasts. The "Reputation Statement of Account" that Tester designed remains one of my favorites; it perfectly encapsulates the idea of social currencies emerging as we reorganize our lives around social relationships.

The statement looks just like an American Express monthly statement, but instead of accounting for your monetary transactions, it tells you how much you've earned by contributing to sites such as Wikipedia or Flickr, how many points you've earned by providing rankings or ratings on various community sites, or how much social currency you've spent by asking someone for advice. Since then, several projects have sprung up that measure people's online contributions and reputations.

The Whuffie Bank, for example, is a nonprofit organization dedicated to building a new currency based on reputation that can be redeemed for real and virtual products and services. The term *whuffie* was coined by Cory Doctorow, a science fiction writer, to denote a unit of reputation-based currency in his novel *Down and Out in the Magic Kingdom*.[23] The Whuffie Bank issues whuffies based on a reputation algorithm that blends information from different social networks. It aims to build a platform that measures the online reputation of contributors on various sites. "As we develop and refine the algorithm that tracks public user activity over the net, the *whuffie* will become an accurate reflection of your web reputation," the site explains. "And as the Internet and social networks become a large part of people's lives, your web influence will become an increasingly accurate reflection of you."[24]

The newest and most striking incarnation of this idea can be found in an online game called Empire Avenue, which simulates a stock market in which shares in individuals can be traded and one can track individuals' market value based on their following in various social media sites, such as Facebook, Twitter, YouTube, and others, as well as demand for their shares by other players.

Commodifying social contributions—turning these into currencies that can be accumulated, hoarded, traded, and invested—may have unintended consequences. It could undermine precisely the kind of exchanges and volunteer contributions that are integral to the gift economies they are supposed to promote. In fact the word *currency* may be the wrong way to describe the incentives for facilitating flows inherent to social creation. The MetaCurrency Project coined the term *current-see* to emphasize the social flows of the exchanges it is trying to enable.[25] Indeed we need to invent new language and new terminology to describe the kinds of exchanges and values that comprise core elements of social production. This puts tremendous responsibility on people who design social platforms, because it is these design elements that will determine whether the platforms will foster gift exchange, competition, generosity, or new forms of greed.

We created social technologies. Our next task is to create social organizations: systems for creating not merely goods but also meaning, purpose, and greater good. Can we imagine a society of "private wealth holders whose main objective is to lead good lives, not to turn their wealth into capital?" asks political economist Robert Skidelsky. Or better yet, might they turn their wealth into a different kind of capital—social, emotional, or spiritual? Our technologies are giving us an unprecedented opportunity to do so.

9

Navigating the Transition

I spent hours talking to, observing, and sometimes working side by side with the amplified individuals profiled in this book. But it was only later, in conversations with Ariel Waldman, that I was able to more fully understand the kinds of skills we will all need in order to navigate the transition to the socialstructed world.

By her mid-twenties Ariel Waldman had accumulated an impressive, lengthy, and variable list of accomplishments. She founded Space Hack, a first-of-its-kind directory that helps thousands of citizen scientists engage in space exploration; created Science Hack Day in San Francisco, a day when hundreds of people come together to work on science projects and that is being replicated in many parts of the world; gave the keynote address to a prominent group of scientists at the 100 Year Starship Study Symposium organized by the Defense Advanced Research Projects Agency (DARPA) of the U.S. Department of Defense; and has become known as one of the top authorities on open science, space exploration, and media issues. This is in addition to having worked in an advertising company for eight years (while still in high school). The list of accomplishments doesn't, of course, include all the projects Ariel has initiated that have not been successful or have not seen the light of day. "I should probably make a list of things I've done that have gone nowhere," she laughs. "The amount of time I've put into Science Hack or Spacehack is probably the same amount of time I've put into things that were total flops."[1]

What are these flops? A blog that seemed funny at the time but didn't get any traction, starting a book and never finishing, a job in a start-up that didn't go anywhere. This ability to fearlessly make things she is passionate about public, without necessarily thinking about the end result, fits a pattern in Ariel's life and is something she considers a key to her success.

"Just put stuff out there" is her motto. "By making and prototyping things, whether it is a blog or a physical event, you are going to get so much that would not otherwise come into your line of view. When people look at your stuff, they might see the application much further than you can, or they see a unique story that would resonate with others. . . . People will start gravitating toward you—they will want to work with you, invite you to speak, give you grant money, or maybe offer a book deal. I just do things because I want to, without caring where they will go. I get excited about them and I am lucky if there are people who also get excited along with me."[2]

When I ask Ariel how a girl from Kansas with a degree in graphic design manages to do the nearly impossible—gain respect of the august community of space scientists—without having a PhD or an academic career, she responds, "I am a bit insatiable about learning new things."[3] Although a straight-A math student in high school, she did not pursue a science career, instead training to become a graphic designer and working as one of the first "digital anthropologists," people studying digital cultures and communities. She got interested in science by watching science channels on TV. In fact she became addicted to watching science programs, particularly space documentaries. "By the time they create the documentary, they have really worked out the story and have made it compelling," she says (unlike what they do in science classes). Her passion for space exploration led her to a job at NASA and to founding Spacehack.org and later Science Hack Day SF. She also reads a lot about science, using her social network as a filter for science knowledge. "It's not that I obsessively consume science news. I don't subscribe to news sites, I subscribe to *people* who are experts in space."[4]

People in her network are her filters and doors to science knowledge. And her science network is quite extensive. The recent open-science weekend meet-up she organized attracted sixty prominent scientists, postdocs, entrepreneurs, science writers, technologists, and designers. Science Hack Days she has organized have brought together hundreds of science enthusiasts, spanning disciplines, organizational affiliations, and levels of expertise. She has about 20,000 followers on Twitter, many of them prominent scientists and science experts.

"I am not someone who is great at coming up with grand ideas," Ariel admits. "Ideas are a dime a dozen. Whatever idea you have, you can Google it, and someone has probably already prototyped it."[5] Ariel considers her unique skill to be community creation. She sees her strength as a combination of having a vision and organizing skills that enables her to prototype the idea and create a community of people around it. Take a crazy idea she had in 2008: combining a BarCamp format (a type of unconference where people self-organize into discussion forums during allotted slots of time during the day) with cupcake tasting. People would bring cupcakes they made or bought, write on the board which ones they brought, and then during different time slots, instead of having BarCamp–type discussion sessions, they would bring out different kinds of cupcakes and talk about them and taste them. A free, fun, but totally ridiculous idea that only a few of her friends would get behind, Ariel thought, as she planned for about forty friends and friends of friends to show up. She rented a small room at Citizen Space, a coworking site in San Francisco, told her friends about it, and made the event public. To her shock, three hundred people showed up for the first Cupcake Camp! Building on the success of the first event, the next Cupcake Camp was held six months later and attracted five hundred people. The last one Ariel herself organized, in 2009, held 730 participants. Since that time Cupcake Camps have become a global phenomenon.

"I could've become a cupcake queen," Ariel laughs. Indeed she was getting interview requests from cupcake blog writers as well as the mainstream media, including the Associated Press. Yet Ariel herself had never made cupcakes and knew nothing about cupcakes except that she liked to eat them and thought it would be fun to bring together people who are into cupcakes. "This fits the pattern of me breaking into industries where I have zero experience. By being passionate and producing prototypes you are being seen as a community leader who brings people together. People start looking to you as an expert."[6]

If you have something you are passionate about, engage a community that is passionate about the same thing, create a platform for this community to come together, think through every detail of community design and management, prototype your idea, then stand back and see if it sinks or swims. This is how Ariel has learned to approach what she does. She has not taken management or leadership classes and does not think of herself as being either a manager or a leader. She is a good old-fashioned community organizer, but a community organizer in the digital age, empowered with tools and technologies that make it possible for her to attract hundreds, sometimes thousands of people to her projects. Community organizing, according to Ariel, involves a lot of cat herding, and she views herself as "lucky to have a combination of vision and attention to detail. It makes me difficult to hire, but it makes it possible for me to have the idea and to prototype as much of it as I can." Like a good social designer, Ariel believes that it is important to not only be a passionate idea person but to also care about details. "I am a bit OCD. Everything has to be thought through. This level of attention to detail is often lacking in open-source communities—people are passionate but don't have great project management skills."[7] However, she admits that she would probably hate having a project management job in an organization because she would not have the freedom to pursue her own ideas and passions.

People like Ariel are not new. Community organizers have been around since time immemorial—they have propelled political movements, led rebellions, created new communities. What is unique is the speed, impact, and scale of what such individuals can accomplish today. Spread a crazy Cupcake Camp idea to sixty cities around the world? Organize worldwide protests around the country and around the globe using the same tactics in a matter of months and sometimes days (think Arab Spring and Occupy Wall Street)? Passionate individuals, amplified with technologies and access to collective intelligence and the resources of multitudes of others they connect to via social media platforms are able to accomplish previously unthinkable things at a speed and on a scale previously unimaginable.

The work that Ariel and others profiled in this book are engaged in is not typical 9-to-5 work assigned by someone else. It is work that resembles art: passionate, self-driven, without limitations of time or organizational constraints. It is best described as the labor of love. In fact, Ariel and others often refer to their projects as such. Lewis Hyde in *The Gift* makes a distinction between work and labor: "Work is what we do by the hour. It begins and ends at a specific time and, if possible, we do it for money. Welding car bodies on an assembly line is work; washing dishes, computing taxes, walking the rounds in a psychiatric ward, picking asparagus—these are work. Labor, on the other hand, sets its own pace. We may get paid for it, but it's harder to quantify. . . . Writing a poem, raising a child, developing a new calculus, resolving a neurosis, invention in all forms—these are labors."[8] Hyde argues that works of art exist simultaneously in two economies: a market economy and a gift economy. A work of art can exist without the market, but where there is no gift, there is no art. I would argue that the products of socialstructing also exist simultaneously in two economies and that what drives people to engage in these efforts is not quantifiable by financial rewards. Socialstructing involves a lot of labor—hours spent solving equations, contributing video footage, doing science projects, creating music. In the process of engaging in such efforts we are engaging in what Hyde calls the Commerce of Creative

Spirit. And in the world in which much of the work can increasingly be done by machines and in which it takes only a few people to produce at enormous scales, we need to turn our time and attention to precisely the Commerce of Creative Spirit, be it in science, arts, health, education, or any other domain.

This is the greatest promise of socialstructing: to bring passion, self-direction, and social connectivity into our lives and into our work. At its best, socialstructing creates a promise to turn what has been directed and ordained by institutions into a labor of love. It is about turning education into a highly personalized and socially embedded experience. It is about making health a participatory process, a partnership between experts and the community that can benefit everyone and amplify our ability to find personalized treatment options. It is about reinventing the governance process that for far too long we have outsourced to professionals. And socialstructing is not just for the heroic few, like Ariel Waldman, Eri Gentry, Paul Radu, and others profiled in this book. Yes, they may be pioneering this new way of working and being in the world. Any transformation starts with a few early adopters paving the way. But what they are doing is highly social and depends on the participation of large groups of people. None of their efforts would survive if they could not engage you and others in contributing.

In the work my colleague Rod Falcon and I did, looking at how young people form and navigate social networks in the age of abundant connectivity, we pointed out that networks take a lot of resources and division of labor to keep them going, with many people serving multiple roles. Specifically, we saw people performing two types of roles: those that maintain the network itself (managing collaboration platforms, sending out group communications, organizing physical spaces for events) and those that provide specific content (doing data analysis, contributing expertise, articles, reviews). The Global Lives Project relies on a large network of Web designers, programmers, videographers, volunteer translators, and others to keep it going. BioCurious couldn't exist without biology experts, statisticians, Web designers, event organizers, and many others. In our observational research we identified many network roles, including:

- Experts: those who provide content knowledge.

- IT support: those who keep the technology infrastructure for the network functioning.

- Brokers: those who connect people or ideas that otherwise might not come together.

- Organizers: those who orchestrate and plan activities for members of the network. The organizer may specialize in certain kinds of activities or know everything that's going on.

- Innovators: those who come up with new ideas for activities, connections, projects, partnerships.

- Edge surfers: people who test boundaries, pushing the limits of the network's usual activities and values.[9]

If you think about your own skills and passions, there is probably something you can contribute to any socialstructed effort. During a Science Hack Day at IFTF, some people who were interested in science but were not scientists or programmers took on the task of making sure there were drinks and food for the team. When the projects were presented at the end of forty-eight hours, they were recognized as part of the team. The difference between what they were doing and how jobs are assigned in traditional work settings or schools is that they self-identified their expertise and chose where they wanted to contribute. Some companies, like Facebook, have adopted the strategy of employees self-selecting tasks they want to work on. People are hired not for specific positions but for their expertise and fit with the culture. After an initial two-week "boot-camp" that all the new Facebook hires go through (where wall signs declare, "Move Fast and Break Things" and "We Hack Therefore We Are"), they decide what project they want to work on.

At IFTF we proudly show people our unusual organizational chart, the result of the visioning effort we undertook in 2007 in recognition of the highly interconnected and fluid external environment, requiring us to adopt a network structure in order to increase our flexibility and amplify our impact in the world. The diagram reflects a set of values we described at the time in our vision document:

> Valuing open collaboration, independence, and the ability of anyone to *rise to the endeavor,* we draw on network leadership models that provide a platform for self-organizing structures. The value of these self-organizing structures is that they can act quickly, responsively, and creatively from the edges. The guiding concepts in this view of leadership are openness, self-election, continuous prototyping, robust platforms, and low coordination costs. Leadership skills focus on community building, consensus building, mediation, commitment, and humility.[10]

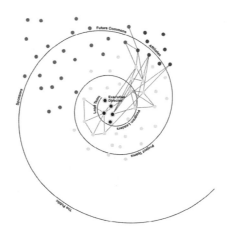

The role of the executive director, my role, was conceived as that of the "speaker for the commons." Our vision document from that time states, "Recognizing that we will have the greatest reach when we can convene a commons for the future, we call on a speaker for the commons—an executive director who is, on one hand, a *primus inter pares* who can step forward to make the final call on decisions when the community fails to agree and, on the other, a guide, mentor, and visionary who leads by convening and inspiring. The executive director balances the interests of individual members of the commons and champions the interests of the whole."[11]

What we wanted to communicate with this swirling cluster of moving stars is the notion of fluid hierarchies, a key feature of many socialstructs that rely on the participation of large networks of people. It is not that such socialstructs don't have hierarchies; it is just that such hierarchies are not based on assigned roles or titles. They are not results of dictates from above. Rather such hierarchies and organizational structures are fluid, emergent, and constantly evolving. They are based on reputation, which is often the result of visible contributions to the effort, as judged by others in the community, either those contributing to the effort or those who are the beneficiaries of its results, or both. In the open-source community, for example, contributors acquire a reputation for the elegance and simplicity of pieces of code they develop. In gaming communities, such as World of Warcraft, players acquire a reputation as a guild master based on their abilities to assemble groups and win battles.

If socialstructing seems overwhelming and confusing, think of it as something you already do as a regular part of your life. Most of us are involved in many social networks, including the ones at work. We have school networks, neighborhood groups, hobby and interest-based networks, or volunteer networks. In each of these we may play different roles. In my son's school network, I may be providing logistics support for afterschool activities; among my friends I may be known as an expert on economics; with my family, I may serve as the social organizer. Our roles and the skills we bring to each one of these communities are different because they are highly context-specific. You can be an innovator in one network and an organizer in another. And your role may shift as the circumstances change.

Soon many more activities will be socialstructed, and people will increasingly come together not in permanent and rigid organizational forms where roles are assigned by the higher-ups but in forms that will evolve to fit the particular needs of a community on an ad hoc basis. The good news is that the kinds of skills we previously reserved for our informal interactions—in social networks, in our volunteer work, with our friends—will be the kind of skills we will have to rely on in whatever work or productive endeavor we will be engaged in. We will be using more of our innate human skills rather than skills learned from management books and management courses. At its best, socialstructing is about humanizing our lives, allowing us to be fully human rather than organizational men and women. Not surprisingly, people who seem to do well in this world are ones who do not fit into the traditional organizational structures; they are difficult to hire and manage because they do not rely on traditional symbols of power, such as organizational titles, monetary rewards, and command of large departments. They are driven by intrinsic motivations and rewards that are hard to measure, and they are capitalizing on their innate skills and abilities and fitting these into endeavors they are pursuing rather than the other way around.

In some ways, then, we can think of the future as a reversal: the skills you learned in your organizations will be less useful, and the skills that you thought were good only for hobbies and volunteer activities are the kinds of skills you will need to succeed in the socialstructed world. What is most important is that the network requires many skills, many abilities and capabilities. There is room for everyone in the socialstructed world!

Concluding Thoughts: Urgent Optimism

In the opening of this book I mentioned that we are living in two worlds: the world of incumbents in which most productive activities are conducted through institutions (corporations, foundations, governments, etc.) and the nascent world in which amplified individuals empowered with technologies and connections with myriad others are able to come together to create, collaborate, and innovate outside of traditional institutional boundaries. This nascent world is the world of socialstructing. It is the curve we have just begun to embark on, and its final destination and shape are not clear. It could lead to a large-scale redefinition of value and meaning, but it also holds the potential to bring with it new types of fracturing and inequalities, as evident in current efforts to monetize the commons and convert social interactions into commodified currencies.

Thinking about the final destination of the nascent curve, however, leaves me with a sense of what my colleague Jane McGonigal calls "urgent optimism." Ariel Waldman, Eri Gentry, Paul Radu, David Evan Harris, and other messengers from the future are sending us signals that leave me with a sense of excitement and hope. I see socialstructing as a way to build a better future by de-institutionalizing production, infusing social ties and human connectedness into our economic life, in the process redefining established paradigms of work, productivity, and value. But there is a sense of urgency in my optimism. If we are not careful, the new curve may also bring with it new disparities. What direction this nascent curve takes is up to us. We are not passive bystanders in the unfolding of the future; we have some responsibility for and agency in shaping the kind of future we want to live in. And we need to urgently get involved in the process of shaping that social-structed future. This involves building a whole new infrastructure for making sure that the potential of the socialstructed world is fully realized and that we avoid some of the potentially negative scenarios, such as digital manor economies. The tasks to resolve are myriad and difficult: creating a regulatory infrastructure that rewards people for doing microwork; putting in place health insurance and benefits systems to recognize new ways of working; and developing new governance systems for what is essentially commons-based production. We need to carefully think about negative impacts of monetizing commons production efforts and the resulting potential income disparities. It is not unreasonable to expect that projects and organizations whose value derives from communities they create (think Facebook, Twitter, and Patients-LikeMe) should incorporate the commons governance principles, as suggested in one of my essays:

- Clearly articulating the promise of the platform to the participants, with all the ensuing rights and responsibilities for members

- Creating a community governance board (without direct financial incentives to the project) to guide and review major policy and strategy decisions

- Crowdsourcing major decisions guiding development and evolution of such platforms

- Ensuring radical transparency around key decisions and financial metrics

- Creating reward structures for management and employees more akin to those of nonprofits or co-ops than those of for-profit entities

In a world where people's jobs will not be given to them, each individual will need to look deeply and understand what she or he is good at, how she or he can contribute to multiple efforts and navigate multiple roles and identities as a part of different communities. Therefore we need to develop new skills and capabilities in our young people. In this largely self-driven and self-directed world, with resources and content widely available on everyday personal devices, we will no longer need to worry so much about the digital divide as about a cognitive divide. Those who are self-driven or whose social networks drive them to acquire more and more knowledge and to consume more and more rich content will be able to increase their cognitive capital, while those who do not possess such drive or whose social settings do not encourage such accumulation of knowledge will be left farther and farther behind. We urgently need to rethink our educational priorities and the kinds of skills we will need in the world of abundant content and rich ecologies of knowledge and information.

These are systemic issues, and we need to start thinking about them now. Instead of trying to solve yesterday's problems—worrying about jobs that will never come back, propping up institutions that are no longer needed, trying to patch up an education system better suited to the waning system of mass production—we need to roll up our sleeves and engage in socialstructing our world. I am afraid that our existing institutions—government bodies, corporations, schools, and labor unions—are legacies of exactly the kind of system that is no longer working, with too many vested interests preventing them from altering course. I believe that the foundations of the new infrastructure for the socialstructed world will be built in meet-ups and unconferences, on community websites, and among the crowds at Occupy Wall Street or whatever its successor is. These entities and movements may appear to be fringe outsiders, but they are the mainstream of the future. Socialstructing requires new levels of engagement in areas that for far too long we have outsourced to institutions and professional elites, from citizenship to education and innovation. We need to give our time, our minds, our energy to the new enterprise of socialstructing. It is a tall order but one that promises a huge payoff: returning richness and human connectedness to our lives. We can take heart in the piece of wisdom I learned from Ariel Waldman: "If something doesn't work, if I see a vacuum, if I think that something sucks, I just go out and do something to fix it."[12] What are you waiting for?

Acknowledgments

Although my name appears on the cover of this book, and I take full responsibility for its content, I feel that throughout the process of writing I have been channeling the voices of many people. First, the people I profile in this book: Paul Radu, Eri Gentry, David Evan Harris, Alex Carmichael, Larry Smarr, Ariel Waldman, and others whom I interviewed and who have so generously shared their time and ideas with me. They are amplified individuals—people who by their deeds are transforming the world and showing others new paths for creating, living, and inventing. These people are just the tip of the iceberg, a small cross-section of the remarkable individuals who are a part of the IFTF extended community. They participate in IFTF workshops, come to share their work with us, and organize meetups and hackathons at the Institute. They are the pioneers of socialstructing who are living the future today. They are my inspiration and my heroes.

In this book I am also channeling my remarkable IFTF colleagues. In working side by side with me, they help me make new connections, challenge my existing frameworks, and push me to think deeply. I feel like every person at the Institute and everyone affiliated with it has had something to do with this book. Special thanks to a few individuals: my brilliant and generous-to-a-fault colleague Kathi Vian, without whose encouragement and support this book wouldn't have come about; IFTF's executive producer, Jean Hagan, whose creativity and daily caring afforded me space for writing; Jane McGonigal, whose infectious, urgent optimism gives me hope for the future; Rod Falcon, who has been a partner from the moment I joined IFTF; Howard Rheingold for pioneering our work on cooperation, which this book builds on. I am forever grateful to Bob Johansen, IFTF's distinguished fellow and former president, for having the foresight to bring me to IFTF and for his continued support and encouragement in my work. He made it possible for me to find a true intellectual home. Lawrence Wilkinson, a longtime chairman of IFTF's board, provided stewardship in reconceiving IFTF as a network organization, a legacy that we live every day. Many thanks to him and to all the IFTF board members for ensuring that the idea and the ideals of the Institute for the Future remain viable today.

Ben Hamamoto was more than a research assistant; he also served as a reviewer and a sounding board throughout the process. I have also been lucky to have the remarkable assistance of Bettina Warburg-Johnson and Sara Skvirsky. Their dedication and unfailing attention to detail set a new standard. My colleagues David Pescovitz, Jason Tester, Jake Dunagan, Nicolas Weidinger, and others have each contributed advice, peer reviews, and inspiration. Many thanks to my husband, Chris Fleischut, a friend, reviewer, partner, and so much more, and to my son, Greg, who inspires me to remake the world.

This book wouldn't have come about if not for my agent, Ted Weinstein, who saw the beginnings of a book in a blog post and convinced me to pursue the idea. Many thanks to my editor, Emily Loose, for her support and stewardship of the book.

Most of all, my deep gratitude to the Institute for the Future and all the people who came before me and who contribute to and help sustain our work. You inspire and provide a space for us to dream the impossible.

Notes

Chapter 1

1. Yochai Benkler, *The Wealth of Networks: How Social Production Transforms Markets and Freedom* (New Haven, CT: Yale University Press, 2006).
2. Eri Gentry, series of interviews by author, Palo Alto, CA, April-October, 2011.
3. ImmunePath Inc., accessed December 11, 2011, http://www.immunepath .com/ (site discontinued).
4. Gentry, April-October, 2011.
5. Cofactor Bio, accessed December 11, 2011, http://cofactorbio.com/ (site discontinued).
6. Paul Cristian Radu, "Adoption Exec Leaves Legacy of Complaints," *San Antonio Express-News,* October 28, 2001, Metro edition, South Texas, 1B.
7. Paul Cristian Radu, series of interviews by author, Palo Alto, CA, April-October, 2011.
8. Radu, April-October, 2011.
9. "Offshore Crime, Inc.," Organized Crime and Corruption Reporting Project (OCCRP), last modified November 20, 2010, http://www.reporting project.net/offshore/.
10. Mihai Munteanu, "Kiss: Police Arrest Kiss," OCCRP, last modified November 20, 2010, accessed December 14, 2011, https://reportingproject.net

/offshore/index.php/kiss-the-downfall-and-arrest-of-kiss; "Offshore Registration Business Forced to Halt Operations," OCCRP, last modified June 28,
2011, accessed December 14, 2011, https://reportingproject.net/offshore/index
.php/offshore-registration-business-forced-to-halt-operations; "OCCRP Wins
Daniel Pearl Global Investigative Journalism Award," OCCRP, last modified
October 16, 2011, accessed December 14, 2011, https://reportingproject.net
/occrp/index.php/ccwatch/cc-watch-indepth/1171-occrp-wins-daniel-pearl
-global-investigative-journalism-award.

11. Radu, April–October, 2011.

12. David Evan Harris, series of interviews by author, Palo Alto, CA, April–
October, 2011.

13. Harris, April–October, 2011.

14. In 2008, the organization received a grant that allowed David to receive a
part-time, minimum-wage salary, which continues today. In 2011, David
hired his first full-time staff member to handle administration and development work for the quickly growing organization.

15. "Mission Statement," Global Lives Project, accessed September 21, 2012,
http://globallives.org.

16. Ben Parr, "Easter Egg: Yelp Is the iPhone's First Augmented Reality App,"
Mashable, accessed September 21, 2012, http://mashable.com/2009/08/27
/yelp-augmented-reality/.

17. Margaret Mead, *Culture and Commitment: A Study of the Generation Gap* (London: Bodley Head, 1970).

18. Ian Morrison, *The Second Curve: Managing the Velocity of Change* (New York:
Ballantine Books, 1996).

Chapter 2

1. Pew Project for Excellence in Journalism, "The State of the News Media
2011," accessed December 5, 2011, http://pewresearch.org/pubs/1924/state
-of-the-news-media-2011.

2. Matthew Fleischer, "AOL Patch to Recruit 8,000 Unpaid Bloggers," Huff-
Post Live, last modified April 26, 2011, accessed September 21, 2012, http://
www.mediabistro.com/fishbowlla/aol-patch-to-recruit-8000-presumably
-unpaid-bloggers_b27409.

3. A decline of 42 percent and a net loss of $14.8 billion: Mark Mulligan with
Laura Wiramihardja, "Music Industry Meltdown: Recasting the Mold," For-
rester Research, last modified January 22, 2010, accessed September 21, 2012,
http://www.forrester.com/rb/Research/music_in-dustry_meltdown_recasting

_mold/q/id/56147/t/2. According to the International Federation of the Phonographic Industry, in 2000 global recorded music sales totaled U.S.$37 billion: "Global Recorded Music Sales Down 5% in First Half 2001," IFPI, last modified September 28, 2001, accessed September 21, 2012, http://www.ifpi .org/content/section_news/20010928.html. In 2010, the total was U.S.$15.9 billion: Richard Smirke, "IFPI 2011 Report: Global Recorded Music Sales Fall 8.4%; Eminem, Lady Gaga Top Int'l Sellers," Billboard, last modified March 30, 2011, accessed September 21, 2012, http://www.billboard.biz/bbbiz /industry/global/ifpi-2011-report-global-recorded-music-sales-1005100902 .story.

4. Jared Moya, "Study: Artists Earn More in a P2P World," ZeroPaid, November 18, last modified 2009, accessed September 21, 2012, http://www .zeropaid.com/news/87267/study-artists-earn-more-in-ap2p-world/; Will Page and Chris Carey, "Adding Up the Music Industry for 2008," *PRS for Music: Economic Insight* 15 (July 2009), accessed September 21, 2012, http:// www.prsformusic.com/creators/news/research/Documents/WillPageand ChrisCarey(2009)AddingUpTheMusicIndustryfor2008.pdf.

5. Daniel Johansson and Markus Larsson, "The Swedish Music Industry in Graphs: Economic Development Report 2000–2008," KTH Royal Institute of Technology, last modified December 2009, accessed September 21, 2012, http://ec.europa.eu/avpolicy/docs/other_actions/col.../kth_annex.pdf.

6. Yochai Benkler, *The Wealth of Networks: How Social Production Transforms Markets and Freedom*, (Benkler.org, 2006), 333, accessed September 21, 2012, http://webyes.com.br/wp-content/uploads/ebooks/book_The_Wealth_of _Networks.pdf.

7. John M. Culkin, "A Schoolman's Guide to Marshall McLuhan," *Saturday Review*, March 18, 1967.

8. Paul Baran and Sharla P. Boehm, "Digital Simulation of Hot-Potato Routing in a Broadband Distributed Communications Network," On Distributed Communications II, (RAND Corporation, 1964), accessed September 21, 2012, http://www.rand.org/pubs/research_memoranda/RM3103.html.

9. Wikipedia, "Donald Davies," accessed September 21, 2012, http:// en.wikipedia.org/wiki/Donald_Davies.

10. Jane McGonigal, *Reality Is Broken: Why Games Make Us Better and How They Can Change the World* (New York: Penguin, 2011), 248.

11. McGonigal, *Reality Is Broken*, 28.

12. James Surowiecki, *The Wisdom of Crowds* (New York: Random House, 2004).

13. "Social Computing Research," HP, accessed September 21, 2012, http:// www.hpl.hp.com/research/idl/.

14. Sitaram Asur and Bernardo A. Huberman, "Predicting the Future with Social

Media," HP Social Computing Lab, last modified March 29, 2010, accessed September 21, 2012, http://www.hpl.hp.com/research/scl/papers/socialmedia /socialmedia.pdf.

15. Ronald Coase, "The Nature of the Firm," *Economica* 4, no. 16 (1937): 386–405.

16. Douglas Rushkoff, *Life Inc: How Corporatism Conquered the World, and How We Can Take it Back*, (New York: Random House Trade Paperbacks, 2011).

17. Pamela Coppola, Andrew Levesque and Ryan Wilmouth, "Production of the Model T: 1908–1927," Bryant College, accessed December 14, 2011, http://web.bryant.edu/~ehu/h364proj/fall_98/coppola/production.html.

18. "Ford Motor Company," Wikipedia, accessed September 21, 2012, http:// en.wikipedia.org/wiki/Ford_Motor_Company#cite_note-6.

19. "Issues: Education," The White House, accessed September 21, 2012, http:// www.whitehouse.gov/issues/education.

20. Clay Shirky, *Here Comes Everybody* (New York: The Penguin Press, 2008).

21. "About Us," *Boing Boing* (blog), accessed September 21, 2012, http://boing boing.net/about.

22. Oliver Chiang, "Twitter Hits Nearly 200M Accounts, 110MTweets Per Day, Focuses on Global Expansion," *Forbes,* last modified January 19, 2011, accessed September 21, 2012, http://www.forbes.com/sites/oliver chiang/2011/01/19/twitter-hits-nearly-200m-users-110m-tweets-per-day -focuses-on-global-expansion/.

23. Christopher Null and Brian Caulfield, "Fade to Black: The1980s Vision of 'Lights-Out' Manufacturing, Where Robots Do All the Work, Is a Dream No More," *Business 2.0,* last modified June 1, 2003, accessed September 21, 2012, http://money.cnn.com/magazines/business2/business2_archive /2003/06/01/343371/index.htm.

24. Choe Sang-Hun, "Teaching Machine Sticks to Script in South Korea," *New York Times,* last modified July 10, 2010, accessed September 21, 2012, http:// www.nytimes.com/2010/07/11/science/11robotside.html?_r=0.

25. Anne Trafton, "Robotic Therapy Helps Stroke Patients Regain Function," *MIT News,* last modified April 19, 2010, accessed September 21, 2012, http:// web.mit.edu/newsoffice/2010/stroke-therapy-0419.html.

26. John Markoff, "Armies of Expensive Lawyers, Replaced by Cheaper Software," *New York Times,* last modified March 4, 2011, accessed September 21, 2012, http://www.nytimes.com/2011/03/05/science/05legal.html ?pagewanted=all.

27. David Autor, "The Polarization of Job Opportunities in the U.S. Labor Market: Implications for Employment and Earnings," Center for American Progress and The Hamilton Project, last modified April 30, 2010, ac-

cessed September 21, 2012, http://www.americanprogress.org/wp-content/uploads/issues/2010/04/job_polarization_report.html.

28. "Future Work Skills 2020," Institute For The Future, (Institute For The Future for University of Phoenix Research Institute, 2011).

29. Teodor Shanin, "How the Other Half Live," interview with Teodor Shanin by Fred Pearce," *New Scientist* 175 (2002): 44–48.

30. Niles Eldredge and Stephen J. Gould, "Punctuated Equilibria: An Alternative to Phyletic Gradualism," in *Models in Paleobiology,* ed. T. J. M. Schopf (San Francisco: Freeman, Cooper, 1972), 82–115.

Chapter 3

1. Edward Castronova, "On Money and Magic," *Journal of Virtual Worlds Research* 2, No. 4, (February 2010).

2. Karma Kitchen, accessed September 21, 2012, http://www.karmakitchen.org/.

3. Bronislaw Malinowski, "Kula: The Circulating Exchange of Valuables in the Archipelagoes of Eastern New Guinea," *Man* 20 (July 1920): 97–105.

4. Bronislaw Malinowski, *Argonauts of the Western Pacific: An Account of Native Enterprise and Adventure in the Archipelagoes of Melanesian New Guinea,* 11th ed. (London: Taylor and Francis, 2005), 68.

5. Malinowski, *Argonauts of the Western Pacific*, 97.

6. Malinowski, *Argonauts of the Western Pacific*, 98.

7. Malinowski, *Argonauts of the Western Pacific*, 98.

8. "Tribe-Anuta," BBC, last modified March 2008, accessed September 21, 2012, http://www.bbc.co.uk/tribe/tribes/anuta/index.shtml.

9. Eric S. Raymond, "Homesteading the Noosphere" April (1998): 8, accessed September 21, 2012, http://cseweb.ucsd.edu/~goguen/courses/268D/noosphere.ps.gz.

10. "Ten Principles," Burning Man, accessed December 6, 2011, http://www.burningman.com/whatisburningman/about_burningman/principles.html.

11. Duran Bell, "Modes of Exchange: Gifts and Commodity," *Journal of Socio-Economics* 20, no. 2 (1991): 165.

12. Bell, "Modes of Exchange: Gifts and Commodity," 166.

13. Bell, "Modes of Exchange: Gifts and Commodity," 166.

14. Bell, "Modes of Exchange: Gifts and Commodity," 166.

15. Castronova, "On Money and Magic," 4.

16. "The History of Money," PBS NOVA, accessed December 6, 2011, http://www.pbs.org/wgbh/nova/ancient/history-money.html.

17. W. Wüthrich, "Alternatives to Globalization: Cooperative Principle and Complementary Currency," trans. Philip Beard, *Current Issues*, 30 (August 2004), accessed December 14, 2011, http://reinventingmoney.com/documents /BeardWIR.pdf.

18. Erik B. Hansch, "Initial Results of WIR Research in Switzerland," New Economics Research, accessed September 21, 2012, http://neweconomics institute.org/publications/initial-results-wir-research-switzerland.

19. James Stodder, "Reciprocal Exchange Networks: Implications for Macro-economic Stability," *Engineering Management Society, 2000: Proceedings of the 2000 IEEE* (2000): 540–45.

20. Jane O'Brien, "BerkShares Boost the Berkshires in Massachusetts," *BBC News,* last modified September 6, 2011, accessed September 21, 2012, http:// www.bbc.co.uk/news/world-us-canada-14814834; the Ithaca Hours, accessed September 21, 2012, http://www.ithacahours.org.

21. Yang Wang and Scott D. Mainwaring, "Incentives in the Wild: Leveraging Virtual Currency to Sustain Online Community," in *iConference 2010 Proceedings,* University of Illinois at Urbana-Champaign, 2010, 270–74; accessed September 21, 2012, http://www.mitbbs.com.

22. Li Yuan, "Web Site Helps Chinese in U.S. Navigate Life," *Wall Street Journal,* last modified October 26, 2004, accessed September 21, 2012, http://online .wsj.com/article/SB109874240593955172.html.

23. Wang and Mainwaring, "Incentives in the Wild: Leveraging Virtual Currency to Sustain Online Community," 270–74.

24. Wang and Mainwaring, "Incentives in the Wild: Leveraging Virtual Currency to Sustain Online Community," 270-274.

25. "Nitro," Bunchball, accessed September 21, 2012, http://www.bunchball .com/nitro.

26. "Nitro Game Mechanics," Bunchball, accessed December 7, 2011, http:// bunchball.design-centric.com/products/gamemechanics.

27. Rachel Donadio, "Battered by Economic Crisis, Greeks Turn to Barter Networks," *New York Times,* last modified October 1, 2011, accessed September 21, 2012, http://www.nytimes.com/2011/10/02/world/europe/in -greece-barter-networks-surge.html?pagewanted=all.

28. Mure Dickie, "Beijing Fears Virtual Money's Influence," *Financial Times,* last modified March 7, 2007, accessed September 21, 2012, http://www.ft.com /cms/s/0/6e4d7c84-cc17-11db-a661-000b5df10621.html#axzz27KQAcgR1.

29. Castronova, "On Money and Magic," 5.

30. Douglas Rushkoff, "Economics Is Not Natural Science," Edge, last modified August 11, 2009, accessed December 8, 2011, http://edge.org/conversation /economics-is-not-natural-science.

31. Rachel Botsman, *What's Mine Is Yours: The Rise of Collaborative Consumption* (New York: HarperCollins, 2010).

32. "CouchSurfing: Mission," Couch Surfing, accessed December 7, 2011, http://www.couchsurfing.org/about/mission/.

33. "CouchSurfing: Statistics," Couch Surfing, accessed December 7, 2011, http://www.couchsurfing.org/statistics.

34. NeighborGoods, accessed September 21, 2012, http://www.neighborgoods.net/.

35. Landshare, accessed September 21, 2012, http://www.landshare.net.

36. RelayRides, accessed September 21, 2012, https://relayrides.com/.

37. 65hours, accessed September 21, 2012, http://www.65hours.com/; Time-Banks, accessed September 21, 2012, http://timebanks.org/.

38. Bag Borrow or Steal, accessed September 21, 2012, http://www.bagborroworsteal.com.

39. A Campaign for Real Milk, accessed September 21, 2012, http://www.realmilk.com.

40. Robin Sloan, "Robin Writes a Book (and You Get a Copy)," Kickstarter, accessed December 14, 2011, http://www.kickstarter.com/projects/robinsloan/robin-writes-a-book-and-you-get-a-copy?ref=live.

41. Sloane, "Robin Writes a Book (and You Get a Copy)."

42. Erick Schonfeld, "Founder Stories (Kickstarter): Going Direct to the Audience for Crowdsourced Funding," *TechCrunch,* last modified January 10, 2011, accessed September 21, 2012, http://techcrunch.com/2011/01/10/startup-sherpa-kickstarter/.

43. Carl Franzen, "Kickstarter Expects to Provide More Funding to the Arts than NEA," *Talking Points Memo*, last modified February 24, 2012, accessed September 21, 2012, http://idealab.talkingpointsmemo.com/2012/02/kickstarter-expects-to-provide-more-funding-to-the-arts-than-nea.php.

44. "Kickstarter Stats," Kickstarter, accessed September 21, 2012, http://www.kickstarter.com/help/stats.

45. Pebble Technology, "Pebble: E-Paper Watch for iPhone and Android," Kickstarter, accessed September 21, 2012, http://www.kickstarter.com/projects/597507018/pebble-e-paper-watch-for-iphone-and-android.

46. Macgregor Campbell, "Bank Says No? Ditch the Bank – Borrow from the Crowd," *New Scientist* (preview of full article), last modified January 12, 2012, accessed September 21, 2012, http://www.newscientist.com/article/mg21228421.300-bank-says-no-ditch-the-bank-borrow-from-the-crowd.html?full=true&print=tru.

47. "Company Overview," Prosper, accessed December 8, 2011, http://www.prosper.com/about/.

48. "About Us," Lending Club, accessed September 21, 2012, https://www
    .lendingclub.com/public/about-us.action.

49. "Why Invest in Peer-to-Peer Lending with Prosper?" Prosper, accessed Sep-
    tember 21, 2012, http://www.prosper.com/invest/; "Earn Steady Returns:
    Lending Club," Lending Club, accessed September 21, 2012, http://www
    .lendingclub.com/public/steady-returns.action.

50. Campbell, "Bank Says No? Ditch the Bank—Borrow from the Crowd."

51. "ScholarMatch helps secure funding for the college-bound," *Western Addi-
    tion,* last modified September 1, 2011, accessed December 8, 2011, http://
    www.thewesternedition.com/?c=117&a=1817; "Impact," ScholarMatch,
    accessed September 21, 2012, http://scholarmatch.org/about/impact/.

52. "About Us," LendFriend, accessed December 8, 2011, https://lendfriend.
    com/about-us/.

53. "Statistics," Kiva, accessed December 8, 2011, http://www.kiva.org/about/stats.

54. "Kiva.org," LinkedIn, accessed December 8, 2011, http://www.linkedin.
    com/company/kiva.org; Statistics," Kiva, accessed December 8, 2011, http://
    www.kiva.org/about/stats.

55. Jonathan Haidt, "Beyond the Book: How to Become Happier," the Hap-
    piness Hypothesis, accessed December 8, 2011, http://www.happiness
    hypothesis.com/beyond-gethappy.html.

56. Elizabeth W. Dunn, Lara B. Aknin, and Michael I. Norton, "Spending
    Money on Others Promotes Happiness," *Science* 319, no. 5870 (2008):
    1687–88.

57. Daniel Pink, *Drive: The Surprising Truth About What Motivates Us* (New York:
    Riverhead Books, 2009).

58. Daniel Ariely, *Predictably Irrational: The Hidden Forces That Shape Our Deci-
    sions* (New York: Harper Perennial, 2010), 79.

59. Dan Ariely, "Money Changes Everything," TEDxBlackRockCity, accessed
    September 21, 2012, http://www.youtube.com/watch?v=oV0cbCFGAtU.

60. Joseph Stiglitz, Amartya Sen, and Jean-Paul Fitoussi, "The Measurement
    of Economic Performance and Social Progress Revisited," last modified
    September 14, 2009, accessed September 21, 2012, http://www.stiglitz-sen
    -fitoussi.fr/documents/overview-eng.pdf.

61. "What are National Accounts of Well-being and why do we need them?"
    National Accounts of Well-being, accessed September 21, 2012, http://www
    .nationalaccountsofwellbeing.org/.

62. "What are National Accounts of Well-being and why do we need them?"

63. Michael Busch, "Adam Smith and Consumerism's Role in Happiness:
    Modern Society Re-Examined," *Major Themes in Economics* 10 (Iowa: Uni-
    versity of Northern Iowa, 2008), 65.

Chapter 4

1. Michael Wesch, "A Vision of Students Today," YouTube, last modified October 12, 2007, accessed September 21, 2012, http://www.youtube.com /watch?v=dGCJ46vyR9o.

2. Mihaly Csikszentmihalyi, *Flow: The Psychology of Optimal Experience* (New York: Harper Perennial, 1991), 4.

3. "National Sleep Foundation 2006 *Sleep in America* Poll Highlights and Key Findings," National Sleep Foundation, accessed September 21, 2012, http:// www.sleepfoundation.org/sites/default/files/Highlights_facts_06.pdf.

4. Nancy Kalish, "The Early Bird Gets the Bad Grade," *New York Times,* last modified January 14, 2008, accessed September 21, 2012, http://www.nytimes .com/2008/01/14/opinion/14kalish.html.

5. Nancy Kalish, "The Early Bird Gets the Bad Grade."

6. Khan Academy, accessed September 21, 2012, http://www.khanacademy.org.

7. Clive Thompson, "How Khan Academy Is Changing the Rules of Education," *Wired,* last modified July 15, 2011, accessed December 8, 2011, http:// www.wired.com/magazine/2011/07/ff_khan/all/1.

8. MG Siegler, "Bill Gates: In Five Years The Best Education Will Come From The Web," *TechCrunch*, last modified August 6, 2010, accessed September 21, 2012, http://techcrunch.com/2010/08/06/bill-gates-education/.

9. Comments on "A Tricky Math Problem: Restricting a in the Equation $a(b^2-1)=c^2+d^2$ to Force $|b|=1$?" *Fluther,* last modified March 4, 2009, accessed September 21, 2012, http://www.fluther.com/36789/a-tricky -math-problem-restricting-a-in-the-equation-ab2%E2%80%931c2d2-to/.

10. John Falk and Lynn Dierking, "The 95 Percent Solution," *American Scientist* 98 (November-December 2010): 486.

11. Eri Gentry, series of interviews with author, Palo Alto, CA, April-October, 2011.

12. Donald L. Finkel, *Teaching with Your Mouth Shut* (Portsmouth, NH: Boynton/Cook, 2000), 8.

13. "Rheingold U," Howard Rheingold, accessed September 21, 2012, http:// www.rheingold.com/university.

14. "What Is Skillshare?" Skillshare, accessed December 15, 2011, http://www .skillshare.com/about.

15. "What Is Skillshare?"

16. 100 Days of Spring Facebook page, accessed December 15, 2011, http://www .facebook.com/pages/100-Days-of-Spring/203559293003754?sk=info.

17. Emily Appelbaum, "One Hundred Days of Spring: As Mid-Market talks, two organizers do," *San Francisco Bay Guardian* online, last modified June 29, 2011,

accessed September 21, 2012, http://www.sfbg.com/pixel_vision/2011/06/29
/one-hundred-days-spring-mid-market-talks-two-youths-do.

18. Shawn Cornally, "'Will This Be on the Test?' An Overemphasis on Grades
    Might Be Killing the Desire to Learn," Good, last modified June 9, 2011,
    accessed December 15, 2011, http://www.good.is/posts/will-this-be-on-the
    -test-an-overemphasis-on-grades-might-be-killing-the-desire-to-learn/.

19. Alfie Kohn, "The Dangerous Myth of Grade Inflation," Chronicle of Higher
    Education 49, no. 11 (2002): B7.

20. Paul R. Sackett, Sheldon Zedeck, and Larry Fogli, "Relations between Mea-
    sures of Typical and Maximum Job Performance," Journal of Applied Psychol-
    ogy 73, no. 3 (1988): 482–86.

21. Jane McGonigal, Reality is Broken: Why Games Make Us Better and How They
    Can Change the World (New York: Penguin Press, 2011).

22. Salman Khan, "Let's Use Video to Reinvent Education," TED Talks, last
    modified March 2011, accessed September 21, 2012, http://www.ted.com
    /talks/lang/en/salman_khan_let_s_use_video_to_reinvent_education.html.

23. "Socrates," Wikipedia, accessed September 21, 2012, http://en.wikiquote
    .org/wiki/Socrates.

24. John Dewey, My Pedagogic Creed (New York: E. L. Kellogg, 1897), 9.

25. Dan Tapscott, "The Impending Demise of the University," Edge, last modi-
    fied June 4, 2009, accessed September 21, 2012, http://edge.org/conversation
    /the-impending-demise-of-the-university.

26. "Bill Gates on in-person vs. online education," YouTube, last modified Au-
    gust 6, 2012, accessed September 21, 2012, http://www.youtube.com/watch?v
    =p2Qg80MVvYs&feature=player.

Chapter 5

1. Jim Dator quoted in Jake Dunagan, "Design: Post-Newtonian Governance," in 2009 Ten-Year Forecast: The Future Is a Chance to Be New (Palo
   Alto, CA: Institute for the Future, 2009).

2. Jim Dator quoted in Jake Dunagan, "Design: Post-Newtonian Governance."

3. Dunagan, "Design: Post-Newtonian Governance."

4. James S. Fishkin, When the People Speak: Deliberative Democracy and Public
   Consultation (New York: Oxford University Press, 2009), 1.

5. "Highlights: Sustainable Business—Impact 1," Landcare Research, last modified October 10, 2011, accessed December 19, 2011, http://www.landcare
   research.co.nz/sustainability/sustainabilty_details.asp?Sustainability_ID
   =161 (page discontinued).

6. MMOWGLI Game, accessed September 21, 2012, https://mmowgli.nps .edu/mmowgli/; IFTF MMOWGLI, accessed September 21, 2012, http:// www.iftf.org/mmowgli.

7. Kevin Kelly, "The Speed of Information," *Technium* (blog), last modified February 20, 2006, accessed September 21, 2012, http://www.kk.org /thetechnium/archives/2006/02/the_speed_of_in.php.

8. Peter Lyman and Hal R. Varian, "How Much Information," University of California, Berkeley, 2003, accessed December 19, 2011, http://www.sims .berkeley.edu/how-much-info-2003.

9. "Open Government Initiative," accessed September 21, 2012, http://www .whitehouse.gov/open.

10. U.K. Cabinet Office, "Building the Big Society" (program proposal), last modified May 18, 2010, accessed December 19, 2011, http://www.cabinet office.gov.uk/sites/default/files/resources/building-big-society_0.pdf.

11. MuniApp, accessed September 21, 2012, http://obapp.com/muniapp/.

12. Naresh Kumar, "Paris Citizens Track Pollution with a Green Watch," PSFK, last modified August 3, 2010, accessed September 21, 2012, http://www.psfk .com/2010/08/paris-citizens-track-pollution-with-a-green-watch.html.

13. Rebecca Costa, *The Watchman's Rattle: Thinking Our Way Out of Extinction* (Philadelphia: Vanguard Press, 2010).

14. Benedetto De Martino et al., "Frames, Biases, and Rational Decision-Making in the Human Brain," *Science* 313, no. 5787 (2006): 684–87.

15. Jonah Lehrer, "Hearts and Minds," *Boston Globe*, last modified April 29, 2007, accessed December 20, 2011, http://www.boston.com/news/globe/ideas /articles/2007/04/29/hearts__minds/.

16. Garry Kasparov, "The Chess Master and the Computer," review of *Chess Metaphors: Artificial Intelligence and the Human Mind* by Diego Rasskin-Gutman, trans. Deborah Klosky, *New York Review of Books*, last modified February 11, 2010, accessed September 21, 2012, http://www.nybooks.com/articles /archives/2010/feb/11/the-chess-master-and-the-computer/?pagination=false.

17. Jonas Salk, "Are We Being Good Ancestors?" *World Affairs* 1 (1992): 16–18.

18. "YAY TAXES!" Summer of Smart San Francisco, last modified June 25, 2011, accessed December 19, 2011, http://www.summerofsmart.org/projects /yay-taxes/.

19. "FamilyScape," Brookings Institution Center on Children and Families, accessed December 19, 2011, http://www.brookings.edu/about/centers/ccf /social-genome-project/familyscape#recent/.

20. "The Social Genome Project," Brookings Institution Center on Children and Families, accessed December 19, 2011, http://www.brookings.edu /about/centers/ccf/social-genome-project.

21. FutureICT, accessed September 21, 2012, http://www.futurict.eu/; Dirk Helbing quoted in Peter Rüegg, "Exploring the Future with Modern Information Technology" ETH Life, last modified May 4, 2011, accessed December 19, 2011, http://www.ethlife.ethz.ch/archive_articles/110504_future_ICT_per/index_EN.

22. "Opinion Space," U.S. Department of State, accessed September 21, 2012, http://www.state.gov/opinionspace/.

23. Tim O'Reilly, The Architecture of Participation, *O'Reilly* (blog), last modified April 6, 2003, accessed September 21, 2012, http://oreilly.com/pub/wlg/3017.

24. Ken Goldberg, "Introduction" (lecture, "The Future of the Forum: Internet Communities and the Public Interest," Berkeley Center for New Media Symposium, December 5, 2009).

25. Maryann Batlle, "Tell us what you really think: '#F---YouWashington' goes viral on Twitter," Storify, accessed September 21, 2012.

26. Magnetic South, accessed September 21, 2012, http://magneticsouth.net.nz/; Landcare Research - Manaaki Whenua, accessed September 21, 2012, http://www.landcareresearch.co.nz/home; Christchurch City Council, accessed September 21, 2012, http://www.ccc.govt.nz/.

27. "Highlights: Sustainable Business—Impact 1."

28. Maureen Kirchner, "Play to Rebuild the Future of Christchurch, New Zealand," Institute for the Future, last modified June 16, 2011, accessed September 21, 2012, http://www.iftf.org/MagneticSouth.

29. MMOWGLI Game, accessed September 21, 2012, https://mmowgli.nps.edu/mmowgli/.

30. "The Great Urban Hack Re-cap," Gray Area Foundation for the Arts, accessed September 21, 2012, http://www.gaffta.org/2010/11/09/the-great-urban-hack-re-cap/.

31. Brendan Moran, "App Watch: This App Could Save Your Life," *Wall Street Journal,* last modified May 27, 2011, accessed September 21, 2012, http://blogs.wsj.com/digits/2011/05/27/app-watch-this-app-could-save-your-life/.

32. Citizen Logistics, accessed September 21, 2012, http://citizenlogistics.com/.

33. Buckminster Fuller, *Anthology for the New Millennium*, ed. Thomas T. K. Zung (New York: St. Martin's Press, 2001), 124.

34. John Hunter, "Teaching with the World Peace Game," TED Talks, last modified March 2011, accessed September 21, 2012, http://www.ted.com/talks/lang/en/john_hunter_on_the_world_peace_game.html.

35. Bruce A. Ackerman and James S. Fishkin, *Deliberation Day* (New Haven, CT: Yale University Press, 2004).

Chapter 6

1. C. P. Snow, *The Two Cultures*, rev. ed. (1959; Cambridge: Cambridge University Press, 1998), 4.
2. Snow, *The Two Cultures*, 4.
3. Alison Gopnik, Andrew N. Meltzoff, and Patricia K. Kuhl, *The Scientist in the Crib: What Early Learning Tells Us About the Mind*, rev. ed. (New York: Harper Perennial, 2001), 85.
4. Dylan Love, "The 10 Greatest Inventors in the Modern Era," Business Insider: War Room, last modified May 6, 2011, accessed December 20, 2011, http://www.businessinsider.com/most-prolific-inventors-2011-5.
5. Derek J. de Solla Price, *Little Science, Big Science*, (New York: Columbia University Press, 1963).
6. *Shapeshifting in the World of R&D* (Institute for the Future, September 2002).
7. John Schwartz, "Fish Tale Has DNA Hook: Students Find Bad Labels," *New York Times*, last modified August 21, 2008, accessed December 20, 2011, http://www.nytimes.com/2008/08/22/science/22fish.html?adxnnl=1&adxnnlx=1348696001-3OUUS6mJUMg6RAvq5d4dAA.
8. "Timeline of PCR and Roche," Roche Molecular Diagnostics, accessed September 21, 2012, http://molecular.roche.com/About/pcr/Pages/PCRTimeline.aspx.
9. Peter Wayner, "Home Labs on the Rise for the Fun of Science," *New York Times*, last modified December 15, 2010, accessed December 20, 2011, http://www.nytimes.com/2010/12/16/technology/personaltech/16basics.html.
10. Ian O'Neill, "18-Year-Old Student Discovers Comet Break-Up," *Discovery News*, last modified September 3, 2011, accessed December 20, 2011, http://news.discovery.com/space/comet-breakup-asteroid-discoveries-18-year-old-110903.html.
11. "Telescope Makers' Workshop," The Eastbay Astronomical Society Website, accessed September 21, 2012, http://www.eastbayastro.org/index/telescop.htm.
12. "Field Expedition: Mongolia," National Geographic, accessed September 21, 2012, http://exploration.nationalgeographic.com/mongolia.
13. Kevin Kelly, *What Technology Wants* (New York: Viking, 2010).
14. Kelly, *What Technology Wants*.
15. John Falk and Lynn Dierking, "The 95 Percent Solution," *American Scientist* 98 (November–December 2010): 486–87.
16. National Research Council, *Learning Science in Informal Environments: People, Places, and Pursuits* (Washington, DC: National Academic Press, 2009).

17. Marni Berendsen, "Conceptual Astronomy Knowledge among Amateur Astronomers," *Astronomy Education Review* 4 (2005):1–18.

18. Wolff-Michael Roth and Angela Calabrese Barton, *Rethinking Scientific Literacy* (New York: Routledge, 2004).

19. Jim Calder, "The Man Behind Make Magazine and Web 2.0: a Q&A with Dale Dougherty," Publishing Executive, last modified August 2007, accessed December 21, 2011, http://www.pubexec.com/article/the-man-behind -make-magazine-web-20-qandamp-a-dale-dougherty-71966/1.

20. Dylan Tweney, "DIY Freaks Flock to 'Hacker Spaces' Worldwide," *Wired*, last modified March 29, 2009, accessed December 21, 2011, http://www .wired.com/gadgetlab/2009/03/hackerspaces/.

21. "About Maker Faire," Maker Faire, accessed September 21, 2012, http:// makerfaire.com/about.html.

22. Marcus Wohlsen, *Biopunk: DIY Scientists Hack the Software of Life*, (New York: Current/Penguin Group, 2011).

23. Meredith Patterson, "A Biopunk Manifesto," presentation, UCLA Center for Society and Genetics symposium "Outlaw Biology? Public Participation in the Age of Big Bio," last modified January 30 2010, accessed September 21, 2012, http://maradydd.livejournal.com/496085.html.

24. "BioCurious: A Hackerspace for Biotech. The Community Lab for Citizen Science," Kickstarter, accessed December 21, 2011, http://www .kickstarter.com/projects/1040581998/biocurious-a-hackerspace-for-biotech -the-community?ref=live.

25. "BioCurious: A Hackerspace for Biotech. The Community Lab for Citizen Science."

26. "OpenPCR: Open Source Biotech on your Desktop," Kickstarter, accessed December 21, 2011, http://www.kickstarter.com/projects/930368578/open pcr-open-source-biotech-on-your-desktop?ref=live.

27. Thomas Lin, "Scientists Turn to Crowds on the Web to Finance Their Projects," *New York Times*, last modified July 11, 2011, accessed December 21, 2011, http://www.nytimes.com/2011/07/12/science/12crowd.html ?pagewanted=all.

28. Fundscience Page, *Meetup.com*, accessed December 21, 2011, http://www .meetup.com/fundscience/ (page discontinued).

29. Cancer Research UK, accessed September 21, 2012, http://www.cancer researchuk.org/home/; http://myprojects.cancerresearchuk.org/.

30. Giridhar Madras, "Scientific Publishing: Rising Cost of Monopolies," *Current Science* 95, no. 2 (2008): 163.

31. Glen S. McGuigan and Robert D. Russell, "The Business of Academic Publishing: A Strategic Analysis of the Academic Journal Publishing Industry

and Its Impact on the Future of Scholarly Publishing," *Electronic Journal of Academic and Special Librarianship* 9 (Winter 2008).

32. Deutsche Bank AG, "Reed Elsevier: Moving the Supertanker," Company Focus: Global Equity Research Report (January 11, 2005): 36.

33. David Colquhoun, "Publish-or-Perish: Peer Review and the Corruption of Science," *Guardian*, last modified September 5, 2011, accessed December 22, 2011, http://www.guardian.co.uk/science/2011/sep/05/publish-perish-peer-review-science.

34. Terrence Tao, *What's New* (blog), accessed September 21, 2012, http://terrytao.wordpress.com/.

35. *Gödel's Lost Letter and P=NP* (blog), accessed September 21, 2012, http://rjlipton.wordpress.com/.

36. Timothy Gowers, "Is Massively Collaborative Mathematics Possible?" *Gowers's Weblog* (blog), last modified January 27, 2009, accessed December 22, 2012, http://gowers.wordpress.com/2009/01/27/is-massively-collaborative-mathematics-possible/.

37. Tom Chivers, "Mendeley: If You Liked That Research Paper, Try This One," *Telegraph*, last modified May 31, 2011, accessed December 22, 2011, http://www.telegraph.co.uk/science/science-news/8546833/Mendeley-If-you-liked-that-research-paper-try-this-one.html.

38. Mendeley, accessed December 22, 2011, http://www.mendeley.com/.

39. "Christmas Bird Count," Audubon, accessed September 21, 2012, http://birds.audubon.org/christmas-bird-count.

40. "111th Annual Christmas Bird Count Current Year Results," Audubon Society, accessed December 22, 2011, http://cbc.audubon.org/cbccurrent/current_table.html.

41. Water Environment Federation, accessed September 21, 2012, http://www.wef.org/; International Water Association, accessed September 21, 2012, http://www.iwahq.org; "About," World Water Monitoring Challenge, accessed December 21, 2011, http://www.worldwatermonitoringday.org/About.aspx.

42. Kevin Schawinksi quoted in Anthony D. Williams, "Crowdsourcing versus Citizen Science," *Wikinomics* (blog), last modified February 9, 2009, accessed September 21, 2012, http://www.wikinomics.com/blog/index.php/2009/02/09/crowdsourcing-versus-citizen-science/.

43. Elizabeth Krasner, "Interview with Daniel Grushkin: Counterbiology" *Volume* 24 (September 2010), accessed September 21, 2012, http://danielgrushkin-press.tumblr.com/post/29306937657/interview-with-volume-magazine-counter-biology.

44. Ellen D. Jorgensen and Daniel Grushkin, "Engage with, Don't Fear, Com-

munity Labs," *Nature Medicine* 12 (2011): 411, accessed September 21, 2012, http://www.nature.com/nm/journal/v17/n4/full/nm0411-411.html.

45. Alan Melchior et al., *Robots 4 Everyone,* "More Than Robots: An Evaluation of the FIRST Robotics Competition Participant and Institutional Impacts," Brandeis University Center for Youth and Communities, Waltham, MA, April 2005, accessed September 21, 2012, http://www.usfirst.org/uploaded Files/Who/Impact/Brandeis_Studies/FRC_eval_finalrpt.pdf.

Chapter 7

1. Larry Smarr, interview by author, Palo Alto, CA, September 28, 2011.
2. Smarr, September 28, 2011.
3. Larry Smarr, "Special Letter: Quantified Health: A ten year detective story of digitally enabled genomic medicine," The Strategic News Service Newsletter, Volume 14, Issue 36, last modified September 26, 2011, accessed September 21, 2012, http://www.stratnews.com/recentissues.php?mode=show &issue=2011-09-29.
4. Nathan Olivarez-Giles, "Foldit Gamers Help Unlock Possible AIDS-Fighting Protein," *Los Angeles Times*, last modified September 19, 2011, accessed September 21, 2012, http://latimesblogs.latimes.com/technology/2011/09 /foldit-gamers-help-unlock-aids-fighting-proteins.html.
5. Robert Martone, "The Neuroscience of the Gut," *Scientific American*, last modified April 11, 2011, accessed September 21, 2012, http://www.scientific american.com/article.cfm?id=the-neuroscience-of-gut.
6. Martone, "The Neuroscience of the Gut."
7. Rochellys Diaz Heijtz et al., "Normal gut microbiota modulates brain development and behavior," Proceedings of the National Academy of Sciences of the United States of America, January 4, 2011, accessed September 21, 2012, http://www.pnas.org/content/early/2011/01/26/1010529108.
8. Michael Gershon, *The Second Brain* (New York: HarperCollins, 1998).
9. Rachel Yehuda et al., "Transgenerational Effects of Posttraumatic Stress Disorder in Babies of Mothers Exposed to the World Trade Center Attacks during Pregnancy," *Journal of Clinical Endocrinology and Metabolism* 90, no. 7 (2005): 4115, accessed September 21, 2012, http://jcem.endojournals.org /content/90/7/4115.full.
10. Rachel Yehuda et al., "Gene Expression Patterns Associated with Posttraumatic Stress Disorder Following Exposure to the World Trade Center Attacks," *Biological Psychiatry* 66, no. 7 (2009): 708–11; C. Sarapas et al., "Genetic Markers for PTSD Risk and Resilience among Survivors of the

World Trade Center Attacks," *Disease Markers* 30, nos. 2–3 (2011): 101–10; Mo Costandi, "Pregnant 9/11 Survivors Transmitted Trauma to Their Children," *Guardian*, last modified September 9, 2011, accessed September 21, 2012, http://www.guardian.co.uk/science/neurophilosophy/2011/sep/09/pregnant-911-survivors-transmitted-trauma.

11. Christopher P. Morgan and Tracy R. Bale, "Early Prenatal Stress Epigenetically Programs Dysmasculinization in Second-Generation Offspring via the Paternal Lineage," *Journal of Neuroscience* 31, no. 33 (2011): 11748–55.

12. Vannevar Bush, "As We May Think," *Atlantic*, last modified July 1945, accessed September 21, 2012, http://www.theatlantic.com/magazine/archive/1945/07/as-we-may-think/303881/3/.

13. Dae-Hyeong Kim et al., "Epidermal Electronics," *Science* 333, no. 6044 (2011): 838–43, accessed September 21, 2012, http://www.sciencemag.org/content/333/6044/838.abstract.

14. "James Young Simpson," Wikipedia, accessed September 21, 2012, http://en.wikipedia.org/wiki/James_Young_Simpson.

15. Stephanie Pain, "This Won't Hurt A Bit," *New Scientist,* last modified February 16, 2002, accessed September 21, 2012, http://www.newscientist.com/article/mg17323304.900-this-wont-hurt-a-bit.html?full=true.

16. Pamela Weintraub, "Discover Interview: The Doctor Who Drank Infectious Broth, Gave Himself an Ulcer, and Solved a Medical Mystery," *Discover Magazine*, last modified April 8, 2010, accessed September 21, 2012, http://discovermagazine.com/2010/mar/07-dr-drank-broth-gave-ulcer-solved-medical-mystery.

17. Mara J. Broadhurst et al., "IL-22+ CD4+ T Cells Are Associated with Therapeutic Trichuris trichiura Infection in an Ulcerative Colitis Patient," *Science Translational Medicine* 2, no. 60 (2010): 60ra88, accessed September 21, 2012, http://www.ncbi.nlm.nih.gov/pubmed/21123809.

18. Ferris Jabr, "Citizen Scientists Eat Worms to Treat Disorders," *New Scientist*, last modified August 3, 2011 (preview of full article), accessed September 21, 2012, http://www.newscientist.com/article/mg21128244.500-citizen-scientists-eat-worms-to-treat-disorders.html.

19. Jabr, "Citizen Scientists Eat Worms to Treat Disorders."

20. My.microbes, accessed September 21, 2012, http://my.microbes.eu/.

21. Nicola Jones, "Social Network Wants to Sequence Your Gut," *Nature*, last modified September 8, 2011, accessed September 21, 2012, http://www.nature.com/news/2011/110908/full/news.2011.523.html.

22. My Daughter's DNA, accessed September 21, 2012, http://www.mydaughtersdna.org/.

23. *Biocitizens and New Media Technology*, Institute for the Future, May 2007.

24. Swati P. Aggarwal et al., "Safety and Efficacy of Lithium in Combination with Riluzole for Treatment of Amyotrophic Lateral Sclerosis: A Randomised, Double-blind, Placebo-controlled Trial," *Lancet Neurology* 9, no. 5 (2010): 481–88.

25. Jay C. Fournier, "Antidepressant Drug Effects and Depression Severity: A Patient-Level Meta-analysis," *Journal of the American Medical Association* 303, no. 1 (2010): 47–53.

26. Jim Fitzgerald, "IBM's Watson delving into medicine," *USA Today*, last modified May 21, 2011, accessed September 21, 2012, http://usatoday30.usatoday.com/tech/news/2011-05-21-watson-medicine_n.htm.

27. Farhad Manjoo, "Will Robots Steal Your Job?," *Slate*, last modified September 26, 2011, accessed September 21, 2012, http://www.slate.com/articles/technology/robot_invasion/2011/09/will_robots_steal_your_job.html.

Chapter 8

1. "About," Khan Academy, accessed December 14, 2012, http://www.khanacademy.org/about.

2. Clive Thompson, "How Khan Academy Is Changing the Rules of Education," *Wired*, last modified July 15, 2011, accessed December 8, 2011, http://www.wired.com/magazine/2011/07/ff_khan/all/1.

3. Jimmy Wales, "Jimmy Wales on the Birth of Wikipedia," TED Talk, last modified July 2005, accessed September 21, 2012, http://www.ted.com/talks/lang/en/jimmy_wales_on_the_birth_of_wikipedia.html.

4. Peter Drucker, "What Business Can Learn from Nonprofits," *Harvard Business Review*, July/August 1989, 88.

5. See BoingBoing's Twitter handle, accessed September 21, 2012, https://twitter.com/BoingBoing.

6. Rob Walker, "Inside the Wild, Wacky, Profitable World of Boing Boing," *Fast Company,* last modified November 30, 2010, accessed December 8, 2011, http://www.fastcompany.com/1702167/inside-wild-wacky-profitable-world-boing-boing.

7. Mark Frauenfelder quoted in Walker, "Inside the Wild, Wacky, Profitable World of Boing Boing."

8. "Laws," Americans for Community Development, accessed December 8, 2011, http://www.americansforcommunitydevelopment.org/laws.html.

9. "What Is a B Corp?" B Corporation, accessed December 8, 2011, http://www.bcorporation.net/about.

10. "Harvard University," Wikipedia, accessed September 21, 2012, http://en.wikipedia.org/wiki/Harvard_University.

11. PatientsLikeMe, accessed September 21, 2012, http://www.patientslikeme.com/.

12. Shayndi Raice, "Facebook Targets Huge IPO: Offering Next Year Could Raise $10 Billion, Valuing Company at $100 Billion," *Wall Street Journal*, November 29, 2011.

13. Yang Wang and Scott D. Mainwaring, "Incentives in the Wild: Leveraging Virtual Currency to Sustain Online Community," *iConference 2010 Proceedings*, University of Illinois at Urbana- Champaign, 2010, 270–71.

14. Wang and Mainwaring, "Incentives in the Wild: Leveraging Virtual Currency to Sustain Online Community."

15. Robert Crease, "Measurement and Its Discontents," *New York Times*, October 23, 2011, New York edition, SR9.

16. Lewis Hyde, *The Gift*, 25th anniversary ed. (New York: Second Vintage Books, 2007), 49.

17. Robert Skidelsky, "Life after Capitalism," Project Syndicate, last modified January 20, 2011, accessed December 9, 2011, http://www.project-syndicate.org/commentary/life-after-capitalism.

18. Skidelsky, "Life after Capitalism."

19. "AOL and The Huffington Post Close Acquisition," AOL press release, last modified March 7, 2011, accessed September 21, 2012, http://corp.aol.com/2011/03/07/aol-and-the-huffington-post-close-acquisition/.

20. Dan Sabbagh, "Bloggers Take Legal Action over Huffington Post Sale," *Guardian*, last modified April 12, 2011, accessed December 9, 2011, http://www.guardian.co.uk/media/2011/apr/12/arianna-huffington-post-sale.

21. Nikolai Gogol, *Dead Souls*, trans. D. J. Hogarth (London: J. M. Dent and Sons, 1915).

22. Marina Gorbis, "Socialstructing: Statement of Social Currency," Boing Boing, last modified July 10, 2009, accessed September 21, 2012, http://boingboing.net/2009/07/10/socialstructing-stat.html.

23. Cory Doctorow, *Down and Out in the Magic Kingdom* (New York: Tom Doherty Associates, 2003).

24. "About," The Whuffie Bank, accessed December 9, 2011, http://www.thewhuffiebank.org/static/about.

25. "Wealth a Living Systems Model," *Doing My Little Part*, last modified December 30, 2011, accessed September 21, 2012, http://finnern.com/2011/12/30/wealth-a-living-systems-model/.

Chapter 9

1. Ariel Waldman, series of interviews by author, Palo Alto, CA, April-October, 2011.
2. Waldman, April-October, 2011.
3. Waldman, April-October, 2011.
4. Waldman, April-October, 2011.
5. Waldman, April-October, 2011.
6. Waldman, April-October, 2011.
7. Waldman, April-October, 2011.
8. Lewis Hyde, *The Gift*, 25th anniversary ed. (New York: Second Vintage Books, 2007), 63–64.
9. *Social Networks in the World of Abundant Connectivity* (Institute for the Future, 2001).
10. *Leading Toward the Future: A Vision of Leadership Structures and Practices for IFTF* (Institute for the Future, 2008).
11. *Leading Toward the Future.*
12. Waldman, April-October, 2011.

Illustration Credits

Index

About the Author

Marina Gorbis is executive director of the Institute for the Future, a nonprofit research and consulting organization based in Silicon Valley. She has worked with hundreds of organizations in business, education, government, and philanthropy, including Procter & Gamble, Deere, the U.K. Office of Science and Technology, and the U.S. Office of Naval Research. A native of Odessa, Ukraine, Gorbis has been a repeated guest blogger on BoingBoing .net and is a frequent speaker on future organizational, technology, and social issues. She holds a master's degree from the Graduate School of Public Policy at UC Berkeley.